The Shattered Spectrum

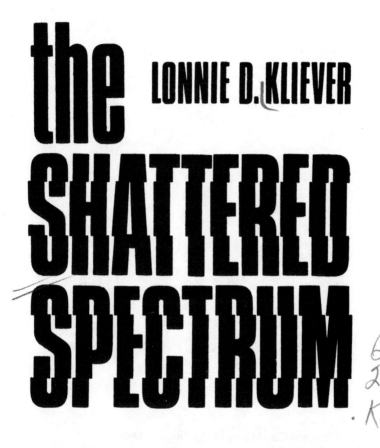

the
SHATTERED
SPECTRUM

LONNIE D. KLIEVER

BT
28
. K558

a survey of contemporary theology

John Knox Press
ATLANTA

Library of Congress Cataloging in Publication Data
Kliever, Lonnie D
    The shattered spectrum.

    Includes bibliographical references and index.
    1. Theology, Doctrinal—History—20th century.
I. Title.
BT28.K558   230'.09'04   80-82184
ISBN 0-8042-0707-0 (pbk.)

For the Austin Circle

Preface

This survey study has a double focus—pluralism and the new theologies. Making sense out of our culture's religious pluralism stands at the center of my research agenda, but the problem of pluralism remains a subsidiary concern in this study. My primary concern is with the wealth of new Protestant and Roman Catholic theologies that have appeared since the end of World War II. This period has been a time of unprecedented experimentation and unrelieved conflict in Christian thought and life. Some comparative order can be found by grouping individual theologians around a shared theme such as secularity, process, liberation, hope, play, or storytelling. But such typological arrangements do not dispel the diversity of belief-systems and life-styles represented in the new theologies. If anything, such analysis underscores their diversity by revealing the remarkable differences among theologians who share a common thematic concern. Seen in this light, recent Christian theology exhibits the same pluralizing trends as the wider culture—trends which, properly understood, portend radical changes in the very form and content of religion in the future. Documenting these trends and forecasting these changes are the burdens of this study.

Perhaps a word is in order about the selection and treatment of the theologians included herein. I have concentrated on the six theological types that seem to have generated the most theological interest and produced the most distinctive results. Each type is analyzed in a threefold manner: a general description of the underlying "root metaphor," an exposition of three representative theologians, and a summary statement of overall strengths and weaknesses.

Personal bias no doubt plays some part in selection and analysis in this kind of study. My choices, however, are intended to reflect the diversity and originality within each theological type, and my analysis is aimed at uncovering the distinctive images, patterns, and even vocabulary of each theologian studied. Others will have to judge how well I have succeeded, but unbiased exposition of each theological type and individual theologian has been my goal. As will be obvious, I lay aside such ideal detachment for more personal judgments in the closing chapter.

There are a number of people who deserve recognition and gratitude for their contributions to this study. I am indebted to R. Donald Hardy, Jr., of John Knox Press for encouraging and enabling me to turn an idea casually mentioned at our first meeting into this book. My departmental secretary, Peggy L. McNear, not only turned my rough drafts into working typescripts, but also freed me from enough administrative routines to enable me to write as well as to teach and chair. Word Processing Services at Southern Methodist University, under the supervision of Kathleen A. Triplett, retyped the manuscript through its several revisions.

My colleagues Thomas W. Moore and Richard M. Zaner of Southern Methodist University and H. Martin Rumscheidt of the Atlantic School of Theology read the manuscript in full and offered useful comments. My wife, Arthiss, proved her indispensable worth again as an unsparing style critic. Her love of common sense and plain talk saved my readers from more complex sentences and theological shorthand than I care to remember. While none of these can be blamed for any of this work's failings, they all have a share in its successes. I also want to express appreciation to the University of Chicago Press for permission to use material from an article I originally wrote for the *Journal of Religion* 59 (April 1979) in the final chapter of this book.

A final debt must be paid to a group of friends from years ago who indirectly and unknowingly contributed to this writing. While living in Austin for a year in the mid-fifties, I belonged to an informal group that met regularly for theological discussion. Their incomparable theological honesty, charity, and irony remain an inspiration and an ideal for me to this day. Dedicating a study on pluralism and the new theologies to them seems especially appropriate. May this book jostle the minds of Ed Bratcher, Riley Eubank, Jess Fletcher, Robert Lovell, and John Lee Smith and honor the memory of Merrill Hutchins, Carlyle Marney, and Blake Smith.

LONNIE D. KLIEVER
Dallas, Texas

Contents

1
The New Pluralism

The last twenty-five years of Christian thought have been a period of intense experimentation if not chaotic change. The revered traditions and towering giants of the theological past have been supplanted by a bewildering variety of theological programs and pundits. Theologies of secularity, process, liberation, hope, play, and story have emerged like the overlapping bursts of a fireworks display. First one and then another of these new interpretations of the Christian faith has captured the center of attention only to be succeeded by yet another explosion of theological energy and illumination. As a consequence, an unprecedented pluralism of belief-systems and life-styles is available today under the heading of "Christian faith."[1]

Of course, theological diversity and conflict are nothing new to the Church. Its long history of institutional schisms, theological reformations, and even religious wars is ample evidence that seldom, if ever, has *anything* been taught by the Church "everywhere and always the same." But, in the modern era, theological disagreements have usually occurred along fairly predicable lines. The varieties of theological outlook roughly took the form of a spectrum, ranging from the conservers on the right to the liberalizers on the left. The theologies toward the right defended the received doctrines of a given tradition in the name of biblical authority, while theologies toward the left modified the old beliefs in the light of new knowledge. These theological differences were usually paralleled by corresponding social attitudes. Theologies on the right were typically more supportive of the political and economic status quo, while those on the left were usually identified with social experiment and change. This conservative-liberal spectrum, though obviously a simplification, has helped locate the major issues and formulate the likely alternatives for almost two centuries of theological debate.

But this venerable theological spectrum has been shattered by the turbulent theological movements of the last quarter century. Actually, as Roger Shinn has observed, the breakup began twenty-five years earlier.[2] The disintegration started with the emergence of theologies that did not neatly fit the conventional patterns of conservatism or liberalism. The leaders of that revolution—Karl Barth, Rudolf Bultmann, Paul Tillich, and the Niebuhrs—were in some ways more biblical and conservative than the conservatives they ignored, in other ways more innovative and radical than the liberals they attacked. Though their theological programs were routinely perceived in terms of the old spectrum, as witnessed by such descriptive titles as "Neo-orthodoxy" or "Chastened Liberalism" being applied to them, the revolution they launched eventually smashed the old spectrum.

To be sure, there are scholasticisms old and new that are still amenable to the classifications of the conservative-liberal spectrum. A latter-day resurgence of evangelical piety has prompted a restaging of the old conservative-liberal debates among evangelical theologians. The mainline theological guild has its coteries of Barthians, Bultmannians, Tillichians, and Niebuhrians whose zealous interpretations of their respective theological masters have the look of the old spectrum. In addition, apart from such scholastic rehearsals of the past, a considerable amount of theological work on the classical loci (God, Christ, Man, Authority, Church, Ministry) is reminiscent of the conservative-liberal divisions because it is done in historical perspective. Nevertheless, these ongoing retrenchments and updatings have been overshadowed in the last quarter century by a kaleidoscope of new theologies that defy classification under the old categories. For these new theologies, there are no established traditions or acknowledged masters to whom homage, whether conservative or liberal, is due.

This new pluralism in theology is largely an outcome of a long process of adjustment to certain structural and ideological changes within the wider culture. That historical process can be helpfully illumined by tracing out the interaction between scientific and theological reflection in the modern period. That the rise of modern science in the seventeenth century played a key role in undermining traditional theology is by now a familiar story. Traditional appeals to an absolutely authoritative Bible and Church, with their exclusive claims for a miraculous history and otherworldly destiny, were slowly but surely undermined by the rival scientific vision of a rationally knowable and uniformly structured universe. The rest of the story, recounting more than two centuries of continuing conflict between modern science and *modern* theology, is less familiar and must be told here to place the new theologies in cultural and theological context. Always at the center of this continuing story of theological efforts to join Christian faith and contemporary culture stands modern science—alternately the arch rival, treasured ally, bad conscience, and benign companion of modern theology.[4]

THE CONFLICT OVER FACTS

At the outset, the central conflict between the new sciences and the old theologies was over matters of natural and historical fact. To be sure, traditional theology was primarily concerned with matters metaphysical and eternal—with the supernatural nature and existence of God and with the supernatural nature and destiny of persons. But these supernatural concerns were intimately linked to certain alleged occurrences in the natural order—to the world's beginning and end and to God's miraculous involvement in the world during the interim. These miraculous interventions in nature and history played a crucial role in this "dualistic" scheme of things since they were the means by which the supernaturals of faith were known and achieved. Accordingly, as scientific explanation and skepticism undermined belief in miracles, much of the basis and content of traditional theology was dissolved.

Theological adjustments to the new sciences were not long in coming.[5] The fundamental strategy of these constructive responses was to relocate the factual elements of faith—those miraculous events in the natural order that were the foundations of faith. Theological rationalists of the seventeenth century had already limited the occurrence of miracles to the biblical era (Tillotson, Locke). This displacement of miracle was carried much further in the eighteenth century by the Enlightenment Deists who limited God's direct and causal activity within the natural order to the beginning and end of the world (Toland, Voltaire, Reimarus). Removing God's miraculous deeds to the distant past or the distant future put such claims about divine activity completely beyond the range of prevailing scientific inquiry, thereby ending the conflict between theology and science for a time. Indeed, the giants of both science and theology in the eighteenth century found this division of ultimate and penultimate facts quite convincing.

This "mutual assistance pact" between science and theology began to come apart in the nineteenth century, however, under pressure of new developments in the geological and biological sciences. These newly emergent sciences fashioned developmental perspectives explaining the vast changes that had occurred in the earth and in living things in the distant past. That such changes in the earth's surface and in forms of plant and animal life had occurred had already been established in the seventeenth century, but for more than a hundred years these great changes were explained by scientists and theologians alike as the consequence of catastrophic interventions by God. In the the nineteenth century these supernatural explanations were swept away—first in geology (Lyell) and then in biology (Darwin)—by scientific explanations of past changes in terms of laws presently in operation. These geological and biological laws used the same kind of universal and mechanistic principles that had proven so fruitful in the new astronomy, physics, and chemistry.

The victory of "uniformitarianism" over "catastrophism" rendered the theological compromises of the eighteenth century untenable. The distant past and remote future could no longer be excluded from scientific investigation and explanation. Even theological claims of a factual kind for ultimate beginnings and endings, to say nothing of events recorded in the biblical materials, were no longer safe from scientific challenge. This jeopardy was redoubled by new developments in historical studies proper. Archeology, anthropology, and history adapted methods of uniformitarianism in their reconstructions of the past which excluded appeals to supernatural causes. The only way to avoid a renewal of the warfare between science and theology seemed to require the surrender of *all* notions of God acting upon the world in some visibly and descriptively obvious way. Precisely that strategy dominated the next hundred years of modern theology.

This theoretical strategy was supported, if not suggested, by certain profound shifts at the level of practical faith that were taking place at this time in the Pietist movement. A more mystical and experiental religiosity appeared, which placed greater emphasis on the miracle of God's indwelling presence here and now than on God's miraculous interventions in the distant past or future. This pietistic relocation of God's activity to a place of personal inwardness proved more helpful in the next stage of theological construction than the rationalistic restriction of God's activity to temporal remoteness, since all periods of the earth's development and mankind's history were now included in the range of scientific inquiry.

THE RELOCATION OF MIRACLE

Following the lead suggested by Pietism and pioneered by Kant, Hegel, and Schleiermacher at the dawn of the nineteenth century, a new theological liberalism emerged that studiously separated theological claims from matters of natural fact. This separation, however, did not eliminate God from the world so much as conceal God within the world. God was henceforth conceived as everywhere present in the world, but within its depths rather than upon its surfaces.[6] This immanent God was especially present within human inwardness and thereby especially manifested in human culture. History rather than nature became the theater of divine activity.

This development meant that a literal sense of theological language was displaced by a symbolic sense. Religious affirmations and assertions became purely figurative, and sharp disagreements over what these symbols meant increasingly divided liberal theologians from one another. Religious utterances were variously interpreted as pictorial expressions of religious experience (the Schleiermacherians), value judgments (the Kantians), or metaphysical truths (the Hegelians). That a time-bomb lay concealed in this turn to the symbolic character of all religious language was clearly signaled by Feuerbach's mid-nineteenth-century reductive interpretation of theological symbols in strictly anthropological terms— an approach that was later developed with such devastating impact on theistic faith by Marx, Durkheim, and Freud. This new-fashioned atheism aside, however, liberal theologians agreed that religious symbols do not furnish or require factual information about the observable world when they are properly understood. They refer only to the noumenal world that underlies but transcends the phenomenal world.

Liberalism's separation of the noumenal and the phenomenal world was, in practice, far from absolute. Indeed, unlike eighteenth-century theology, which increasingly separated the being of God from the being of the world, nineteenth-century Liberalism merely separated knowledge of God from knowledge of the world. God and the world remained intimately related ontologically, though categorically separated epistemologically. But even

this epistemological sundering was not complete. Liberal theologians derived strong reassurances of God's hidden activity within
the world from the natural and historical sciences since the world-
picture they presented was one of marvelous development and
progress. Reciprocally, Liberalism's world-picture of a divine presence and meaning within all things offered strong sanctions and
reassurances for the unfettered scientific investigation of nature and
history. Seen in this light, Liberalism was actually a highly successful refinement of the eighteenth-century pact between science and
religion. Though contributing nothing to one another directly, theology and science remained mutually supportive for most thinkers
well into the twentieth century.

    Cultural circumstances and further scientific developments, how-
ever, rapidly brought this arrangement to an end. Culturally, the
apocalyptic events that ushered in the twentieth century laid waste to
liberal theories of cosmic and historical progress. Although biological
evolution remained firmly established, the nonscientific character of
all theories of progressive and purposive evolution, whether in nature or in history, was rudely brought home by the events of the
times. Political, economic, moral, and religious turmoil made a mockery of Liberalism's confidence in an immanent and purposive deity.

    This experiential challenge to liberal faith was reinforced by new
theoretical challenges from the emerging social sciences. As suggested above, the nineteenth century's "symbolic turn" opened the
door to what Paul Ricoeur has called "the hermeneutics of suspicion."[7] With the turn away from the literal meaning of religious utterances to their symbolic meaning, the hermeneutical question of their
proper interpretation became a radically open question. In a situation
where neither empirical facts nor dogmatic authorities could help set-
tle questions about the proper interpretations of symbols, a whole
new approach to the character of religious beliefs became possible.
Seen as symbolic, the supernatural claims of religion could now be
interpreted as *disguised* expressions of something other than they appear to be. In the late nineteenth and early twentieth centuries, this
"suspicion" led to a variety of reductionist interpretations of religious
beliefs. The central symbols of religion were variously rendered as
societal representations (Durkheim), ideological deceits (Marx), and
neurotic projections (Freud). These purely naturalistic explanations
of the inner life and religious symbols had momentous consequences
for theological reflection. They signaled the disappearance of the last
inviolable "place" for God's personal presence and causal action.
Henceforth, the "inner" space and time of human experience became
just as open to scientific inquiry as the "outer" space and time of nat-

ural phenomena. Indeed, religion itself, in both its public and private expressions, became a subject of scientific inquiry.

The combined impact of cultural turmoil and scientific reductionism on Christian thought and life shattered the liberal synthesis of the scientific and Christian worldviews. As the nineteenth century had driven a wedge between the direct activity of God and natural occurrences, so the early twentieth century laid a caveat against appeals to God's presence in historical events. Once again, modern faith was put to flight by scientific advance and changing circumstance.

THE RETREAT TO REVELATION

In this crisis situation, nothing less than radical measures seemed appropriate. A new theology arose devoted to diastasis rather than synthesis, to separating finally reason and revelation, culture and faith, science and theology. This "neo-orthdox" theology reestablished the absolute priority of divine revelation and the autonomy of theological reflection by separating the finite and the infinite ontologically as well as epistemologically. Neo-orthodoxy still spoke of the "mighty acts" of God within the affairs of selves and of nations, but these actions had no empirical basis in the events within which they occurred. Neither scientific nor philosophic analysis of these events could ever discover or disprove the divine presence, because faith's encounter with God happens in a dimension other than ordinary natural process and human knowing. The faithful "see" and "hear" God only when God reveals himself through events, as he did decisively in the Christ event and as he does repeatedly through the biblical witness to that event. Here at last, all possible conflicts between science and theology, between human circumstance and theological certitude seemed resolved. Theology, based on revelation and faith alone, could henceforth remain untouched by the changing fortunes of scientific theory, historical reconstruction, or existential circumstance.

This theological ban on constructive alliances between faith and reason was matched by equally stringent prohibitions within twentieth-century philosophy, though hardly for the same reasons or with the same results. On the Continent, essentialist philosophies that stressed the fundamental rationality of human beings and their total environment were overwhelmed by an existentialism that stressed nature's otherness, history's absurdity, and humanity's impotence. In a very different mood, but with similar results, British-American philosophies mounted a programmatic attempt to purge philosophy of meaningless assertions and idle disputes. Under their various criteria for meaningful assertions, all transcendent claims about divine and human reality were treated as humanistic projections at best and as linguistic nonsense at worst. Thus, Neo-orthodoxy's exclusive appeal to revelation received indirect confirmation from contemporary philosophy. The dominant philosophies of the time concurred with the reigning theologies that there are no rational or experiential bridges from man to God and that claims for such bridges can only be a matter of illusion or revelation.

Despite its methodological severity, Neo-orthodoxy dominated Christian thought and life for more than a generation. This preeminence was no doubt due in part to the intellectual climate and existential mood of the times, which were ripe for a theological emphasis on a revelation and redemption coming from beyond all merely human knowing and doing. But Neo-orthodoxy's power and influence were more a matter of the imaginative ways it correlated divine transcendence and deliverance with human disorder and impotence. Though methodologically disavowing any dependence of theological reflection upon human knowledge, in point of fact Neo-orthodoxy made full use of the best scientific and philosophical insights into human and historical affairs in its application of biblical themes to the human situation. By arguing *from* the Christian revelation *to* the human situation, Neo-orthodoxy provided a highly effective interpretation of the Christian faith for two generations of modern believers.

As surely as Neo-orthodoxy effectively addressed the existential and reflective situation of the early twentieth century, just as surely did that voice fade with the passage of time. This loss of effectiveness can be attributed in part to increasingly aggressive challenges to theistic faith from philosophical and social-scientific accounts of religious experience and discourse. But these challenges would not have had their devastating impact apart from the pyramiding effect of certain social and existential developments long under way. Modern social differentiation and existential alienation brought on a massive crisis in personal faith. The "death of God" controversy in the nineteen-sixties gave symptomatic expression to this deep spiritual malaise within the Christian communion following World War II. Faced with this crisis, Neo-orthodoxy lost its commanding voice because its covert experiential legitimations became problematic.

THE LOSS OF FAITH

This mid-century crisis of faith was partly a side effect of certain changes in the social structures of modern life that were brought about by the scientific revolution. Most telling of all the changes was the loss of the Church's thousand-year monopoly on defining the nature of reality, the order of society, and the destiny of individuals. Other thoroughly secular social groups claimed a share in these tasks of "world construction" and "world maintenance."[8] Paramount among these structures were such distinctively modern developments as democratic government, mechanized work, bureaucratic order, mass communications, and public education. Each of these shapers of human thought and energy, along with a variety of voluntary groups including the Church, was a separate and often separating force of reality definition, social integration, and personality formation.

Nowhere was such differentiation and diffusion among the social processes for establishing and maintaining human order more evident and influential than in public education, since academic institutions had become the primary formative agents of contemporary culture. The educational franchisement of the masses put new and troublesome knowledge in the hands of a public ever increasing in size and discernment. Well before mid-century, academic institutions were no longer merely training an elite destined to teach the masses, but had begun to teach the masses themselves. The Second World War and its aftermath greatly extended access to education across geographic, ethnic, and economic lines, dramatically increasing the growth of the intellectual classes. Moreover, the knowledge thus disseminated to the masses became increasingly specialized and fragmented. Gone were the days when academic institutions conveyed a unified and unifying body of knowledge to their students. Public education became a civil war of competing perspectives without defining center or circumference—a situation that today reaches from the research universities, through the secondary schools, and into the curricula of the primary schools.

This democratization and specialization of knowledge equipped the many for the highly professional roles increasingly required by a bureaucratic and industrialized culture, but it also burdened the many with the unfocused and unfinished character of all human knowledge. Such socially reinforced cognitive dissonance, coupled with the social mobility and anonymity of modern life, created a situation ripe for existential alienation from traditional patterns of belief and behavior. The occurrence of just such alienation on an ever-expanding scale became evident in the postwar years of the fifties and sixties. To be sure, the war's end had been celebrated by a short-lived religious revival, but this outburst of fervor mirrored rather than mitigated the inner turmoil and doubts that beset the times.

The inner frame of mind for this withering of faith at the roots—like the social context in which it occurred—was largely a product of the scientific revolution. Over the years, the unchecked advance of scientific understanding and control of the natural and human world had rendered a transcendent problem-solving and need-fulfilling God less and less necessary. More and more, the world and life within it became intelligible and worthwhile quite apart from some supernatural "otherworld" or "afterlife." Indeed, this secularizing process was so pervasive that modern theologians were compelled to relocate God and faith within *this* world and *this* life. But even this inward God became progressively less credible as an account of the inner life. Modern scientific inquiry and historical research had furnished a variety of alternative accounts of the life force, of the moral imperative, or of the religious sense. No longer were uncritical appeals to the contents and certainties of a Christian inwardness convincing since these had now to be understood at least in part as culturally relative expressions of certain natural processes of socialization and individualization.

Yet the twentieth century's progressive secularizing and relativizing of human consciousness cannot alone account for the pervasive doubt of the fifties and sixties. Both Liberalism and Neo-orthodoxy had incorporated these altered perceptions of human experience and understanding in their reformulations of faith. The postwar disaffection from faith was less a failure of intellectual imagination than of moral credibility. Indeed, radical doubt arose only when the very idea of a personal God active in history became morally untenable as well as intellectually superfluous.[9]

Belief in God lost its moral credibility in two very different ways. One was a consequence of the modern world's radically altered concept of what constitutes a responsible belief, whatever that belief might be about. The eighteenth-century Enlightenment introduced a new "morality of knowledge," which had progressively dominated the thinking of the educated person. The central tenet of this morality of knowledge was that it is wrong to believe anything (whether scientific, historical, moral, or religious) on insufficient evidence.[10] Once this demand for evidence became an operative assumption in the thinking of ordinary people, theological reflection took on a new urgency and gained a new audience. While no theology can create faith, it could possibly preserve faith by furnishing credible grounds to those whose beliefs had become problematic. In the absence of a theology that supplied such reassurances, believing in God became a compromise of personal integrity that growing numbers of clergy and laity were no longer willing to make.

The other blow to the moral credibility of believing in a personal God active in history came from a heightened sense of the sheer magnitude and absurdity of human suffering.[11] Faith's old conundrum of why the innocent suffer in a world supposedly created and governed by an all-powerful and all-loving God took on fresh insistence in a world newly acquainted with the horrors of human cruelty and natural catastrophe. Such twentieth-century spectacles as racial genocide, obliteration bombing, massive starvation, seismic disaster, and ecological destruction brought all suffering and evil into dramatic focus. Many people came to share Albert Camus's moral revulsion of "any scheme of things in which children are put to torture."[12]

Here then—at the point of the morality of believing in a hidden God without sufficient evidence or manifest decency—the distinctive character and challenge of modern doubt becomes clear. This is no mere intellectual doubt about the adequacy of certain theological formulations; this is radical doubt about the very existence of a personal God. Seen in this light, the "death of God" controversy was anything but a media event manufactured by a few misguided academics and opportunistic journalists. It signaled a radical break with the theological past—a break confirmed by subsequent developments in religious thought and life both inside and outside the Church.[13]

Against this kind of experiental doubt, Neo-orthodoxy was utterly powerless. Of course, Neo-orthodoxy had methodologically finessed the whole question of experiential evidence and counterevidence by grounding faith and theology in the transcendent Word of God given through, but not contained by, the words of Scripture. Theological appeals to biblical language, human nature, historical inquiry, scientific thought were methodically ruled out by Neo-orthodoxy's separation of faith and theology from all scientific knowledge and philosophic speculation. Indeed, a part of the staying power of Neo-orthodoxy is that it methodically built doubt into its system by making the absence of evidence a necessary condition of the presence of faith.[14] But in practice Neo-orthodoxy could not avoid appeals to inward personal experience. There was no other recourse for deciding when the Word spoke through the words than an appeal to some kind of self-authenticating encounter within. Thus, as these inward personal experiences of "seeing" and "hearing" the Word of God became problematic, Neo-orthodoxy's concealed dogmatism and pietism were exposed and discredited.

THE DILEMMA FOR THEOLOGY

Modern theology was brought face to face with the dilemma of scientific origin that had long troubled it.[15] One of the sticking points of that dilemma was the scientific picture of a "closed universe." The scientific vision of an interrelated and constant system of natural causes and effects had been relentlessly and successfully extended to the whole cosmic and historic process. Consequently, modern faith and theology were progressively deprived of an assured factual basis. The effort to find "room" for God in first one and then another area of natural order or human experience as yet untouched by science seemed doomed to fail. The successive intrusions of scientific inquiry into such "inviolable bastions of mystery" discouraged, if not prevented, further search for the factual grounds of faith.

The second point of scientific challenge to theological reflection was the scientific paradigm of responsible thinking. Scientific accounts of the world prevailed simply because they had been shown to be true, often against the "received" truth of religious belief, common sense, and even prevailing scientific understanding. How these demonstrations occur has been endlessly debated by philosophers, but the essentials of scientific thinking seem clear enough to its practitioners. Scientific thinking appeals to a particular kind of evidence (publicly available and, in some sense, empirically given data) and a particular kind of explanation (systematically interdependent and universally reproducible structures.)[16] Because of the demonstrated power of this kind of thinking, these standards have pervaded the whole modern culture and become the ideal canons of cognitive behavior. Thus, theological claims that invoke neither public evidence nor reproducible structures are cognitively suspect at best, cognitively empty at worst.

With the horns of theology's dilemma thus clearly exposed, the troubled history and spectacular collapse of modern theology can be recapitulated more precisely. Under the pressures of scientific advance, Liberalism had surrendered the factual world of nature to the sciences. But at that time the distinctively human world of history remained "open" to theological explanations of a causal and confirmable kind. Inward experiences of the sacrality, morality, or rationality of historical events functioned as data for both theological reflection and confirmation. This direct appeal to "inner facts" was buttressed by the indirect evidences furnished by scientifically sanctioned views of a purposive cosmic order. Liberal theology thus managed to avoid that horn of the dilemma which demanded "scientific" evidence for all responsible thinking. However, it was soon impaled on the other horn because twentieth-century science and circumstance stripped Liberalism of its presumptive evidence for the indwelling presence of God in nature and in history.

To avoid this dilemma, Neo-orthodoxy surrendered the factual world of history as well as nature to the sciences. Faith and theology were grounded in an entirely different order of divinely given and guaranteed revelation. But, as suggested above, Neo-orthodoxy's actual power to inform and confirm the faithful lay in its greater fidelity to the cultural circumstances and individual needs of the times. Nineteenth-century liberal progressivism and activism no longer spoke to the cultural chaos and individual paralysis of the early twentieth century. But, as Neo-orthodoxy's covert experiential warrants dissolved in turn, its essential groundlessness became evident. Having seized neither horn of the modern dilemma, Neo-orthodoxy managed to fall on both. If ever a theology was at dead end, it was this theology without explicit factual basis *or* rational grounds.[17]

Modern theology thus reached a radical impasse in its two-centuries-long search for constructive alliances with modern science and contemporary culture. Theology could neither align itself with nor isolate itself from science. Efforts at alignment had required the relocation of the facts of faith in special "places" beyond the reach of science, first in nature and then in history. But this "theology of the gaps," to use Dietrich Bonhoeffer's memorable phrase,[18] was progressively undermined by the further extension of immanent and mechanistic explanations to the whole of cosmic and historical process. Efforts at isolation freed theology from competition with science by separating faith from all factual occurrences and explanations. But this "revelational positivism" was defenseless against challenges from rival accounts of human experience or from existential doubts about Christian meaning. Confronted with this dilemma, many sought to go around the problem by letting go of modern science (the new mysticisms) or by surrendering cognitive theism (the "death of God" theologies).[19] Others sought a way through the problem by reexamining the horns on which constructive theology lay impaled. That reexamination has given rise to the new pluralism in theology today.

THE SEARCH FOR GROUNDS

The classical way to overcome a dilemma is to show that the two undesirable alternatives posed by the dilemma are either ill-formulated or not the only options available. Precisely this course of action has dominated the most recent stage of modern theology. Underlying all of the new theological experiments is the effort to reconceive the relationship between facts and faith, between scientific claims and theological utterances. Put more directly, contemporary theology is a series of frontal attacks on the omnicompetence of the scientific notion of a closed universe and the scientific paradigm of responsible thinking.

Counterattacks on the scientific vision of a closed universe seek variously to demonstrate either that the universe is itself more open than nineteenth- and early twentieth-century science assumed or that the scientific picture of a closed universe is a highly useful but by no means exhaustive way of conceptually ordering our personal experience and total environment. Other equally helpful ways of "imaging" the world from perspectives based on different data and models from those of science are permitted and demanded by our experience. Similarly, counterattacks on the scientific paradigm of responsible thinking seek to show either that the operative standards of scientific truth are applicable within other domains of rational discourse, including religious and moral utterances, or that these scientific standards operate alongside other criteria of meaningfulness and truth. The entire scientific enterprise may itself rest upon such "nonscientific" standards. Whichever tack is taken, recent theological construction has concentrated on discovering new factual and logical grounds for faith in God.[20]

For understandable reasons, this new quest gave first priority to the problem of theological criteria. The new linguistically oriented philosophers had raised serious questions about the cognitivity and veracity of theological claims precisely at the point of the criteria of these claims. Logical Positivists insisted that only those statements which are in principle testable by scientific means can be considered meaningful and verifiable. Linguistic Analysts, working with a more flexible definition of meaning and truth, acknowledged that language can be used legitimately in ways other than scientific description and prediction. But they insisted that these ways imposed their own distinctive goals and rules of proper usage. In short, common to both programmatic challenges to religious language was the demand that religious thinkers make clear just what the functions and norms of religious discourse are if they want to be taken seriously.

Theologians and philosophers of religion were quick to take up the challenge. Philosophical theology of the fifties was utterly dominated by questions of linguistic use and verification.[21] Sustained attention was given to delineating the functions and norms of ordinary realms of discourse (scientific, historical, moral, legal, literary, promissory, hortatory) and to comparing these to religious language. Out of these comparisons came numerous revisionary proposals for what religious people are "really saying" when they speak of God, Christ, heaven, hell, and the like, modeled on one or another of these less problematic domains of discourse. But, for all the brilliance and insight of these proposals, no convergence or consensus about the proper functions and norms of religious utterance was forthcoming. In fact, rival theories of religious language proliferated as first one and then another linguistic doorknob was turned in search of new room for meaningful speech in religion.

Given this widening disagreement over theological norms, a decided shift in the sixties away from questions of criteria to questions of substance was hardly surprising.[22] This shift was more than a reaction of impatience or embarrassment over the disarray among theories of religious language, however. It grew out of a recognition of the anemia of the theological language under review in these linguistic studies—whether orthodox, liberal, or neo-orthodox. In virtually every case, arguments for a particular set of theological criteria were couched in the language of a given reading of faith. But a growing number of religious thinkers were convinced that these theologies "in place" had in one way or another lost touch with historic faith or contemporary experience. They were equally convinced that theology's "loss of speech" was more a problem of relevance than of assurance. Existing words had simply lost their connections with vital human needs, concerns, and beliefs. Consequently, theological energies were redirected to seek out new connections between religious language and ordinary experience. Put another way, contemporary theologians took up the other side of the dilemma posed by modern science: What are the experiential data of faith in a scientifically explainable world? Efforts to answer that question have dominated theological inquiry to the present day.

The renewed search for the experiential grounds of faith and language is no mere "return to Liberalism," despite the centrality of religious experience to both. Liberalism's conception of the autonomy of religious experience can no longer be maintained. Religious experiences are no more exempt from scientific explanations in terms of physical, social, and psychological dynamics than any other human experiences. While admitting that all human experience, including religion, is amenable to scientific inquiry, these latter day "experiential" theologians insist that such scientific accounts of experience are not exhaustive. There are aspects of reality within common experience that transcend the scientifically knowable and explainable. Organizing those aspects in terms of Christian symbols is the central task of these new ventures in theological construction.

This rapprochement with experience must also be distinguished from neo-orthodox apologetics. As we have seen, the practical power of Neo-orthodoxy lay in its ability to relate the great biblical themes to the human situation. But these correlations always moved from the explicit answers of faith to the implicit questions of existence.[23] In the new appeals to experience, the conversation between faith and existence has become a genuine dialogue. Indeed, the new theologians of experience listen before they speak. They explore the ways in which our experience reshapes faith before they explain the ways in which faith transforms our experience. Human experience has become a source of theological construction as well as an object of theological criticism.

The new theologies of experience are also distinctive in terms of the experiences they select for theological exploration. For the most part, they pass over such human concerns as worship, trust, guilt, conscience, and dependence which have long been associated with religion.[24] Their search for new experiential and interpretive bridges between Christian faith and contemporary sensibilities is concentrated in two broad areas: in contemporary cultural preoccupations thought to be inimical to faith (such as science, technology, secularity, process, liberation) or in universal human activities heretofore ignored in theological reflection (such as fantasy, creativity, hope, play, storytelling). The apologetic strategy here is obvious. If the very elements of contemporary life that have undermined past expressions of the faith can be shown to contain dimensions of transcendence or underpinnings of faith, then the cultural renewal of Christian thought and life becomes genuinely possible. Better still, if transcendence and faith can be discerned in human activities found the world over, then the universal relevance of Christian thought and life becomes credible once again. Precisely because of their mundane nature, these experiences are thought to furnish strategically decisive data for theological construction and criticism.

Theological analysis and use of such experiences vary greatly. Some "foundational" theologians, who are concerned with establishing the rational possibility of faith, invoke one or more of these experiences in laying the groundwork for a systematic interpretation of the Christian experience of God.[25] A much larger number of "constructive" theologians, who systematically develop the thematic content of faith, have built entire theologies around one or another of these experiences. They have chosen some well-known feature of our experience, such as secularity or storytelling, as a new "root metaphor" for rethinking all the symbolic experiences and expressions of faith.[26] Herein lies the rich diversity of contemporary theology. Not only are we confronted with theologies of secularity, process, liberation, hope, play, and story (to name only the most prominent). Within each of these new types of theology, further differentiations occur because the root metaphor is variously elaborated in the hands of different theologians. As a consequence, contemporary theology is pluralistic through and through.

This runaway pluralism has pervaded but not preempted the last twenty years of theological reflection. As noted earlier, "theology as usual" continues in some quarters without serious regard for the theoretical and practical challenges to faith outlined above. But even theologians who are convinced of the need for thoroughgoing reformulations of belief and behavior are divided over what to make of these "new type" theologies. This division was eloquently voiced in a 1975 symposium on "Whatever Happened to Theology?" sponsored by *Christianity and Crisis.* For example, Van Harvey laments the ill health of Protestant theology in America since the sixties:

> The lack of serious dialogue among peers, the subsequent narcissism (the theology of autobiography) and faddism (the theologies of atheism, hope, play, revolution and, most recently, polytheism tailgating one another like automobiles on a California freeway) are all bleak testimony to a pervasive loss of vocation and the breakdown of a once noble intellectual discipline.

Gordon Kaufman holds these rapid-fire "theologies of ..." in even greater contempt:

> As each new turn of this sort was made, it became embarrassingly clear that anyone and everyone could dress up his/her new cause in language and ideas drawn from the Christian tradition and proclaim one more "new theology." Theology apparently had no integrity or standards or demands of its own; its symbols could be used as a kind of decoration for and legitimation of almost any partisan position found in the culture. The once proud queen of the sciences, having lost a sense of her own meaning and integrity, had become a common prostitute.

But, in predictable fashion, Harvey Cox gives a very different reading of these "impure" theologies:

18 THE SHATTERED SPECTRUM

What has happened to theology? When I hear the plaintive requiem being sung and see the crepe-draped bier of the queen, I smile. I know there is a Tom Sawyer peeking over the bannister, enjoying the spectacle, aware that the laments are a trifle previous. Theology is being done today—in curious places, under unusual sponsorship, by unauthorized persons, unnoticed by those who read only the right journals. The queen is dead? The hell, you say. Long live the queen!

Roger Shinn concurs by stressing that our cultural situation permits nothing more than theological fragments and forays:

Perhaps another generation will regain a metaphysical confidence and a comprehensive vision denied us. Yet I, personally, do not regret that lack of the panoramic theological assurance. I believe that our kind of situation is the more characteristic and the more authentic human situation. It is, I think, closer to the biblical situation than are the ages of speculative confidence. It appreciates the confession: "I believe; help my unbelief" (Mark 9:24). This is a good time to work at theology.[27]

What then of this new pluralism in theology? Is it a mitotic differentiation of living faith or a malignant multiplication of dying faith? Does it suggest a new theological "Dark Age" of lesser minds and lesser faith than the past? Does it signal a new era of experiential religion and theological creativity? Does it mean a temporary loss of dominating thinkers and established traditions? Does it spell the end for all monolithic cultures and traditions? Needless to say, these questions cannot be answered apart from a study of new theologies themselves. Accordingly, the following chapters are a survey introduction and invitation to such study.

Our inquiry will concentrate on six new types of contemporary theology: theologies of secularity, process, liberation, hope, play, and storytelling. These are the root metaphors that have proven most fruitful for theological reflection—and that for a reason beyond their inherent suggestiveness. These experiences are readily available and common to all—believers and nonbelievers, educated and uneducated, rich and poor. While such cultural activities as science and technology have not been ignored in the new search for transcendence, their religious implications are clear only to those who understand these highly complex systems of thought and action.[28] By contrast, secularity, process, and liberation are cultural preoccupations that suffuse everyday life and thought for the masses. Though such human capacities as creativity and fantasy have been put to inventive theological use, the widespread indifference to art and the mystifications surrounding fantasy limit their apolegetic impact for the most part to an elite familiar with aesthetic and psychoanalytic sensibilities.[29] But the human experiences of hope, play, and story-telling are familiar elements in the experiences of all. In short, theological concentration on just these cultural and human activities reflects a new *populist* sensitivity within theology. Theology is no longer strictly reserved for the scholar in the academy. Theology is being done for the person on the streets. The new pluralism in theology is also a new populism.

In this study a chapter will be devoted to each of the six types of theology. Within each chapter a similar format will be followed. First, a description of the underlying root metaphor will be broadly sketched, showing how it requires and inspires new patterns of belief and behavior. Then significant variations on each type will be set out through summary descriptions of representative thinkers. It should be noted here that these descriptions are not offered as complete or even current accounts of a given theologian's position. One of the fascinating features of the new theological pluralism is the fluidity and tentativeness (some would say instability) of the thought of individual theologians. They may work with a given root metaphor for a time, only to move on to an entirely different way of doing theology later.[30] I hope this arrangement of the material will encourage thematic and developmental comparisons. The book will conclude with a chapter that critically engages questions like those above about the present and future significance of these new types of contemporary theology.

2
Secularity as Threat and Opportunity

John A. T. Robinson, Harvey Cox, Paul van Buren

There is no more dominant and obvious feature of modern existence than its preoccupation with *this* world and *this* life. That people and cultures have not always found this world meaningful and
this life worthwhile is obvious to anyone familiar with traditional cultures. The religions and even the sciences of traditional cultures were
dominated by an otherworldly outlook. Traditional Christianity was
certainly no exception as is evident from the most casual acquain-
tance with early and medieval Christian iconography, liturgy, and
theology. For the traditional Christian, existence in space and time
derived its meaning and worth from some "otherworld" and "afterlife." In sharpest contrast, the beliefs and actions of men and women
of the modern world reflect an affirmation of the final intelligibility
and importance of our lives here and now, within nature and history.
This *secular* outlook suffuses all of modern life, even the thought and
behavior of people and institutions that officially condemn it.

There are many in this country who readily admit the secularization of "once-Christian" Europe but deny that of "Christian"
America. Our sustained church attendance, political prayer break-
fasts, outspoken Christian celebrities, and religious opinion polls are
cited as proof that America has not gone the secular ways of the Old

World. But such religious and political jingoism betrays a misunderstanding of American history and piety. In a recent study, Martin E. Marty has shown that the secular dissolution of otherworldly and authoritarian faith has taken very different forms in the three major centers of modern Christendom.[1] On the continent of Europe, the secularizing process took the form of an unrelenting attack on God and Church and a studied effort to replace them with humanistic ideals and institutions. England's historic turn to the mundane order was more a matter of simply ignoring God and the Church, leaving them to those declining few who preserve the old traditions for reasons of personal need or public decorum. But in the American culture, the inherited traditions were preserved by subtly isolating and segregating religion. Institutional religion thereby survived and even flourished by limiting itself to the personal, familial, and leisured sectors of life while surrendering the political, social, economic, and cultural dimensions of life to secular tutelage.

This territorial separation of religiosity and secularity worked well for more than a century. But in the last hundred years the private churchly culture has been bent increasingly toward sanctioning and serving the public secular culture. This subordination of personal faith to secular concerns is as prevalent in today's evangelical Christianity as it was in yesterday's social-gospel Christianity. In both cases, the Christian and the American ways of life are inseparably merged.[2] Thus, both the empty churches of Europe and the full churches of America are monuments to the pervasive secularization of life in the modern world.[3]

Seen in this light, the American experiment in accommodating Christian faith to modern secularity is not unlike past theological efforts to come to terms with modern science, which we reviewed in the opening chapter. This similarity is far from coincidental. For one thing, modern science is a prime cause and manifestation of the secularizing process. Theological responses to modern science are thus efforts to come to terms with a secularized understanding of the natural and human worlds. More important, the American and theological adaptations to a secular-scientific world shared at base a common strategy. In both instances, modern challenges to faith were met by *relocating* God and faith in some special place unsullied by scientific or secular encroachments. This underlying strategy led to seemingly opposite results, but both were equally ruinous to historic Christianity. As a theological strategy, the search for "unsecular" places eventually emptied faith of all cultural relevance. As a social strategy, the confinement of faith to "unsecular" places finally subordinated faith to cultural concerns. In each instance, the vision of a personal God active in history—creating, judging, and renewing a kingdom of justice and love—was lost. Faith became an empty echo of a past culture or a pious reflection of a present culture.

By the late fifties, a number of theologians had seen through this impasse of cultural irrelevance versus cultural compromise. They saw that the problem lay in the attempt to restrict faith and understanding to some unsecular data or domain, whether within or beyond the world. They saw that Christians must somehow find God *in* the secular without reducing God *to* the secular. These insights gave rise to a new type of theology—a "theology of secularity" that sees, beyond the threat of secularity, an opportunity within secularity itself for the recovery of a faith both authentically Christian and consistently modern.

THE SECULAR OUTLOOK

We have already caught a glimpse of the meaning of the secular outlook, but we need a fuller definition to understand the new secular theologies that began to appear in the early 1960s. The word "secular" has an ancient and changing lineage of meanings, but running through all of them is a fundamental stress on *this* world.[4] The Latin term *saeculum* meant "of this age" or "related to this world." As such, the word carried no special value connotations since it merely referred to the given world or the present generation. In the late medieval and early modern period, the word took on moral overtones when it was used to describe the process of transferring property from the Church to the state in settlement of the religious wars that shattered the Holy Roman Empire. Buildings and lands that had been set aside for "holy use" were spoken of as "secularized" when they were returned to ordinary ownership and use. Something of this same movement away from the Church and into the world was also implied in describing priests who left the priesthood as "becoming secularized."

In the nineteenth century, "secularism" came to denote a moral life-style based on human reason and devoted to humanitarian service. Some theologians thought this secular morality was compatible with Christianity's otherworldly faith, but others saw it as a rival to the moral demands of faith. The word "secular" took on decidedly negative connotations in the early twentieth century among theologians who saw the Church's uncritical adoption of cultural forms of thought and value as "a secularization." For them, any theological confusion of the categories of faith and culture was a lamentable compromise of the Gospel's integrity and the Christian's responsibility. Only recently has the secular move "from the Church to the world" been accepted as an irreversible historical process and acclaimed as a positive human good. Today the term "secularization" denotes an intellectual, social, and existential outlook free from all ecclesiastical controls and supernatural worldviews. Secular persons and secular societies define themselves quite apart from all "other" worlds and "priestly" mediators, finding within themselves life's principles of order and meaning.

As such, the secular outlook stands in marked contrast to the ways individuals and groups have understood and conducted themselves for millennia. From primitive times, people have oriented their thinking and managed their affairs "from above," so to speak. They have assumed that the world of time and space is surrounded by an eternal and transcendent world. Life in the time-space world is derived from, governed by, and fulfilled in the eternal-transcendent world. Furthermore, for this perspective, the connection between these separate worlds is established and maintained only through special means. Miraculous occurrences and religious authorities link the physical and the spiritual worlds. Consequently, in this traditional scheme of things, people have depended upon supernatural happenings and institutions to define reality, prescribe morality, and control society in this world while looking forward to the world to come for the final resolution of life's mystery, suffering, and meaning.

Against this thinking and living "from above," the secular outlook views the world and approaches life "from below." This loss of interest in otherworlds and afterlives as sources for understanding and resources for living has been making inroads in social and mental structures for centuries. But the secularizing process has dramatically accelerated in the twentieth century, and what was once the arrogant vision of an educated elite has become the common sense of the masses. The perspective of thinking and living "from above" has slowly but surely been squeezed out of the modern world by the rise of science, by the reach of technology, and by the power of revolution.

Modern science has taught people to explain things "from below." Appeals to otherworldly powers, metaphysical postulates, and miraculous interventions have become logically unnecessary as people have learned to explore and explain the natural world and human life without them. Using their own powers of observation and imagination, human beings have pulled more and more of the real world into an intelligible and functional explanation of the ways and whys of the universe. First the world around and then the world within have come under human investigation and naturalistic explanation. In the process, the boundaries "beyond which science cannot go" have continually receded. In the physical world, the conquests have been spectacular—motion, matter, energy, space, vitality. In the human world, the boundaries of thought, relationships, want, and guilt have been breached, and even the frontiers of life and death are being explored. Of course, the secular world is full of unanswered questions and residual mysteries. But, to the extent that these can ever be resolved, secular men and women need no help "from above" to explain their world.

Modern technology has equipped people for controlling things "from below." Human beings will always be dependent upon a natural environment, but they are less and less plagued by the limitations, discomforts, fickleness, and ravages of their environment. Mechanical technology has transformed life and society by harnessing energy and creating tools almost beyond imagination. Medical technology has made great strides in extending life's enjoyment, productivity, and longevity. Environmental technology is making dramatic breakthroughs in more efficient use of natural resources and in regulating natural processes. Of course, all these technological marvels have multiplied the world's risks and problems—accidents, warfare, pollution, and overpopulation to name a few. Even these liabilities of technology, however, are believed soluble by technological means yet to be developed and enacted. Secular men and women need no help "from above" to control their world.

Finally, modern revolution has enabled people to change things "from below." Persons will always live within a social order, but no longer do kings rule by divine right or enjoy amnesty from public redress. No longer must the oppressed endure injustice as a whim of Fate or a judgment of God. The modern era was ushered in as much by social and political revolution as by scientific discovery and technological advance. The masses have learned how to be victors rather than always victims of history and society. They have learned that organized power exercised in a variety of ways can bring about social, political, and economic changes. To be sure, the achievements of revolution are neither perfect nor permanent, and this lesson has profoundly altered the structures of society. Representative and pluralistic societies variously place final power in the hands of the people and build orderly revolution into the very fabric of political institutions. But, whatever the prevailing social philosophies and institutional embodiments, people no longer wait for otherworldly recompense for or delivery from indignity, suppression, and exploitation. Secular men and women need no help "from above" to change their world.

Obviously, this secular outlook proved radically incommensurate with the authoritarianism and supernaturalism of traditional, orthodox Christianity. Though less dramatically, secularism proved just as subversive to Liberalism and Neo-orthodoxy. These modern reinterpretations of the faith were eventually domesticated or desiccated by the very secular encroachments on Christian thought and life that they sought to avoid. Even before midcentury, a number of nominally neo-orthodox theologians were probing for ways beyond the impasse of the liberal fusion and neo-orthodox separation of faith and culture. They were convinced that Neo-orthodoxy had seen the problem rightly—liberal attempts to reserve special places in history or inwardness were doomed to fail because these places would be secularized as surely as Orthodoxy's nature miracles had been. But Neo-orthodoxy had failed to solve the problem. By separating the content and the grounds of faith from all secular experiences and evidences, Neo-orthodoxy emptied faith of all practical assurances and relevance.

Accordingly, these neo-orthodox "revisionists" sought new ways to relate Christian faith and secular experience in positive ways. The most influential and thoroughgoing programs were worked out by Paul Tillich and H. Richard Niebuhr. Both called for the faithful to discover and serve God in and through the secular. Both sensitively probed modern man's cultural and personal experience for dimensions of ultimacy (Tillich) or manifestations of faith (Niebuhr) that furnished concrete points of contact for understanding and enacting Christian faith. But these impressive correlations of faith and culture (and others dependent upon or similar to them) did not break completely with the theological strategy of the past. Even these formulations finally required a mystical validation of ultimate concern (Tillich) or a historical revelation of radical faith (Niebuhr). Though they moved Christian thought and life into the secular arena, their theologies still rested upon special, unsecular places for God and faith.

One theologian prior to the midpoint of the twentieth century did call for an uncompromising acceptance of the secularizing process. Dietrich Bonhoeffer, in the fragmentary writings that became known only after his death at the hands of the Nazis in 1945, claimed that only a "religionless Christianity" could survive in a "world come of age." By this he meant that the Church must put away all concepts of God as the solution to problems that arise when human understanding fails and human resources end. Reserving special places for God, such as moral consciousness, boundary situations, or religious depths, is a last-ditch effort to make room for God and is doomed to fail. The wave of the future for a world freed from adolescent dependence upon religious worldviews and authorities belongs to a faith freed from the symbolic and ritual garments of "religiousness." By religiousness Bonhoeffer meant something more radical than simply traditional otherworldly piety and inwardness. He meant a Christianity freed from the view of God as a miraculous problem-solver (whether in the natural or the human order), from the view of Christ as the miraculous fulfillment of a spiritual depth (whether a moral or a religious depth), and from the view of the Church as the miraculous custodian of a saving power (whether a revelatory or sacramental power).

Bonhoeffer did not live to produce a consistent theology, ecclesiology, and liturgy for such a religionless Christianity, though his posthumous writings are filled with tantalizing suggestions and tentative sketches.[5] Moving through all of his works are two different and perhaps contrary assessments of secularism. Sometimes the secularizing process is viewed as God's way of teaching people to live in and for the world without him. More typically, Bonhoeffer sees secularism compelling us to confront God where he has always been—in the midst of life rather than on the fringes, in the ordinary rather than in the extraordinary. As we shall see in the following discussion, both views of the secularizing process were developed within the new "theologies of secularity," which took Bonhoeffer's mandate to heart.

THEOLOGIES OF SECULARITY

Virtually all theological explorations of a secular mode of Christian life and thought begin by drawing a clear distinction between secularization and secularism. "Secularism" involves a commitment to a closed worldview. As such, secularism clothes itself in many guises: in such philosophies as materialism, positivism, existentialism, and empiricism; in such quasi-religious movements as nationalism, fascism, and communism; in such ideological causes as humanitarianism, egalitarianism, rationalism, and liberationism. Common to all these symbolic and social embodiments of secularism is a fundamental point of view that reduces reality to what is empirically given, naturally caused, and scientifically known.

"Secularization," in contrast to utter secularism, remains open to the discovery of fundamental dimensions, structures, or processes of transcendence *within* the secular. To be sure, such transcendent aspects are not separable from the secular, but neither are they identical with it. They lie beyond the physicalistic conceptions of reality, mechanistic conceptions of causality, and positivistic conceptions of knowledge that are employed in the sciences and enshrined in secularism. Secularization affirms that the empirically given and scientifically known world is the real world, but asserts that it is not *all* of the world that is real. This notion of "something more" than the secular opens up new possibilities for understanding God's relation to the world and humankind's relation to God. Thus, while secularism, as a closed ideology, is incompatible with any theistic form of Christian faith, secularization, as defined here, imposes no such categorical strictures on theological reflection.

Whether or not experiences of such "inner-worldly" transcendence do indeed provide a new location and language for faith cannot be determined apart from theological explorations of the experiences. This means a return to experiential starting-points for theological understanding, to a reflection upon and clarification of just those putative experiences of transcendence. Such experience-based thinking may be guided by the trustworthy witnesses to faith from the past, especially the normative witnesses of Scripture and creed. But these witnesses can only be instructive if they can be translated into the distinctive language and needs of our time. Thus, theological explorations of the "religious" dimensions and depths of secular experience must be rendered in language and concepts appropriate to secular sensibilities. Among such efforts to speak the Gospel to the world as it is today, the secular theologies of John A. T. Robinson, Harvey G. Cox, and Paul M. van Buren are clearly the most important. Not only have they dominated the disussion of secular theology, but also they exhibit the range of approaches within this type of theology.

Christianity as Worldly Holiness—John A. T. Robinson
In a real sense, John A. T. Robinson must be credited with setting off the explosive chain reaction of new theologies that continue to fill the horizons today. His *Honest to God* helped alter the context and content of contemporary theology in ways that he neither foresaw nor approves. That impact was certainly not due to the originality of his thought since *Honest to God* is basically a synthesis of certain key ideas from the theologies of Tillich, Bultmann, and Bonhoeffer.[6] The synthesis is not without its own merit and originality because it does

create a new theological whole of the ideas of God as "depth dimension" and faith as "this-worldly love." The revolutionary impact of
this tract, however, is due more to the fact that it charts an Anglican
bishop's struggle toward a more adequate understanding of faith and
that it has been read by tens of thousands of people. Robinson's secular updating of theology actually contained nothing very surprising to
theologians, but it took the believing and unbelieving public by
storm. That storm not only let the public in on theology, it brought
the public *into* theology in the sense that theologians began to pay
more attention to the everyday experiences of common people rather
than to depend merely on philosophical definitions of human nature.
Without doubt, today's theological populism and pluralism owe much
to theology's having gone public in the "Honest to God Debate."[7]

Robinson gives a secular cast to what remains an essentially neo-
orthodox theology by stressing its divergence from traditional Orthodoxy and by suggesting its relevance to everyday experience. The
first concern of this theological reformation is to show that the reality
of God is separable from the "two-story" worldview within which
both biblical and orthodox Christianity were expressed. Adumbrated
in *Honest to God* and developed more fully in *Explorations into God*
and *The Human Face of God*,[8] the essence of Christian faith,
Robinson argues, is the affirmation that "the personal" is the ultimate
matrix and meaning of human life and world order. Traditional Christianity expressed this central conviction by picturing God as the
world's personal Creator, Judge, and Redeemer. Given the mythological and prescientific thought patterns of earlier times, the image of
God as a Super-Person was an appropriate way to communicate the
truth of faith. But speaking of God as a person overseeing and sometimes overriding the world process has been rendered irrelevant and
untenable for increasing numbers of modern Christians.[9] Honesty to
the modern world and fidelity to historic Christianity require a new
conception of God, a new way of expressing the ultimate reality of
"the personal" at the heart of things. Fortunately, that way is readily
available in the secularist's depth experiences of love and scientific
terminology of systems.

Though acknowledging that the idea of God as a supernatural person has died for secular men and women, Robinson insists that the
reality of personal love as a lived experience remains very much
alive.[10] This depth experience of love *is* the experience of God—the
same for us as for our fathers and mothers. What we need is a new
language about God to understand and describe this experience properly.[11] The language of traditional theism will not do since theism

finally separates God and the world. Nor will the language of classical pantheism do since pantheism ultimately equates God and the
world. These perennial ways of speaking about God's reality and relation to the world fail because the experience of God as Personal
Love is neither separable from nor identical with the love we experience in company with others and with nature. What is required is a
panentheistic conception of God that can simultaneously relate and
distinguish God and the world.[12] Robinson finds such dynamic and
organic terminology in the field theories of the natural and life sciences. God is the "interpersonal field," at once in and beyond all
things and persons, that unifies and energizes all things within a living Whole. Because that energy and unity has the character of personal love rather than impersonal mechanism, God's presence and
power are most clearly manifest in experiences of human community.
Thus, belief in God is the conviction that the "being of things deep
down *is* Love" and that all experiences of love are, at depth, encounters with God.

The other burden of Robinson's theological reformation is to trace
out the ripple effects of this new panentheistic conception of God.
Christologically, the emphasis on Christ as the "Son of God" shifts to
Jesus as "the man who lived God" by being " the man for others."[13]
As such, Jesus perfectly embodied and perennially discloses Transcendent Love in our midst. Indeed, the word of God through the
man Jesus reveals that the life of love is life in God.

Ecclesiologically, sacred practices are redirected to the building
up of communities of interpersonal love.[14] Neither worship nor
prayer is an opportunity to withdraw from the world "to be with
God." Rather, both are occasions to respond to "the beyond in our
midst." Liturgy must be put to the service of love—to seeking out the
lonely in accepting love, to helping out the needy with enabling love.
The Church is the community that makes "the human face of God"
manifest in the midst of life's work and play, triumphs and failures,
joys and sorrows.

Ethically, the emphasis shifts from divine laws to situational decisions.[15] Biblical mandates and moral principles are not timeless directives that must be obeyed in every concrete situation. Rather, they
are vivid illustrations of the kind of demands Unconditional Love
makes in concrete situations. But, because love is always relational
and practical, the faithful must determine anew in each moment of
decision what such love permits and what it requires. An ethics of
love can only be a "situational ethics." Thus Robinson recasts all the
doctrines and disciplines of faith in a secular mold of "worldly holi-

ness" that discovers, reveres, and serves God as human love's ultimate ground and goal.

Christianity as Political Discipleship—Harvey G. Cox

A very different approach to a secularized Christianity is offered by Harvey Cox though there are interesting parallels between him and Robinson. Both wrote best sellers in the early sixties that still enjoy multiple reprintings and translations. *The Secular City*, like *Honest to God*, made a profound impact on the style and substance of all subsequent theological endeavor.[16] Though both are academics by training and profession, they are churchmen who write with a pastoral concern and personal urgency. Their books are tracts for the times rather than systems for the ages. Finally, their secular theologies are both heavily indebted to Bonhoeffer. Each sketches out a "religionless Christianity" for "a world come of age." But how different those secular theologies! Cox calls Christians into the urban and secular society from which Robinson seems to withdraw with his stress on intimate and interpersonal love. Indeed, Cox insists that the faithful must fully inhabit the "secular city."[17]

To be sure, life in "technopolis"—shaped as it is by anonymity and mobility, devoted as it is to pragmatic and profane ends—calls for a new kind of Christianity.[18] But this new way of speaking and doing the truth can prove quite compatible with biblical religion because secularization is, in large measure, a latterday consequence of the biblical faith.[19] Cox spells out this surprising claim in terms of the impact of three pivotal biblical "events" on the secularization of Western culture.

The biblical account of creation prepared the way for secularization by "disenchanting" nature. The belief that God created the heavens and the earth *ex nihilo* dispelled all magical and mystical views of natural things (sky, stars, mountains) and processes (generation, birth, growth, death). Henceforth, the world could be treated as a finite thing rather than as a sacred presence. Such disenchantment was a necessary precondition for the emergence of science and urbanization since it allowed for an instrumental approach to nature and society.

Similarly, the biblical event of the Exodus led to the "desacralization" of politics. This people's revolt against a harsh and repressive rule pioneered the founding of society on revolution rather than on birthright. This desacralization set in motion a process that eventually delivered political life from its primitive identification with nature (static order, kinship systems) and immersed it in the dynamics of history (social process, public consent). Political arrangements and alliances became social contracts and compromises worked out by human beings for human beings rather than shadow images of a "Heavenly City" or an "Inscrutable Power."

Finally, the biblical covenant at Sinai prepared the way for the "deconsecration" of values. The heart of the Law is the prohibition of idolatry. The prohibition denies finality to all earthly goods and goals since God alone is absolute. The relativizing of values that has accompanied the process of secularization is but the historical and philosophical complement of biblical iconoclasm. In other words, these central demystifying strands of the secularizing process can be traced back to their beginnings in biblical religion. Ancient faith and modern secularity alike give humankind the freedom *and* responsibility for tending nature's garden, for fashioning political systems, and for forging human values. Thus, rather than bewail or oppose secularization, Christians are called to celebrate its liberties and undergo its disciplines by learning to speak of God in a secular fashion.

Cox is under no illusion about the difficulties of this task. Fashioning a secular theology is in part a sociological problem.[20] All words have meaning according to how they are used in their sociocultural setting. Words inevitably lose their meaning when that setting changes unless they are redefined to fit the new situation. This transformation usually happens gradually and imperceptibly unless changes in setting are abrupt or ignored. Even in new settings, efforts at redefinition become extremely difficult because stereotyped images of past meaning and use linger.

The word "God" is no exception to this process. It has undergone profound changes of meaning as is evidenced by the shift from primitive, mythological images of God as Personal Being to medieval, metaphysical conceptions of God as Unifying Principle. Unfortunately, all these earlier ways of speaking about God still lie buried in the minds of modern Christians like the fossils that they are. Because these old ideas are clearly out of place and out of touch with the contemporary sociocultural scene, "God" has been reduced to an escapist magical being or an irrelevant explanatory system. Moreover, even the theologians and preachers who challenge these distorted understandings of the word "God" are misunderstood, because they are still perceived in terms of the cultural roles and public pronouncements of past theologians and preachers. Thus, Cox counsels, the first move toward redefining God is altering the social context in which speaking of God occurs. Those who speak of God must refuse to play out the old roles of "medicine man" and "answer man" which would trivialize whatever they say. Only be relocating speech and speaker in the secular world can the word "God" take on meaning for the secular world.

This means for Cox that speaking of God today becomes primarily a political issue.[21] If theology is to make any sense, it must leave behind metaphysical worldviews and mythological modes. It must plunge into the political life and language of urban-secular persons. The reason for this imperative is that political symbols and institutions do for modern secular society what mythology and metaphysics once did for primitive and medieval societies: They define the horizons of human unity and meaning, of human disorder and despair. If Christian faith cannot address life-and-death political issues in a political mode, then "God" is dead to the real world in which modern people live.

Of course, the word "political" in this context is understood in a far broader way than the legislative or judicial process of a given society. In fact, it carries a decidedly normative connotation. "Politics" includes all that is involved in making and keeping human life *human* in the world. Thus, Cox declares, we speak of God politically when we locate God within the web of interhuman reciprocity that gives and sustains all human life. More importantly, we speak of God in a political way when we place ourselves where the restoring, reconciling activity of God is going on, where the proper relationship between people is appearing or trying to appear. Speaking of God politically is more than pledging "one nation under God"—it is creating one nation under God "with liberty and justice for all." Giving the word "God" a secular meaning will come about only through demonstrating the relevance and necessity of God in political speech *and* political action.

Even for a "theology of social change," however, speaking of God comes down to a theological question.[22] How can he bear witness to a Political Power in history beyond all the political powers of history when that "Politician-God" remains utterly hidden? Cox admits that the reality of the biblical God cannot be conclusively established over against reductive or sceptical accounts of religious belief. The biblical God is no more available for human certitude than for human manipulation. The difference between the serious believer and the equally serious unbeliever is not a matter of discrete data. Both encounter the same reality, but they interpret and, hence, respond to that reality in radically different ways. In fact, both encounter in the political system that which lies beyond the social conventions, legal mandates, and institutional structures of human making. The Christian names that "something not ourselves" God. By naming that which transcends us in the political process God, rather than Fate or Drive or Energy, the Christian responds to a *personal* integrity, dependability, receptivity at the heart of human life and historical events. Herein lies the demonstrable difference between the believer and the nonbeliever: Different names for reality evoke different responses to reality.

Cox toys with two metaphors for explaining how God meets us in the world. The "work team" image suggests that God is experienced in a relationship of "alongsideness."[23] God neither needs nor compels individuals to focus interest and attention on himself. He wants them to concentrate their concern and energy on the shared task of building up a human community without walls and woes. By contrast, the image of God as the "coming future" suggests a temporal, rather than a spatial, mode for distinguishing God's presence in human history.[24] Speaking of God as the one who lures and leads selves and nations into the future abolishes once and for all the two-story dualism, the static absolutism, the otherworldly escapism, and the human belittlement so typical of traditional theism by dynamically relating-while-distinguishing God and history. But, whether "alongside" as partner or "ahead" as future, God remains hidden in the dynamic processes and wounding limits of personal and social existence.

Moreover, whatever metaphors are used (new or old, temporal or spatial), speaking about God takes on life and power only through the efforts of a people who locate and participate in God's action in the world. The Church's task, says Cox, like the ministry of Jesus which it continues, is threefold—*kerygma* (proclamation), *diakonia* (reconciliation), and *koinonia* (demonstration).[25] The people of God must bear witness to the coming of a new era, already begun but not yet complete, in which the liberating rule of God will set the captives free. And the Church must broadcast this "seizure of power" in deeds as well as words. The Church has the task not only of exhibiting human wholeness in its own communal life but of entering into every struggle for human wholeness in the world at large. As such, the Church truly serves as "God's *avante-garde*"—embodying the powers of life and exorcizing the forces of death in the City of Man which is the Kingdom of God.[26]

Christianity as Historical Perspective—Paul M. van Buren

In a series of essays, Paul van Buren explores the secularization of Christian language and life in ways that differ remarkably from both Robinson and Cox. His theological reflections have an acknowledged experimental air about them precisely because today there are no clear understandings of what Christianity and secularity mean considered separately, much less how they are and can be related to one another. Understand and relate them we must, however, if we wish to be persons of historic faith and contemporary sensibilities. We do, for better or worse, live in a world deeply interested in questions of human life on this side of any supernatural or metaphysical "beyond." If we want to be Christians in our world, we must learn to "secularize" Christianity and "Christianize" secularity. Thus, van Buren undertakes his theological explorations with the hope that the meaning of both the Gospel and secularism will become clearer when they are conjoined.

More exactly, van Buren explores the interface between two twentieth-century responses to secularism—neo-orthodox theology and linguistic philosophy.[27] Though these responses developed independently and seem inimical to one another, they share certain common features which need only to be explicated further to yield a secular understanding of Christian faith that is at once theologically proper and philosophically credible. Van Buren's "rearrangement" of biblical theology and analytic philosophy came in an enormously controversial book, *The Secular Meaning of the Gospel*. Here he attempts what Harvey Cox had only lightly suggested—to declare a moratorium on using the word "God" because of widespread confusion over its proper meaning. In later theological explorations, culminating in the publication of *The Edges of Language*, van Buren lifts this moratorium.[28] But, as we shall see, he never takes sides on the question of whether or not "God exists" since he believes this question misunderstands the biblical faith as deeply as it mystifies the modern mind.[29]

In *The Secular Meaning of the Gospel*, van Buren sets out to interpret Christianity as a this-worldly empirical faith and to show that this secularized interpretation is both philosophically necessary and biblically correct. His argument takes two general forms. Negatively, all talk about God, much less dependence upon God, is ruled out from the start.[30] Modern-day "empirical attitudes," which for van Buren are given normative expression in the rigorous standards of Linguistic Analysis, limit meaningful statements to scientific assertions about things or to historical and ethical assertions about persons. Thus, people who suppose that the word "God" refers to some supernatural being or metaphysical structure are simply mistaken. More accurately, such descriptive language about God is literal *nonsense*, since only those claims that are in principle verifiable by empirical data have to do with some objective and knowable state of affairs. Because there are no empirical data that count conclusively for or against claims about God, statements that seem to attribute reality and activity to a divine entity are literally meaningless.

Van Buren, of course, admits that biblical and theological language is replete with such statements and that such language had meaning in the past. But that meaning had nothing to do with a transcendental being or structure, person or process. These literal-sounding claims were in fact oblique or poetic ways of expressing one's total commitment to a total "perspective" on human life.[31] Unfortunately, this proper use and meaning of the word "God" has again and again been lost. The concrete imagery of biblical language and the descriptive form of theological statements have repeatedly misled Christians and non-Christians alike into thinking that talk about God is about something "out there" rather than about ourselves. Consequently, since "God-talk" (and all circumlocutions such as "Transcendence," "Being-Itself," "Ultimate reality," and the like) is both literally meaningless and religiously misleading, van Buren counsels that it be avoided entirely in theological construction.

The positive side of van Buren's secularized Gospel is that the Christian faith is a distinctive expression of a "historical perspective"—a shared way of life modeled on the man Jesus.[32] Echoing his Barthian background, van Buren finds Christology at the center of the biblical Gospel and classical theology.[33] But, unlike Barth, he explicates the logic and intention of Christology strictly in terms of human attitudes, commitments, and relationships. Jesus is the man whose freedom from anxiety and freedom for love called forth a community of women and men devoted to living and sharing that freedom with others. Stories about the freedom of Jesus still evoke that same kind of response and devotion today. In the past, these stories were couched in theistic language because no other way of conveying Jesus' centrality for faith was available. But we need no longer speak of his life and work in divine terms to understand and communicate his importance today. Accordingly, van Buren briefly sketches how all the major doctrines (christological, soteriological, and ecclesiological) and practices (preaching, sacraments, and prayer) of Christian faith can be reinterpreted in terms of this view of the meaning and mission of Jesus of Nazareth.[34] He concludes that the secular meaning and the biblical meaning of the Gospel are one and the same, though they are expressed in very different languages.

Partly in response to the storm of criticism—both philosophical and theological—that this book loosed, van Buren continued his explorations of how "a Christian who is himself a secular man may understand the Gospel in a secular way." The pivotal themes of *The Secular Meaning of the Gospel* remain central: the important shifts in human sensibility in our cultural context, the unnecessary alienation of many educated Christians from their religious heritage, the analysis of the Christian faith as a "historical perspective" covering the totality of life, the history of Jesus as showing and giving the way for all people to be in the world, and even the rejection of any objective reference for the word "God." But these commitments were refined and restated in subsequent writings by virtue of a clearer grasp of the many things human beings do with language. Most significantly, van Buren's new appreciation of the versatility of language led him to place the experience of wonder at the heart of religion and to reinstate the word "God" as the linguistic expression of those experiences of wonder.[35]

This reconstituted understanding of Christian faith comes to clearest expression in *The Edges of Language*. Van Buren begins this linguistic analysis of the religion of "educated Christians" by arguing that the debate between theists and atheists does not exhaust the options open to contemporary Christians. All parties to this debate have uncritically accepted a widespread view of language, that is, the idea that words name or describe things or persons. It makes no difference whether the language of reference in theology is construed literally or analogically. If the model of factual God-talk is assumed, van Buren sees no possible escape from atheism for modern men and women—whether the "hard" atheism of rejecting outright all such God-talk, or the "soft" atheism of reducing all God-talk to a moral way of life. But this whole quarrel between factual theism and hard or soft atheism can be circumvented (not ignored but literally bypassed) by adopting a more adequate view of language and its workings.[36]

Van Buren envisions language as a platform with a center field and with edges.[37] Language at the center is governed by clear rules, while speaking at the edges extends the various rules of unambiguous usage right up to the point of breaking them, of lapsing into nonsense or silence. While these conventional rules can be amended and these edges extended through innovative usage and by social consensus, there can be no going *beyond* language in thought, action, or feeling. Language is a necessary condition (and inevitable conditioner) of all human experience. Language at the center gives form to conventional, predictable, and efficient behavior. Center field linguistic behavior includes not only empirical assertions, scientific generalizations, and logical operations but also moral reasoning, historical judgments, and political directives. By contrast, the edge-use language of jokes, poetry, paradox, and religion are occasions for those imprudent, unpredictable, and visionary human experiences of humor, love, beauty, and wonder. In short, literal language (center field usage) and figurative language (edge usage) give form to radically different ways of being in the world.

Religion, according to van Buren, is distinguished from other linguistic activities at the edge by intense concern and passionate wonder over some aspect of our linguistic existence.[38] All religions share this feature of linguistic behavior, although they differ from one another over which aspect of language is stretched to the limits—whether talk about the self, or society, or history, or nature. Thus, "God" is not the object or ground of religious experience but a linguistic way of expressing profound awe and commitment toward some domain of human experience. "God" is that word which marks the outer edge of human speaking and living.[39]

What then of Christian religion? Van Buren acknowledges that Christianity has come in many different forms, but he regards history as the chief area of religious concern for biblical religion and contemporary Christianity.[40] To be a Christian means to stretch the solid, rule-governed speaking about the history of one man and one people out to the edges. To call this "God's history" is a linguistic way of holding this history in awe and devotion. The Christian religion is that linguistic behavior which "arises from the urge to say the utmost concerning the past and future of Jesus of Nazareth, of his people Israel, and then of others, including the speaker, who consider themselves associated with that people." Living this history religiously binds all human times and places into a single story of the struggle of faithfulness, love, justice, and mercy against betrayal, self-love, injustice, and vengeance.

Van Buren concludes by briefly relating his analysis to those linguistic approaches that reduce religion to a moral or quasi-metaphysical point of view.[41] Christian religion is connected with morality, but morality inspired by wonder shatters the conventional behavior of "center field morality." Christian religion does involve a way of seeing history's meaning and context, but this seeing does not involve making cognitive claims or developing comprehensive systems on the nature of all things. In short, though intimately related to both, the Christian religion is no more metaphysics than it is morality. Christian religion is life on the frontiers of language where wonder, passion, and commitment shape historical behavior and beliefs.

SECULAR THEOLOGIES IN QUESTION

Here then are three very different expressions of a secularized Christianity. All share the conviction that the secular dismantling of traditional Christianity's otherworldly and authoritarian outlook need not be ruinous to Christianity itself. Indeed, Robinson, Cox, and van Buren variously argue that this challenge actually prepares the way for a full recovery of the essentials of biblical faith in our time. But exactly what these essentials of belief and behavior are finds no common resolution in their secularized versions of the Gospel. The overall contrast among Robinson's intimate and interpersonal "holiness," Cox's aggressive and prophetic "discipleship," and van Buren's measured and reserved "perspective" mirrors deep divisions about the meaning of both secularity and Christianity. Small wonder that they offer no consensus theology of secularity.

What do modern-day theologians and lay persons make of these secular theologies? This study cannot include a critical rehearsal of the distinctive insights and oversights of individual theologians. But something of the collective strengths and weaknesses of each theological type must be noted to help us understand the proliferation of theological types over the last quarter century and assess their impact on the future theory and practice of religion.

Considered broadly, there can be no doubt that secular theologies like those of Robinson and Cox give Neo-orthodoxy's "hidden God" a new lease on life for many contemporary Christians.[42] This reprieve, however, is scarcely due to their reformulations of the doctrine of God, which remain as experientially nebulous and philosophically vulnerable as their neo-orthodox prototypes. The real power of these theologies lies in their applications of the biblical faith to secular life. By defining the core of faith as "interpersonal love" or "social action," Christian symbols are joined to vital human relationships and concerns. Interpreting the experienced ultimacy that naturally accompanies these vital interests as experiences of God gives instant relevance to the word "God." Perhaps equally important to the attractiveness of these theologies is their explicit attention to liturgy and ethics. Their humanized liturgy and contextualized ethics relieve the troubled minds of those Christians for whom the traditional forms of devotion and duty have become meaningless. In short, Robinson and Cox exemplify a kind of secular theology that offers strong support for those whose biblical faith is still essentially intact. By lending religious legitimacy to certain

preoccupations of secular life and by giving the disciplines and doctrines of faith a secular form, they give the faithful a renewed sense
of vitality and integrity. But they do not speak to the deeper
problems of existential doubt and religious understanding outlined
in the first chapter.

The merit of secular theologies like van Buren's is that they seek
to address these deeper challenges to faith.[43] They seek to articulate
the meaning of the Gospel within the operative assumptions of secular thought. For these secularizers of Christianity, the "rhetoric of relevance" of a Robinson or a Cox falls on deaf ears. What is needed
today is not a way from the Church into the secular world but a way
from the secular world back into the Church. Modern alienation from
the biblical heritage as well as from the traditional practices of Christianity must somehow be overcome for faith to be authentically Christian and unflinchingly secular.

Given the challenge of unbelief on top of irrelevance, the typical
christological focus of these more radical versions of secular theology seems inevitable. The historical and symbolic importance of
Jesus furnishes a common denominator for transposing the biblical
tradition into the historically relative and linguistically limited
structures of modern consciousness. Though narrow, those structures still permit personal and communal experiences of wonder
and obligation that are historically evoked and humanly exemplified. Thus, "Jesus is Lord" can be confessed by secular man as
surely as by biblical man, though that confession will necessarily be
voiced in different words and deeds. Yet just this christological focus, which is so central to these forms of secular faith, proves un-
convincing and irrelevant to many people today. Why this man?
Whence his power? Such questions are as puzzling to truly secular
sensibilities as the old myths about a divine being and a supernatural redemption. A christological faith requires either more (Jesus
somehow discloses transcendent structures of reality) or less (Jesus
is one among many human heroes available for personal emulation).
As they stand, these secular christologies are neither convincingly
secular nor Christian.

This admixture of strengths and weaknesses has sent other theologians, who also broadly affirm both secular and Christian sensibilities, in search of a better way of conjoining them. Something more is
required to revive a flagging faith than labeling secular experiences
of self-transcendence as encounters with God or as embodiments of
Jesus. Such theological claims are vulnerable to the challenge that
they only cast a pious glow on personal love, social passion, radical

freedom, and the like. Worse yet, they can be charged with lending ideological sanction to life-styles and social orders that are inherently restrictive and repressive. Whether it is God or Jesus that is molded in the image of middle-class, liberal, pragmatic sensibilities matters less than that either "object" of faith lacks religious depth and cultural breadth. Troubled by these weaknesses in the secular theologies, a number of theologians have sought a deeper reading of the Christian past and the secular present.

Deeper soundings of the secular spirit of modernity have concentrated largely on two profound shifts in attitude that have come out of the collapse of otherworldly and authoritarian systems of belief and behavior—the celebration of *change* and the affirmation of *autonomy*. Throughout most of human history, people have feared change and yearned for permanence. God has been traditionally conceived of as unchanging and unchangeable. Values have been thought to be absolute and eternal. Correspondingly, the finite and the temporal have been downgraded as unstable and imperfect. But a growing sense and understanding of burgeoning life, historical development, and creative variation have brought a new attitude toward flexibility and innovation.

Similarly, throughout the past our Western religious traditions have denounced autonomy as the primal sin. Claims by individuals to decide their own existence, fashion their own values, or create their own meaning were seen as a denial of divine sovereignty and ecclesiastical authority. But the dismantling of hierarchical worldviews, religious institutions, and social systems has conveyed an inalienable sense of freedom to modern men and women. In fact, the secular outlook goes far deeper than merely affirming this life's meaning and this world's worth. It embraces variableness and creativity as fundamental characteristics of all thought and life.

Recent theological explorations of these modern preoccupations with change and autonomy have generated at least two more distinctive types of contemporary theology: theologies of process and theologies of liberation. While both types are necessarily interested in questions of development and freedom, their energies are heavily invested in one or the other of these. Process theologians are, by and large, preoccupied with questions of development. They search out the ways in which our new sense of change inspires a process vision of God that is at once compatible with scientific, philosophical, and biblical understanding. By contrast, liberation theologians are more directly concerned with matters of freedom. Capitalizing on the affirmation of autonomy, they direct their theological energies toward an actual revolution of personal identities, social structures, and historical processes. Both of these new types of theology, however, seek firmer experiential grounds for faith than those offered by the theologies of secularity. How they proceed and how well they succeed will be our concern in the next two chapters.

3
Process as Critique and Construct

John Cobb, Teilhard de Chardin, Thomas Altizer

Ours is a world that values new things. Alvin Toffler, in his cele-brated study of modern cultural change entitled *Future Shock*, shows how the taste for the new time and place, the new product and experience, the new opportunity and relationship is transform-ing our lives.[1] He contends that the accelerated thrust of change within our "super-urbanized" and "super-industrialized" world has created a "throw-away society" of "new nomads." The law gov-erning both human-thing and human-person relationships in this society is conspicuous and compulsive consumption. Not only are our foodstuffs "pre-processed," our manufactured products "planned-obsolescent," and our living spaces "modularized," but also our communications systems have become "kinetic," our social institutions "ad-hocratic," and our family structures "atomistic." We are a populace devoted to ever-increasing consumption, ever-multiplying distractions, and ever-accelerating mobility. Indeed, Toffler warns that our love of novelty has gone so far and so fast that our psychic and social capacities for change are being overloaded and the future is breaking in on us with devastating effects. Toffler's description of this "future shock," like most apocalyptic visions, is somewhat overdrawn. But his study does reveal how deeply committed to change the modern world has become and how remarkably life and thought are changing as a consequence.

This affirmation and internalization of change have put severe strains on our Christian heritage, which has long centered in an unchanging and absolute Deity, a unique and final Incarnation, and an infallible and authoritative Scripture. This strain is especially obvious in those militant orthodoxies that barricade a defined core of belief and practice against all changes, but it can also be seen in less conservative theologies such as Liberalism and Neo-orthodoxy. These latter theologies did, of course, introduce dynamic elements into the Christian faith with their stress on history over nature as the context of humankind's relation to God. But, for all of their stress on the historical revelation and reality of God, absolutistic images of Jesus and God prevail. In these theologies, Jesus is not fully historical since he remains a unique event in human history. He is made absolutely normative for all of history. Though God is "personalized" in liberal and neo-orthodox thought, he is not fully personal because he is in no way constituted by his relations with the world. He finally remains absolutely untouched by the world. In short, the reigning theologies of the modern era have systematically excluded the revelation and reality of God from all real change.

As we have seen, however, such claims for the absolute finality of Christ and the absolute transcendence of God are at odds with the cognitive and moral standards of the modern mind. Indeed, notions of a timeless Christ and a changeless God have compelled many modern individuals to surrender all belief in the reality and revelation of God. Nevertheless, there are contemporary theologians who accept the modern critique of all religious absolutes, but who find in the very idea of change a constructive principle for a new theism. They variously insist that a changing God who really risks his life and shares his power in the world process can come alive to faith once more. Indeed, their conviction has given rise to a whole new type of contemporary theology—a theology that finds in the root metaphor of process not only a powerful critique of all absolutistic conceptions of the Christian faith, but a foundational construct for a new theism at once thoroughly modern and essentially biblical.

THE PROCESS TRADITION

The new "process theologies" are part of a wider breakdown of the static sensibilities that have dominated Western culture since early Greek thinkers followed Parmenides rather than Heraclitus in affirming the primacy of being over becoming. As noted earlier, Western thinkers have for the most part valued fixed permanence over dynamic process. Of course, they have been aware of the transience of life, the flux of history, and the variations among cultures, but such changes have not been accorded the weight of ideality or reality. Change as *growth* was regarded as the accidental alteration of an immutable and underlying essence; change as *decline* was seen as the inevitable dissolution of an imperfect and ephemeral existence. In neither case did change really belong to the world of stable reality and ideal perfection. Gradually and inexorably, however, this rejection of change has been dissolved by modern discoveries of a universe in process and human interaction with it.

This dramatic shift in sensibilities is clearly visible in scientific thinking since Darwin and Einstein. Darwin's theory of evolution replaced the static world of fixed species with a dynamic world of evolving life forms, bringing temporal novelty into the heart of the life sciences. Einstein's theory of relativity revolutionized the working models of the "harder" sciences of physics and chemistry. The classical physical sciences had long been dominated by Newton's vision of the world as a machine with discrete parts interacting according to mechanistic laws. But quantum mechanics and field theory reconceived the subatomic world, which underlies the world of seemingly fixed and separate objects, as a flux of energy in a network of relations. This development brought temporal relationships into the heart of the physical sciences. So swift and sure were the Darwinian and Einsteinian revolutions in their own fields that their operative assumptions soon spread, and interaction, temporality, and novelty became regulative categories in all the sciences.

The triumph of process categories in scientific reflection is paralleled by the similar revolution in the way life is experienced in the twentieth century.[2] One characteristic of contemporary life is a deep sense of the contingency of all things. We know ourselves to live in an interdependent world in which each event must be seen as part of an endless flow of preceding causes and succeeding consequences. We have learned enough about these interrelations through patient searching to trace many of their recurrent features. This enables us to predict and to control the flow of events with a fair degree of success. Nevertheless, our humanly ordered and ordering actions take place in an ever-expanding matrix whose principles and trajectories of interaction are by no means fully understood. Our acceptance of this interdependent and mysterious matrix marks a profound shift from the way contingency was understood in the past to the way it is experienced by women and men today. Classical thinkers saw all experiences of contingency pointing beyond themselves to a noncontingent reality on which all things contingent depend. For them, contingency drove the finite mind beyond the arbitrary givenness of the natural world to a realm of necessary being, beyond the inherent limits of sequential reasoning to a realm of sufficient explanation. By contrast, the modern sense of contingency denies both the necessity and possibility of just such a move to an "other" world. There is no world of "necessary being" and "sufficient reason" beyond the one world that we human beings sense and shape in our limited ways.

A second feature of contemporary existence is our sense of the transience of all things. We live in a world of becoming where things, events, societies, and especially persons come to be and pass away. The consecutive flow of all things from the past into the future makes development and death the fundamental rhythm of all processes. Here again we see a sharp difference between modern and earlier views of transience. Earlier theological, philosophical, and even scientific traditions never considered attributing temporal process to reality *as a whole*. Just as in the past the contingency of all things pointed beyond themselves to a realm of necessity, so the transience of all things implied an eternal being or order on which all things in passage depend. For that eternal ground, growth and change were as impossible as perishing and death. In striking contrast, human beings now see time as a fundamental structure of the whole as well as of the parts of that whole. All is becoming, all is changing. This modern emphasis on passage out of the past into the future refocuses attention on developmental processes *in time* rather than upon recurrent cycles *of eternity*. Furthermore, the time-bound character of all processes redraws the boundaries of human hope and fear. The relevant environment for human life is now seen to be the temporal contexts of nature and history.

The third shift in contemporary existence, reflecting a process view, is the relativity of all things. A sense of relativity follows from the experienced contingency and transience of all things. The interdependence of all things means that each entity, whether object or organism, is a nexus of relations within a given context. Given the transience of all such links, each context is itself a constellation of interactions and transactions in process. Thus, no entity, experience, or achievement can be absolute. Everything is conditioned by its distinctive environment, and everything is relative to that particular environment. The implications of this temporal and situational dependence are especially telling for all modern understanding of cultural achievements and belief systems. Because these are seen as relative to a particular context, they embody no permanent form or universal authority. The art, literature, philosophy, religion, and even science of a given culture can make no claim to finality or universality. Needless to say, the acknowledgment of cultural relativism represents a decisive break with the classical past where certain occurrences, traditions, and institutions were accorded a timeless relevance and universal authority. Such absolutism has given way to a pluralism of social arrangements and worldviews.

What room is there for faith in God in this kind of changing universe? Granted that human beings have gained some sense of their own powers of change and growth in this scheme of things. How can the acceptance of life's contingency, transience, and relativity lead to anything other than rebellion or despair about the human situation? Many people have drawn such conclusions. Antimetaphysical philosophies and death-of-God theologies summon us to carve out human meaning and order within a universe ultimately devoid of purposeful process and destiny. Mystical and evangelical religions counsel withdrawal from a world corrupted by error and burdened with death. Such declarations of tragic humanism, on the one hand, and revivals of escapist religion, on the other, seem to have dominated this century's thoughts about living in a changing world. Against these calls for "heroic rebellion" or "world negation," however, some thinkers have placed the world's flux into a larger context of the world's "creative becoming." For them, the world exhibits organic unity, purposive striving, and emergent novelty. As we shall see, their metaphysical visions of a universal, creative becoming have blazed the way for the new theologies of process.

Process categories began finding their way into metaphysical reflection at least two centuries ago.[3] Idealistic and romantic thinkers alike brought the Absolute out of its unchangeable and unchallengeable heaven, joining it to all finite reality and immediate experience. The Absolute was thereby reconceived as the Whole, containing and in a sense contained in each and every particular part (Hegel, Schleiermacher). These reconceptions were not clear-cut breaks with older ideas of static and absolute Being because the Whole was still perceived as ultimately immutable and determinative. But, by taking finitude and freedom *into* ultimate reality, these thinkers showed how permanence and unsurpassability could be understood anew. They prepared the way for the process philosophies that emerged in the late nineteenth and early twentieth centuries.

Process thinking did not surface in a single school of thought but among a variety of original and influential thinkers. Process themes were deployed in visions of the dynamic unfolding of history (Herbert Spencer, Auguste Comte, Karl Marx) and of self-creation (Charles Peirce, William James, John Dewey). They were further extended into comprehensive visions of reality as evolutionary process (Henri Bergson, Samuel Alexander, C. Lloyd Morgan) and as creative process (Alfred North Whitehead, Henry Nelson Wieman, Charles Hartshorne). Though diverse, these thinkers do form a loosely knit tradition of process philosophy since they all see the universe as some kind of developmental process. In this process, the new comes into being as the present dies away to what has been past for the sake of what will be in the future. Thus, for these process philosophers, every entity (whether self, universe, or God) is at any moment a creative integration of inner and outer, of past and future, of self and other.

Seen in these terms, this process tradition is of obvious importance to contemporary theological reflection. It makes available a whole new conception and vocabulary for speaking about humankind, world, and God in processive and purposive interaction. As such, it offers to contemporary theology what such great philosophical traditions as Neo-Platonism, Aristotelianism, and Kantianism gave to theologies of the past—a framework for integrating the biblical heritage and the cultural sensibilities of the time. As in all such weddings, the "organismic" models of process philosophy require a thoroughgoing reinterpretation of Christian beliefs and practices. But a theology modeled on process categories promises not only to reconcile Christian faith with modern science but also to rescue the biblical conception of God as a social and personal reality. Little wonder that the process tradition in philosophy has inspired a cognate process tradition in theology.

THEOLOGIES OF PROCESS

Process theologies have taken the formulation of a new understanding of "God and world" as their central task. Of course, every theology's first task is defining God's reality and relation to the world. That priority has often been overlooked in the past because theological controversies have usually turned on questions of lesser moment. But the modern challenges to Christian faith that we outlined in the first chapter center on the problem of God. In the last analysis, whatever can be said about nature or history, self or society, Christ or

Church depends on what is first said about God because God is for the Christian faith the Ground and Goal of all things.

In a real sense, all the new theologies that we are studying in this book address themselves to the problem of God and world. Certainly all offer new ways of discovering God within the world. But process theologians engage the question of the fundamental nature of a changing world and a living God more directly than any of the other new theologies. Process theologians contend that an understanding of God and world intelligible to modern humanity and faithful to Scripture must meet two requirements: The being of God must be such that he not only affects but is affected by the world's change, and the power of God must be such that he not only shares but suffers the world's power. In short, only a processive and relational view of God can combine biblical faith and modern sensibilities in a manner both philosophically responsible and religiously satisfying.

Generally, the term "process theology" is only used to describe those theologians who interpret Christian thought and life within the framework of Whitehead's metaphysics. Without question, followers of Whitehead have formed a powerful school that dominates process thinking in theological circles today. Within this study, however, the "Whiteheadians" represent only one distinctive style of process theology.[4] They make use of only one of several concrete expressions of the broad root metaphor of process that underlies this type of theological reflection. As we shall see, followers of Whitehead draw upon the processive experiences of selves for their new understanding of God (John Cobb, Schubert Ogden). Others within the process circle model their reinterpretations of God on principles drawn primarily from evolutionary processes in nature (Teilhard de Chardin, Ian Barbour) or emergent processes within history (Thomas Altizer, Langdon Gilkey). The works of John B. Cobb, Pierre Teilhard de Chardin, and Thomas J. J. Altizer offer the most complete and systematic accounts of process theology to date. Therefore, we will concentrate on their thought for gaining a fuller understanding of the similarities and differences among theologies of process.

God as Creative Advance—John B. Cobb, Jr.

Since the early sixties, John B. Cobb has been advocating a renewal of natural theology—a theology that grounds the Christian faith in data and norms which are not dependent on Christian revelation. Not unaware of the difficulties of such a task, he fully appreciates why Neo-orthodoxy abandoned the quest for natural theology. The modern world's secularized and relativized outlook has undermined all available views of God as purposeful Power and personal Presence. Nevertheless, Cobb is convinced that natural theology cannot be abandoned without disastrous results. Severing Christian faith from scientific knowledge and ordinary experience leaves faith devoid of experiential or logical grounds. Thus, the very circumstances that seem to invalidate natural theology also necessitate it. Confronted with this paradox, Cobb sees only one way out for theological renewal. The only way faith in God can be put on a solid experiential and logical footing is through conjoining a revised theistic vision and a revised modern cosmology.[5] The prevailing views of God and of nature in philosophy and theology must be reformulated for any natural theology to gain a hearing in the modern world.

Cobb's search for this new understanding of God and world begins with a critical study of *Living Options in Protestant Theology*. This study focuses on the formative role of philosophy in theology, because Cobb contends that every theology, at least implicitly, builds on certain underlying philosophical assumptions about the world. He draws several conclusions from this study.[6] Christian theologians, he says, should self-consciously develop a natural theology since theological reflection always implies assumptions about language and logic, nature and history that are not derived from faith alone. Classical natural theology is no longer possible because the very notion of a universally accepted philosophical system is a thing of the past. Nevertheless, the impossibility of classical natural theology does not exclude the possibility of a reconceived natural theology. Cobb calls this new approach "*Christian* natural theology," insisting that a metaphysical outlook which is historically and conceptually indebted to the Christian faith can achieve philosophic excellence and acceptance if it illumines human experience generally and grounds its metaphysical claims responsibly. Metaphysical thinking, like scientific thinking, is less concerned with the origin of ideas than with their explanatory power and evidentiary basis.[7]

Cobb further insists that a theologian may create his or her own philosophical vehicle for a Christian natural theology or may borrow another's philosophy provided that it is compatible with historic faith and contemporary science. He finds precisely such a vehicle in the process philosophy of the late British-American scholar Alfred North Whitehead.[8] Whitehead breaks with the static and dualistic categories that long dominated classical thinking in theology, philosophy, and science by taking the processive character of subjective experience as the fundamental clue to the ultimate nature of things. He reasons that we know the inner world more directly than we do the outer world and that we must finally conceive of reality in a way that makes sense of this inner world. Because metaphysical reflection must start and end with our own experienced life, Whitehead chooses to derive his metaphysical principles from that life.

If subjective experiences of life really hold the key to the nature of all things, then the essential characteristics of life must somehow belong to each and all of the real things comprising the universe. Accordingly, Whitehead defines the fundamental elements of reality as "occasions of experience." Each such occasion is a "concrescence," or synthesis, of its own relevant past and reachable future. The relevant past of each emerging occasion constitutes its "physical pole" and contains the inheritable achievements of preceding occasions. The reachable future of each burgeoning occasion constitutes its "mental pole" and presents the achievable possibilities for immediate actualization. Thus, each actual occasion "prehends," or takes hold, of these two poles in a pure moment of creative attainment. The more the physical pole dominates, the more the synthesis replicates the past. The more the mental pole prevails, the more novel the resulting concrescence. Whatever the balance, all actual occasions conjoin the physical and the mental, the past and the future, the actual and the ideal, and the recurrent and the novel in a distinctive moment of experienced "enjoyment."[9]

Given their "dipolar" character, not all the elemental building blocks of reality enjoy their achieved unity in the same way or to the same extent. Discrete occasions always occur as parts of more encompassing and enduring wholes. They come into being and surrender their being in a network of interconnected and ongoing occasions. These wholes, which Whitehead called "societies" of occasions, actualize and organize their member occasions in distinctive ways. Indeed, as we shall see more fully below, the commonplace distinctions we make between the inanimate and the animate, between the natural and the human, and between the earthly and the divine correspond to different societies of occasions, each with its own distinctive function and coherence. We shall also see that some of these societies are structured in the same way as their member occasions—as dipolar concrescences of the physical and the mental, of the past and the future, of the actual and the ideal, of the recurrent and the novel. Thus, Whitehead did not collapse things into an undifferentiated process of occurrences on either the microcosmic or the macrocosmic scale. But he did insist that all things, whether elemental occasions or encompassing societies of experience, do have in common the formal qualities of temporality, relationality, vitality, and creativity. Whitehead did join all things—from the proton to God—in a single dance of life!

Though but a thumbnail sketch, this summary suggests why Cobb and others find Whitehead so important for theological reflection today. Whitehead's dipolar thinking provides a metaphysical framework within which all the ancient and modern splits between mind and matter, fact and value, reason and faith, world and God can be overcome. Cobb finds in Whitehead's revised theistic vision and scientific cosmology a remarkable basis for the renewal of theological understanding and existential confidence demanded by our times.

But Cobb is no slavish follower of Whitehead. Despite its obvious Christian background and widely recognized excellence, Whitehead's philosophy is not always fully adequate for Cobb's theological purposes. He thus freely modifies Whitehead where the requirements of faith demand it.[10] He has worked out the framework of his own "Whiteheadian Christian natural theology" in A Christian Natural Theology and in God and the World. More recently, he has gone far beyond Whitehead in working out the systematic implications of a Whiteheadian theology in The Structure of Christian Existence, Christ in a Pluralistic Age, and Process Theology.[11] Recognizing the originality and scope of Cobb's continuing theological work, we now briefly explore his use of Whitehead in redefining the reality of God.

Cobb begins with a generic definition of the word "God" as "a unitary actuality supremely worthy of worship and commitment."[12] This highly general phenomenological definition of God allows for worldviews and life-styles that either affirm or reject the existence of a God while still permitting great leeway to those who do affirm the reality of God in how they concretely conceive of God and connect God with ordinary experience. Cobb notes that a variety of concrete conceptions of God as Supremely Worthy Being has been maintained within the Christian tradition. The four conceptions of God which have dominated Christian thought through the centuries have been those closely linked to certain fundamental human experiences—experiences of absolute dependence (God as Creator), of cosmic order (God as Lord), of moral obligation (God as Lawgiver), and of cosmic awe (God as Holy One). He further observes that these different approaches have often been in tension with each other and that these tensions are reflected in the diversity of theologies and communions within the Christian heritage. But even if these several strands are theologically woven together, as they surely have been in such great theological systems of the past as Thomism and Calvinism, they do not furnish an adequate approach to God and world for our day.

These traditional conceptions of an overtowering and overpowering God have at best only a tenuous foothold in contemporary experience. They are manifestly out of touch with today's emphasis on process and change in the natural and the social sciences. At a deeper level, these traditional images of God have become morally problematic. Not only does the conception of an all-powerful God ruling the universe raise the age-old problem of why there is so much natural evil and human suffering in the world, but it robs individuals of the very freedom, responsibility, and creativity that lie at the heart of both the biblical tradition and modern sensibilities. Little wonder that people in and out of the Church have trouble seeing a God "supremely worthy of worship and commitment" in the traditionally portrayed roles of Creator, Lord, Lawgiver, and Holy One.

Cobb sees a way around these outmoded conceptions of God with the help of Whiteheadian categories—a reconception of God at once more faithful to biblical personalism and more compatible with contemporary science. Whitehead's thought connects with a common element found in both the preaching of Jesus about the Coming Kingdom and the scientific picture of an evolving universe. Though surely for different reasons and in different imagery, the ancient Jesus and the modern scientist both direct our attention to the *processive* aspects of experience and reality. Using Whiteheadian metaphysics, Cobb integrates this ancient eschatology and today's scientific cosmology in a new conception of God as "The One Who Calls."[13]

Focusing attention on the processive character of human experience, Cobb asks three questions: Can we identify our experience as selves in the world as a "call forward"? If so, does this call forward direct us to something beyond itself? If it does, is it appropriate to name that which calls things forward "God"? In addressing the first question, Cobb notes that scientific accounts of natural process routinely appeal to antecedent conditions only as determining causes and sufficient explanations. But this mechanistic model of causation and explanation does not stand up as an exhaustive account of the dynamics of human experience. This kind of causal account of human behavior in terms of prior conditions simply does not explain our personal experiences of disinterested concern for truth and disinterested love for others. These normative experiences, which "lure" us beyond what the past alone would dictate, point to an aspect of human experience that even non-Christian philosophers and social scientists are now recognizing—the purposive and intentional character of human behavior. This aspect of human experience is what Cobb labels "the call forward."

Cobb next asks whether there is something that calls all things forward or whether this "teleological pull" is found only in human experience. Here Whitehead's vision of a universe alive becomes decisive because it enables Cobb to show how all things are dependent upon what is received from the past, but not totally determined by that past. Whitehead's dipolarity is by no means limited to those societies of occasions that can consciously entertain future possibilities and ideals. The pull and power of unrealized possibilities is as visible in an evolving universe as it is in the consciously planned projects so typical of human behavior. Cobb insists that nature, no less than human nature, answers to something more than our pasts and beyond ourselves since both are realms of emergent complexity and coherence. Whatever its ultimate character, that "something more" calls all things forward (whether electrons or galaxies, cells or animals, selves or civilizations) toward ever new and richer possibilities of becoming.

Can that pull forward be named "God"? Does it have the unity, actuality, and worthiness to merit our worship and commitment? Certainly some kind of "force" seems to move the teeming universe forward, but can we speak of that force in terms of personality—of purposive will and loving reciprocity? Cobb is convinced that we not only can but must speak of the call forward in this fashion. Nothing short of a Cosmic Person could supply the persuasive power and supportive love that a universe of inherently free and ultimately coordinated occasions requires.

Cobb, of course, speaks of God as personal in the Whiteheadian sense of the person as a distinctive society of occasions. Cobb's conception of God as a *personal* society of occasions depends on a series of distinctions that he draws between the ways societies of occasions are organized.[14] Some societies are organized as aggregate wholes that lack any coordinated experience or centered enjoyment as wholes. These "corpuscular societies," which include all the mere objects of the universe, are simply the sum total of their constituent occasions. Other societies are organized as organic wholes whose parts serve and are served by the whole. Within such organic societies, Cobb further distinguishes between "democracies" and "monarchies." He regards all forms of plant life as "democratic societies" because none of their functionally coordinated occasions is central to the life of the society as a whole. By contrast, all animals are seen as "monarchical societies" because they are functionally organized around "dominant" or presiding occasions. Monarchical societies do consciously experience their inner and outer environments and, thus, do act on those environments in a conscious way. Among these animal organisms, Cobb makes yet another crucial distinction. Human beings are those remarkable monarchical societies who self-consciously remember their past, anticipate their future, and weave the two together in continuous and creative harmony. Cobb's final distinction is drawn between human persons and the Divine Person. Human persons are coordinated and centered societies of occasions that are finite in a double sense. Their experience includes only a limited past and future, and their lives endure through only a space and time. The Divine Person, by contrast, is that one unbounded and perdurable society of occasions who self-consciously remembers *all* the experiences and envisions *all* the possibilities of the entire universe by weaving them together in an everlasting process of self-actualization.

Cobb further explains the relation between God's life and the life of all things in God in terms of God's dipolar nature. The mental pole of the divine life, which Cobb calls the "primordial nature" of God, envisions all the unactualized possibilities for every entity in the universe. God primordially gives each entity in every moment of becoming an "initial aim" toward actualizing its own optimum possibilities. But God does not bend all becoming occasions to his primordial nature in a way that destroys their relative independence. Rather, God "lures" each moment of experience toward its highest and best actualization without absolutely requiring that result of a given actual occasion. In a similar fashion, Cobb explains that God's physical pole, which he calls God's "consequent nature," remembers all the experiences of every occasion and society of occasions in the universe. God consequently assimilates all these passing actualizations into his own becoming as part of his own unending life. In so doing, however, God does not absorb these entities into his consequent nature in a way that destroys their relative integrity. Each occasion and society of occasions has its own finite life and worth and makes its own distinctive contribution to the abiding experience and unsurpassable worth of God. Thus, in Cobb's grand vision of reality, every real entity has its own becoming life, but every real entity depends upon and contributes to some more inclusive and enduring life. Ultimately all entities receive their life from God and return their life to God. God is that "Creative Advance" who inspires the creative becoming of all things through tender persuasion and who treasures their achieved values in his own everlasting life.

God as Omega Point—Pierre Teilhard de Chardin

The most celebrated Roman Catholic theologian of process is the late Pierre Teilhard de Chardin. Whether he should be included for study in this volume can be questioned because he died in 1955 and his major works were written between the twenties and the forties. But the unusual circumstances of his background and career properly place his work in the context of our discussion. Though born in 1881, Teilhard knew full well the threats of Modernity since nowhere were secularism and relativism more advanced than in his native France.[15] Determined to combine Christian piety and scientific learning in "bringing France back to God," he became a Jesuit and studied philosophy and biology under the influence of the great evolutionary scientists and philosophers of the day (Darwin, Lamark, and Huxley; Spencer, Bergson, and LeRoy). Unfortunately his own early teaching and writing on evolution brought him into conflict with the Roman Catholic Church, and he was assigned in 1926 to a teaching post in China where he remained in virtual exile for twenty years. His paleontological discoveries and publications during the China years, including an important share in identifying the famous Sinanthropus skull in 1929, made him a world citizen of the scientific community.[16]

During these same years, he wrote a number of highly original works that synthesized Christian faith and evolutionary science. He was, however, forbidden by the Holy Office to publish any of these despite his strenuous efforts to secure Rome's approval. Apart from private distribution to friends and superiors, none of his important philosophical and theological works were known until they were published by his friends after his death in 1955. Thus, through the vagaries of history, Teilhard became a genuine contemporary of the postwar theologians we are surveying in this book.

Teilhard, like Cobb, calls for a new theology that combines a revised understanding of both God and world. The "fixist" and "dualist" categories of classical science and theology have been swept away by twentieth-century advances in scientific learning and social alterations of human life. Neither the changeless God of St. Thomas Aquinas nor the "block" universe of Sir Isaac Newton seems real anymore. Neither the Platonic antinomy nor the Cartesian dichotomy between matter and mind makes sense anymore. All are dissolved in our newly discovered universe of "energy-events" in continuous change. Like Cobb, Teilhard explores how a processive view of God and world affects religious thought and life, but, unlike Cobb, he also explores how this new view of God and world affects scientific thought and practice. Herein lies Teilhard's audacious originality—he claims nothing less than that modern science needs Christian faith as much as Christian faith needs modern science to make complete sense of things as they really are.

Teilhard's daring apologetic program is structured around the idea that there are two complementary ways to gain knowledge of God—through science and through theology. In the special terminology of Teilhard, evolutionary science followed to its summit arrives at "matter become mind." Christian theology traced to its heart ends with "Logos become flesh." Rightly understood, evolutionary science sees all things from their primal beginning as a process of "Cosmogenesis"—the ascent of matter to God. Properly interpreted, Christian theology views all things from their final end as a process of "Christogenesis"—the descent of God into matter. Cosmogenesis and Christogenesis meet in God, the "Omega Point" where the two trajectories of time and eternity bend into one great circle. Apart from the new terminology, Teilhard's position may on the surface sound little different from earlier versions of Logos Christology or natural theology, and he readily admits kinship with these earlier classical syntheses of reason and faith. But Teilhard's striking modernity and originality become clear when the structure and content of his apologetics are examined more closely. He claims to "spiritualize" matter and to "materialize" spirit in such a way that the actual convergence of science and religion is achieved.

Teilhard explores this convergence in writings that run the gamut from theological exercises in mystic devotion (*The Divine Milieu, Hymn of the Universe*) to theological comments on current events (*The Future of Man, Science and Christ*). But his masterwork is found in *The Phenomenon of Man* and in a shorter restatement entitled *Man's Place in Nature*.[17] In these, Teilhard lays out a grand design of God and world becoming that is neither empirical science nor deductive metaphysics, but what he calls a "hyperphysics"—a higher science that takes into account all the structural processes and causal energies at work in the natural and human world.[18]

The titles of Teilhard's most important works suggest that persons stand at the center of his thought, and in a sense they do. Human experience does serve as a model for interpreting all things, but only insofar as human experience discloses the "axial direction of the evolutionary process."[19] Human life as we know it today stands at the halfway mark of a process that stretches back to the "prehistory" and forward to the "posthistory" of the universe. From our vantage point, we are compelled to believe in a "protoconsciousness" within all things from the beginning and a "superconsciousness" within all things at the end. In other words, for Teilhard the "phenomenon of man" is the crucial clue to the evolutionary process, but the evolutionary process is the final key to reality. In Teilhard's own words, "[evolution] is a general condition to which all theories, all hypotheses, all systems must bow and which they must satisfy henceforward if they are to be thinkable and true. Evolution is a light illuminating all facts, a curve that all lines must follow."[20]

The importance of evolution to Teilhard's thought goes beyond marshalling evolutionary theories in biology, paleontology, geology, and astronomy. These evolutionary schemes serve as factual exemplification and verification of a universal law of the world process. The most fundamental axiom on which Teilhard builds everything else is what he calls "the cosmic law of complexity-consciousness."[21] This law states that there is a tendency for the organization of matter through time to become increasingly complex, increasingly centered, and, thus, increasingly conscious. Clustered around this law are three corollaries that underwrite Teilhard's entire scientific and religious outlook.

The first corollary emphasizes that all things have a "within" and a "without," an inner driving force and an outer expression of it.[22] The within corresponds to the spiritual aspect of a thing, the without to the material. The without reflects the structured complexity of an entity, the within the centering consciousness of that entity. In structurally simple entities (molecules, objects), an infinitesimally small level of consciousness is required for organization and maintenance. In entities more complex structurally (cells, organisms), the much higher level of consciousness that we ordinarily call "life" is demanded for sustaining growth and stability. In the most "ultracomplex" entity yet to appear (human beings), the requirements for centered existence are so great that consciousness breaks through to self-consciousness, and what we call "mind" or "spirit" comes to full appearance. Thus, for Teilhard, cosmic history is an ascending spiral of material complexity and spiritual awareness where each new level builds on and transcends what has gone before.

The second corollary of Teilhard's "cosmic law of complexity-consciousness" further refines his idea of a "psychic energy" at work within all things. This energy takes two forms and serves two functions—"tangential energy" and "radial energy."[23] Like his distinction between the within and the without, these two kinds of energy always exist in polarity and can be ascribed in varying ratios of dominance to every entity and every stage of cosmic history. Tangential energy denotes the level of inner consciousness required for an entity to organize and maintain itself in the universe. This is the energy that accounts for all of the "local" movements and changes that an entity undergoes as a matter of course. As such, tangential energy may be spoken of as "material energy" because it manifests itself through material structures and is measurable by the empirical scientists. But there is, also, in everything a tendency toward greater complexity and centricity, and radial energy is that pull of consciousness within every entity toward novelty and advancement. This is the energy that is responsible for the ongoing directive process of evolution that is everywhere exemplified in cosmic history and tacitly recognized by evolutionary scientists.[24] Radial energy may be thought of as "spiritual energy" because it discloses itself in spirit's creative advance through all things. Thus, Teilhard posits two kinds of energy to make sense out of the interdependence of material forces and spiritual powers within all things and to explain how the highest reaches of the spiritual life emerge from the lowest levels of the material world.

A third corollary of Teilhard's cosmic law of evolution explicates the manner of the movement of all things toward ever-increasing complexity and consciousness. There is for Teilhard an unmistakable continuity of movement in cosmic history, but nowhere is this a straightforward, linear progression. Rather, each evolutionary advance passes dialectically through successive phases of "divergence, convergence and emergence."

The first phase of every evolutionary advance is always one of divergence. Because all things tend toward increasing complexity-consciousness, every replication of an entity through time is in fact a process of ramification. Teilhard sees this process as a "bushing out" that produces many variations in form and function from the original. Some of these "gropings" toward greater complexity-consciousness prove to be creative advances, some to be abortive failures.[25] But, at a given point, the inherent possibilities for variation within a given divergence reach a limit, and, concurrently, a convergence phase begins. Those diverging gropings that successfully branched out from their root stock become the "axial line" for consolidating new achievements of material and spiritual unification. As this converging process of "psychic compression" and "material cohesion" reaches a critical mass, a "cosmic recoil" propels a new breakthrough of spiritual and material organization. This emergence phase occurs when a "new creation" appears, surpassing all that has gone before by completing and exceeding all preceding possibilities for unification. Thus, Teilhard tracks each upward turn of the evolutionary spiral as a movement of "opposition in divergence, composition in convergence and transformation in emergence."

Armed with these principles, Teilhard works backward and forward in elaborating the history of cosmic evolution. He extrapolates three ascending stages that have dialectically emerged to date. He begins with the subatomic "stuff of the universe," which by proliferation and combination into various forms over eons of time produced the molecules and sidereal masses that constitute the "geosphere." The next grand level of critical complexity emerged when cells and organisms superimposed a "biosphere" on the geosphere. The multiplication and variation of these life forms, in turn, over millions of years propelled a convergence from which humankind emerged, and a zone of intelligent life that Teilhard calls the "noosphere" covered the geospheric-biospheric reality of the world. On this lattermost level, the evolutionary process became conscious of itself, and humankind became self-consciously involved in the further evolution of the universe.

Not surprisingly, Teilhard concentrates most of his analysis on the emergent evolution of the noosphere.[26] He sees the first dialectical phase of the "hominization" of earth beginning with the branching out of Neanderthal hordes from their prehominoid predecessors and a convergence countless thousands of years later on one stem from among the Neanderthaloids called *homo sapiens*. This stem in turn proliferated into different phyla, and these Neolithic groups gradually covered and conquered the earth by forging their own geographical and tribal identities. This diversification phase reached its critical limit almost simultaneously in five areas, and the convergence of civilizations began. The Mayan, Polynesian, Chinese, Indian, and Mesopotamian civilizations in time became yet another divergence as each great center of life developed its own skills, institutions, and traditions. The Mayan civilization was apparently too isolated and the Polynesian too dispersed to survive. Continued evolution of the Chinese and Indian cultures was stymied by their own social and religious traditions. Only the more Western zones experienced a creative convergence of factual knowledge and active religion that produced a world empire and deepened the bond between matter and spirit. Christendom in its turn exploded in a chain reaction of divergence that culminated in the advent of modern nationalism and individualism.[27] These new constellations of matter and spirit reached the critical limit of divergence along this axial line in modern relativism and pluralism, and evolving life has once again begun a convergence that is already visible in our time.

Teilhard's evolutionary account of cosmic history leads to the present day and a new phase of evolutionary emergence which he calls "planetization."[28] The modern earth's pressures of populations, colonizations of territories, advancements of technology, even wagings of war have increasingly brought individuals and peoples together. Indeed, global interchanges of trade, travel, communication, and knowledge are weaving the material substructure for a new advance in consciousness. Just what that advance will be like and how it will be reached cannot be fully known by inference from past achievements of the evolutionary process. We can extrapolate from those achievements a trajectory of growth toward a greater unification of persons and a greater development of mind. We can further surmise that this trajectory will not be realized without our cooperation and contribution. Putting the two together, we can conclude that we are moving toward a goal that will unite people without overriding their freedom or obliterating their individuality. But the means and the meaning of that "Omega Point" cannot be determined from studying the past.

Are we then left to guess and grope toward the final planetization of earth? Could that goal be missed because of human ignorance and weakness? Such might be the fate of earth and of ourselves were things dependent on human understanding and effort alone. The emergent character of the evolutionary process means that it can only be understood from *end to beginning*. Thus the crucial principles for interpreting and guiding that process cannot simply be inferred from the observed phenomena, though once these principles are known the factual world everywhere suggests and sustains them. Rather, the interpretive principles must either be discovered *at* the end or revealed *from* the end. That discovery is always out of reach, but the revelation of those principles is at hand. For Teilhard, the "Omega Point" of cosmic history is revealed to us in Jesus Christ and is present to us *in nuce* in the Church as the God who draws together a universal community of love.

Here at last we discover the real means and meaning of Teilhard's vision of cosmic evolution. Evolutionary science finally receives its first principles and final chapter from the Christian faith.[29] What actually began in Jesus Christ and has become manifest in our time is the fourth and final stage of cosmic history—the final transubstantiation of matter into spirit. The geospheric, biospheric, and noospheric reality of the world is being taken up and transformed into a "Christo-sphere." At the center and circumference of that sphere is God—the "within" making all things make themselves, the "radial energy" drawing all things forward and upward, and the "emergent" Super-consciousness that personalizes and spiritualizes the whole universe. "God is at the birth, the growth, and the goal of all things."[30]

Though a converging planetary consciousness presaging this last great change seems under way, Teilhard warns that its final consummation may lie thousands or even millions of years away. The End of ends will come only when everyone is "perfectly united with God while perfectly remaining oneself." That such a consummation will come is, however, assured by the presence in world history of the First Person to be so united to God and of a Pioneer Community in which that union among persons united by God is happening. When at last that communion between God and persons is spread throughout the earth, Teilhard sees yet another emergence, since even a fully "Christified" earth is not the final goal of cosmic history. In that final consummation, the centering of minds in the "Mind of minds" will reach a critical point where human beings so break out of themselves that they will break free from matter. In this final "ex-centration" and "re-creation," God will somehow raise up the whole creation to a new level of life even as Christ was raised from the dead.[31] The evolved earth is but the prelude and precondition of an eternal heaven.

For Teilhard, therefore, the Alpha and the Omega of cosmic history are inseparable. Cosmogenesis and Christogenesis describe the same process from different directions—the spiritualization of the world and the personalization of God. Nevertheless, Teilhard does not merge his scientific and his theological writings into one language and logic. Rather, he seeks to show the limitations of either one taken by itself and to center both in God. His whole concentric system of evolutionary science and mystical theology is a call to believe wholly in God and wholly in the world, the one through the other. For Teilhard:

> The Christian . . . is at once the most attached and the most detached of men. Convinced in a way in which the "worldly" cannot be of the unfathomable importance and value concealed beneath the humblest worldly successes, the Christian is at the same time as convinced as the hermit of the worthlessness of any success which is envisaged only as a personal advantage (or even a general one) without reference to God. It is God and God alone whom he pursues through the reality of created things.[32]

God as Total Immanence—Thomas J. J. Altizer

That Thomas Altizer should appear among Christian theologians concerned with a processive view of God and the world may seem strange to those who associate him only with the death-of-God radicals of the sixties. Did they not advocate "taking *God* out of the dictionary" of modern Christianity? Did they not collapse all talk about God into talk about human perspectives or historical processes? Did they not leave God and theology behind for other ways of talking about the human situation? While affirmative answers to these questions apply to some of the death-of-God radicals, none applies to Altizer. He has consistently interpreted the "death" of God as a decisive moment in the *life* of God. He has unfailingly proclaimed a God of Total Immanence beyond the disappearance of the God of Absolute Transcendence. All this he has done in a continuing series of provocative theological writings. Indeed, John Cobb and others have hailed him as the most "influential" and "creative" American theologian of the postwar era.[33] Far from having come to an end, both Altizer's God and his theology are in a lively process of development.

But what a strange process! For Altizer, both the life of God and the life of thought move in a distinctively dialectical way. He acknowledges that some form of dialectical movement and understanding is present in all the higher expressions of mystical and prophetic religion. But the particular form of dialectic that Altizer embraces is derived from the radical tradition of the nineteenth century—Freud, Nietzsche, Dostoevski, Marx, and especially Hegel and Blake. From these modern visionaries, Altizer learned to search out the deepest movements of Spirit and moments of truth precisely in historical crises of total reversal or dissolution. The total negation of past forms of consciousness and experience is the very means of their total transformation into new forms of consciousness and experience.

Herein we already see Altizer's divergence from other processive views of God and world. Both Whiteheadian and Teilhardian theologies embody a dialectic of sorts between God and world and between past and future, but in neither of these process theologies does God change in any essential way. For them the world changes, and thereby God's experience of the world changes. The fundamental structures of the being of God and the being of the world in God never change. Nor is the past essentially negated in either of these theologies. Whiteheadian and Teilhardian theologies preserve the past in God since the past is the earnest of each entity's abiding identity and worth. By contrast, Altizer's dialectical thinking and vision hold to a radical transformation of God as well as of the world.[34] In his scheme, there can be no real change in the world unless there is real change in God. Indeed, God undergoes a series of radical changes. Because each change represents a *total* break with the past, Altizer speaks of each change as a "death" of God. Moreover, unlike Cobb and Teilhard, Altizer envisions a coming Kingdom where all distinctions and separations between God and the world will be totally overcome. The final death of God will leave behind "all those polarities and antinomies which isolate and alienate all individual centers of experience."

Altizer works out this dialectical vision in a three-cornered conversation among the "Coming Kingdom" of biblical eschatology, the "All in All" of oriental mysticism, and the "Radical Atheism" of modern consciousness. Each of these elements figures prominently in every one of his major writings, though the weight and place given to each have undergone a kind of dialectical change during his career.

Schooled in the University of Chicago's famous program in History of Religions, his first book on *Oriental Mysticism and Biblical Eschatology* assimilates the biblical faith in a Coming Kingdom into oriental mysticism's vision of a return to Primordial Unity.[35] Altizer thought he saw in Buddhist world-rejection a way to overcome simultaneously every person's ontological separation from God and the modern world's loss of belief in God. But subsequent study of a similar pattern of world-negation within primitive religion, which Altizer published in 1963 as *Mircea Eliade and the Dialectic of the Sacred*, suggested that the relationship between the Sacred and Profane, between the past and future is more deeply dialectical than he had first imagined.[36] This study convinced him that primitive and Buddhist paths of world-rejection and time-reversal are closed to people of the West and doubly so to Christians for whom history is the realm of all things real, whether human or divine. Only a theology based on the *historical* phenomenon of faith can be true to the biblical tradition and modern consciousness. God must be found in history—even in a history as devoid of God as nineteenth-century radicalism and twentieth-century secularism suggest. Thus, in a dramatic reversal of his earlier espousal of world-negating mysticism, Altizer began to explore modern atheism as a profoundly new experience of God and expression of faith—first in *The Gospel of Christian Atheism* and, subsequently, in *The New Apocalypse, The Descent into Hell*, and *The Self-Embodiment of God*.[37]

At the heart of these later explorations stands a highly original processive view of God and the world. Altizer envisions God in a continual process of self-expression and self-fulfillment. This process is not a linear movement shadowed in an evolving universe or an eternal recurrence embedded in a cyclical universe. Rather, God lives and moves and has his being through a succession of dialectical self-embodiments in world history. God moves toward self-fulfillment through a series of self-expressions that negate and transmute his own earlier self-expressions. Reminiscent of primitive religion and oriental mysticism, Altizer speaks of this process as a "coincidence of opposites"—as the dialectical identity of the Sacred and Profane, of the past and future. But, unlike the primitive and oriental negation of the profane world by the Sacred Totality, Altizer heralds a total immersion of the Sacred in the Profane. Instead of a backward movement of world-negation toward an Original Totality, Altizer acclaims a forward movement of world-affirmation culminating in a Total Immanence. Instead of an ultimate identity of opposites that finally annihilates the profane, Altizer anticipates an ultimate unity of opposites that fully joins the Sacred and the Profane. In short, unlike all forms of primitive religion and oriental mysticism, Altizer's understanding of the life of God is *apocalyptic as well as dialectic*—it is forward-moving and world-completing.[38]

One conviction that Altizer does take from oriental mysticism is the belief that, ultimately, God is the only Reality: In the Beginning and in the End, God is All in All. Any separation of the world from God represents a fall away from this Original and Final Unity. But, in Altizer's apocalyptic vision, the world separate from God is not an unreality or an illusion born of human ignorance or craving as the Eastern religions maintain.[39] The world is as real as our common sense suggests, and God's transcendence of the world is as genuine as our theistic heritage avers. Moreover, in further distinction from the oriental mystics, Altizer sees the world's reality and God's transcendence as a consequence of a divine rather than a human fall into separateness. The world owes its separate being to God's fall from unity into transcendence.[40] The more God differentiates himself from the world by transcending it, the greater the individuation of all things in the world. In Altizer's dialectical vision, the Fall of God from Primordial Oneness and the Creation of the world of separate entities are one and the same.

In this dialectical identity of the Fall of God and the Creation of the world, Altizer sees the first meaning of the "death" of God. The same transcendence that releases the actuality of the world empties the reality of God. Seen from the world's side, the Fall of God frees the world from all transcendent constraints. Viewed from the side of God, the Creation of the world empties God of all concrete reality. As God becomes ever more distant and the world becomes progressively more autonomous, the total transcendence of God and the total disappearance of God come together. The God who becomes Totally Spirit as the World becomes Totally Flesh thereby becomes Totally

Empty.[41] Somewhat like the wise parent whose controlling and commanding reality progressively dies away so that the child might become an adult, the Creator God progressively draws away from the world into Total Nothingness. In short, a radically transcendent God gives birth to the world through his own death.

How can God be All in All if he dies away into Total Nothingness? Does the dialectic of God's life come to rest with the transcendent dissolution of a Primordial Unity, or is this reversal but the obverse of an immanent realization of a Final Totality? Altizer sees the latter occurring through a "coincidence of opposites" unfolding itself in our history. The process by which the world is emptied of a transcendent God is the very same process by which God is emptied of transcendent Spirit. The world taking on actuality coincides with God taking on flesh. Here the death of God is seen as a process *within* history rather than beyond history—the emptying of God's transcendent self-expression into an immanent self-realization, the emptying of the Sacred into the Profane.[42] This pouring out of divinity into humanity began in Jesus Christ, but only the long history of Christendom has made this death of God in Christ Jesus manifest. Unfortunately, the early Church partially obscured the radical reality of God's mergence with human flesh by affirming Christ's resurrection from the dead and his ascension to the heavens. Those images once again separated divinity from humanity, heaven from earth, life from death. Only the historical decline of Christendom and the rise of secularism has finally stripped Christianity of this otherworldly outlook. Christians at last *can*, because they *must*, face the radical significance of Jesus Christ: God *is* everywhere in our world, especially in "every human hand and face."

For Altizer, this means that a genuinely "Kenotic Christology" is finally possible.[43] St. Paul's great hymn to the Cosmic Christ who empties himself (*kenosis*) is actually being realized in our time—God's transcendent Spirit is being totally emptied into human flesh. Altizer speaks darkly of this kenotic process as a "descent into Hell." Only a total reversal of Heaven (God's transcendent self-expression) by a total descent into Hell (God's immanent self-realization) can bring God nearer than thinking or breathing. This is why a Cross of Suffering and Death stands at the very heart of Christian faith—Incarnation and Crucifixion are one and the same! The living God, nowhere more present than in the death of Christ, is present for today's Christian in the death of Christendom and in the brokenness of humanity that confronts us on every hand. This darkening of transcendence is but the dawning of an immanence that the Christian knows as God. It is God himself who is here being actualized as Total Immanence.

Thus, Christians can joyously affirm the death of God because thereby they share in the living God's presence and each concrete moment's eternity. God's total submersion in the world, however, is not the end of the divine life. Dialectical through and through, Altizer looks still further ahead to another reversal of Total Immanence when God will once again be All in All. This final death of the cosmos need trouble us no more than our own death.

> Once Christ is known as the source and ground of a total transformation of consciousness and experience, then the loss of all we have known as identity and selfhood can be accepted and affirmed as the realization of the presence and compassion of Christ. True darkness can then be known as the fruit of compassion, and the actual death of an individual center of consciousness can be celebrated as the self-annihilating presence of the universal Christ.[44]

Kenosis and Apocalypse—God's and our own—are one and the same!

PROCESS THEOLOGIES IN QUESTION

Like the secular theologies discussed in the last chapter, we have found similarities and differences among theologies of process. All share in common the view that the static and otherworldly cosmology of earlier forms of Christian thought lies at the roots of modern doubt. Not only are those understandings of God and world out of touch with the scientific and historical sensibilities of the day, they also fail to illumine the central human experiences of love, suffering, and responsibility. Only a processive view of God and world can redress these failings and revitalize biblical faith for our time. But how "process" is defined and how God and world interrelate are matters of sharp disagreement within the process camp. The contrasts between Cobb, Teilhard, and Altizer give clear indication of the variety of ways the metaphor of "process" can be deployed in theological work.

Acknowledging this variety, what has been the impact of process theology considered broadly? Has it established a significant constituency among professional theologians, and, more important, has it made an impact at the grass-roots level of faith and practice? Without a doubt, process theologies like Cobb's and Teilhard's have won wide respect in theological circles, and they enjoy an articulate following among younger North American theologians. These theologies are prized for their theoretical and practical value. They are permeated by scientific understanding, philosophical awareness, and Christian imagination. They provide a meaningful place for human effort in a universe where both man and God are at home. By contrast, Altizer's influence thus far has been overwhelmingly negative in two ways. His theological critique has stimulated theological experimentation and has generated theological opposition. Nevertheless, Altizer's constructive work—often allied with the fine arts and depth psychologies—represents a dynamic mysticism on the margins of mainstream theology that employs Christian symbols to interpret human yearnings to experience life deeply and to embrace death fully. Yet for all their metaphysical daring, scientific sophistication, and moral sensitivity, the process type of theology exemplified by these three thinkers has not been granted preeminence in theological circles. Nor has it made as much impact on everyday belief and practice among the masses as have some of the other theologies we are surveying.

Critics of process theology offer many reasons for its failure to gain widespread acceptance in Christian circles. Even those theologians who do not hold to a normative Christian orthodoxy frequently charge that the process transpositions of Christology, ecclesiology, and eschatology are at odds with the Christian tradition. Critics of a more modern persuasion question the possibility of any metaphysical system-building or mystical utopianism in a world as relativized and secularized as our own. Surpassing all these criticisms are those having to do with the process vision of God. Here complaints are made that the process God is too abstract to be lovable, too limited to be worshipped, and—most importantly—too remote from the daily affairs of individuals and groups. For all their talk of a God of change who sustains freedom and redeems suffering, the process theologians offer little hope and guidance for immediate change to the masses whose worldly circumstances thwart freedom and inflict suffering relentlessly. For all the breathtaking sweep of their theologies, Cobb's measured realism, Teilhard's cosmic optimism, and Altizer's mystical quietism leave the world very much as it is for the time being.

In the next chapter, we will examine a very different kind of theology, also devoted to change, which does address the practical problems of personal and political existence. "Liberation theologies" grow out of the same soil as process theologies. They too exchange a vertical model of divine transcendence for a horizontal one. They too see God and people as copartners in the process of world-making.

But, rather than looking for God in a world of change, they find God by changing the world. They locate and identify God for the world today in the same place where he has always been most visible and powerful—in the struggles for liberation among all the earth's oppressed.

4
Liberation as Challenge and Response

James Cone, Mary Daly, Gustavo Gutiérrez

Modern thought and life were born out of the struggle to free individuals from the heavy hand of past traditions and authoritarian institutions. Modern concepts of personal autonomy had their early roots in the Renaissance and Reformation where individual powers of mind and rights of conscience were asserted against theological, philosophical, and political authorities previously thought to be absolute. These protests against authority were developed further in the Enlightenment struggle for intellectual and political freedom and in the Romantic emphasis on personal inwardness and uniqueness. But a full sense of life's openness to autonomous thought and action came out of the technological and social changes brought about by the free exercise of reason and conscience in the realms of science and politics. The progressive dismantling of static orders within nature and history that has come with modernization has opened up the natural and cultural world to radical change. Indeed, the deeper the discovery of the world's contingency, temporality, and relativity, the wider the range of human freedom, competence, and responsibility. Each successive overthrow of a fixed structure of human existence has been hailed as an advance in human liberation.

Of late this celebration has not been unmindful of what has been gained and lost in this advance. There was a time, especially in the nineteenth century, when only the credit side of the ledger was acknowledged. The combined impact of scientific progress, technological achievement, religious toleration, and world peace produced a euphoric confidence that all human ills and ignorance would soon be conquered. But the sobering events of the twentieth century soon dispelled such naive optimism. The burdens of autonomy have been brought home with a vengeance by rapidly growing problems of political conflict, economic instability, expanding populations, vanishing resources, and exploding knowledge. Gone are the simple assurances of the past when an inscrutable Providence or an irreversible Progress insured a happy outcome for all humankind. A world open to real change permits failure as well as success. A world decisively shaped by human actions can become better or worse. The price of human freedom is the possibility of human folly. Whether we achieve peace or destroy civilization, whether we share wealth or protect privilege, whether we control growth or overcrowd the planet, whether we temper consumption or plunder earth, whether we discipline knowledge or outstrip wisdom lies in our own hands.

Yet, for all of this weight of responsibility and uncertainty, most modern individuals stoutly affirm autonomy as a primary fact and value of human experience. In fact, the struggle for personal freedom has been dramatically extended in the last twenty-five years. Not only have marginal peoples and underdeveloped countries risen up to demand freedom for themselves, but individuals in advantaged groups and countries have significantly enlarged personal freedom in the areas of societal roles and personal life-styles. Liberation movements the world over are stirring up individuals and groups to use their increasing knowledge and power to change their environment, their society, and themselves. Among these movements is a new type of theology—a "theology of liberation"—that places a mandate on the Christian and the Church to free all the earth's oppressed.

THE LIBERATION MANDATE

To be sure, there are doom-sayers who see in these liberation movements the beginning of the end of the modern world's experiment in autonomy. Critics are deeply troubled by a narrow individualism and introversion visible in these movements, especially in liberation movements among the advantaged. Christopher Lasch has chronicled and named this collapse of autonomy into egoism in his book *The Culture of Narcissism.*[1] Focusing broadly on American life,

Lasch discerns a "new narcissism" at work in an amazing variety of regimens promising personal salvation—health foods, psychic self-improvement, Eastern meditation, sex therapy, alternate life-styles, assertiveness training, exercise programs, adult education, arts and crafts, wilderness camping, spiritual healing, charismatic ecstacy. Mass movements as different as the revival of evangelical religion and the cult of expanded consciousness are seen, at bottom, to share a narrow concern for self-improvement and self-fulfillment. This new narcissism is more than mere selfishness. Lasch warns that it signals a deep sense of inner emptiness and a broad loss of social connection. Beneath our narcissistic society's ideology of personal growth and happiness lies a festering pessimism and fear of life. The nuclear family or solitary individual thus turned in on itself finally weakens rather than improves, destroys rather than fulfills itself. Lasch concludes his jeremiad with a call to return to the "moral discipline" formerly associated with the work ethic, the hierarchical family, the free market, and the basic curriculum.

A full discussion of Lasch's diagnosis and cure need not detain us here, though we will return to the question of narcissism in the final chapter. But two observations on his study are in order for present purposes. First, there is no doubt much truth in what Lasch says. A *pathological* narcissism that cuts off individuals from their neighbor and their community and from their past and their future can be seen in much of the frantic activity surrounding our "meaning industries." This kind of self-regard has all the emptiness, repressed rage, unsatisfied craving, uneasy performance, pseudo-insight, calculating seductiveness, and fashionable acclaim that Lasch attributes to the American way of life as a whole. This kind of narcissism does bring the modern ideal of autonomy to grief in a bathos of self-destruction.

On the other hand, what Lasch has called the culture of narcissism is not all of a piece. It is not simply a matter of autonomous individualism gone sour. For all its pathological excesses and social introversion, the new narcissism also represents a revolutionary extension of the modern ideal of autonomous existence. The new narcissism is deeply symptomatic of a larger process under way that Thomas Hanna has rightly called "the *somatic* revolution."[2] That this quest for fully embodied existence should do violence to received traditions and established institutions is hardly surprising since revolutionary change often rides the waves of excess. Seen in this light, even our culture's excessive concern with self-improvement and self-fulfillment is part of this revolutionary quest to liberate the body as well as the mind from all oppression.

This somatic revolution will be misunderstood, if not missed entirely, if it is construed in a narrowly physiological and hedonistic way. To be sure, the sexual revolution and the drug culture are a part of "bodies in revolt." The freedom to feel what the body feels is a fundamental freedom of embodied existence, though such sensate liberties have surely claimed more attention from liberators and commentators than they deserve. But the somatic revolution also includes the freedom to think, act, make, play, enjoy—even suffer and die—*as* bodies think, act, make, play, enjoy, suffer, and die.

In other words, the somatic revolution represents the overthrowing in theory and in practice of all body-mind dualism. Though long alienated by common sense and traditional wisdom from flesh and matter, we are finally beginning to understand that we *are* our bodies and our situations—that we believe, hope, and love as well as sense, feel, and act in a bodily and earthly way. There are powerful forces working against full acceptance of such incarnate and situated existence. As far back as we have record of human efforts at self-understanding, flesh and spirit as well as time and eternity have been divided. Inevitably this dualistic approach has made the body inferior to spirit and the earth anterior to heaven. This denigration of the sensual and the temporal—enforced theologically and reinforced philosophically for centuries upon centuries—is deeply engrained in our speech and sensibilities. Modernity's secularizing and historicizing of personal and social existence have slowly but surely undermined these dualisms, however. Scientific understanding, technological competence, and political change have put us in touch with ourselves and in command of our world in radically new ways. Little wonder that after centuries of loathing the body and fearing the earth we should be so fascinated with bodily "highs" and material "goods." But we are learning through these primitivist experiments and other more refined explorations of full-embodiedness to take possession of our physical lives and to claim that share of earth's body that such life requires.

For understandable reasons, the Church has not exactly been in the forefront of the somatic revolution. Christian ideas of God and practices of faith have too long been tied to the separation of flesh and spirit, of world and God to welcome their fusion. The great gains in embodied life have come through the secular revolutions that have changed the face of the earth and our place on it. Indeed, from our present-day vantage point, we can see that all the modern world's great revolutions—technological, political, economic, and social— have been somatic revolutions of sorts since all have furthered the cause of happy and healthful life in the world. They have all operated at some level on the assumption that unless bodies are free and have free access to earth's body, the minds and souls of all remain enslaved. Moreover, most of the significant advances in body liberation have been the work of the disadvantaged and disaffected of our civilization. Those who have been routinely excluded from full bodily life are the ones who have put their bodies on the line in dramatic enactment of the value of embodied existence. Those who have systematically been alienated from bodily freedoms are the ones who have attacked the political, economic, social, and ideological barriers to happy and healthful life in the world. The modern world's "resurrection of the bodily" has, like most resurrections, come out of bodily turmoil and suffering.

As so often happens, the Church has at last begun to assimilate the somatic revolution—even to claim biblical warrants, if not historical credit, for this "re-discovery" of the incarnate and situated character of human life. Of course, traditional Christianity had long seen prosperity as a sign of divine favor and charity as a mark of human compassion. But seldom did prosperity and charity become ideals of social order and policies of social action until Liberal Protestantism pioneered a "social Christianity" that bent Christian faith in service to such causes of human betterment. The social implications of faith were not forgotten in Neo-orthodox revisions of Liberalism nor have they been absent from the Roman Catholic thought of the last hundred years. Even latter-day evangelical theologies have come to affirm embodied existence in a new way and to care for the quality of human life in the wider culture. Thus, as strange as it may sound, books as far apart in time and thought as Walter Rauschenbusch's A Theology for the Social Gospel and Marabel Morgan's The Total Woman share a common denominator.[3] They reflect a somatic revolution under way within the thought and life of the Church.

The Church's reassessment of embodied existence has taken an unexpected turn of late. Insistent and angry voices have been raised in the Church against the confinement of bodily liberation to certain privileged circles. These protestors variously charge that the freedom to be at home in the body and in the world has largely been a one race (white), one sex (male), and one class (upper) affair. Nonwhites, nonmales, and non-upper-class North Americans have been routinely denied the right to take full possession of their bodies and their earth. The perception of what is afforded to one race, sex, or class but not to another has generated one of the most explosive and influential theological movements of our time—a "liberation theology" that cries out for the deliverance of all the bodily and earthly oppressed.[4]

THEOLOGIES OF LIBERATION

The new liberation theologies rise from a growing wave of secular liberation movements the world over. These movements represent a broad range of ethnic, sexual, and socioeconomic concerns. Drives for black, brown, and red power are staking out their own race's claims to full dignity and opportunity. A many-faceted women's movement dealing with everything from equal pay to abortion rights is shaking cultural institutions and male psyches to their foundations. Third World peoples in Latin America, Asia, and Africa are battling their way out from under colonial rule and capitalist domination. Though their specific struggles are different, at bottom these liberation movements share a common cause. They seek the freedoms of fully embodied existence. This is especially obvious in the case of Third World struggles against the bondage of grinding poverty, chronic disease, dismal ignorance, and economic exploitation, but somatic revolution is just as central to ethnic and women's movements. The feminist revolt, like the black, chicano, and Indian rebellions, must be seen not only as a quest for identity but as an expression of body consciousness pointing toward the full acceptance of different styles of bodily life. The same can be said for a host of less celebrated movements (from Gay to Gray Liberation) that have spun off from these core revolutions. Members of each oppressed group are striving to take full possession of their own bodies and their own earth.

According to theologies of liberation, these secular freedom movements present a dual challenge to the Christian faith. Negatively, they offer a devastating critique of the Church's racism, sexism, and colonialism. They show that any religious belief, practice, or institution that identifies with the world's powerful or disregards the world's powerless is a source of oppression and an obstacle to liberation. Echoing Marx, Freud, and Nietzsche, they call for the total overthrow of all religions of privilege and all religions of escape. Positively, these secular liberation movements offer the Church an opportunity to recover its true faith and regain its true voice. By their very opposition to establishment and escapist religion, they turn faith to where God is and return theology to what the Gospel is. The God of the Bible is always at work among the "marginalized"—among those who are left by the economic, political, and social wayside. The God who became incarnate in Jesus preached good news to the poor, release to the captives, liberty to the oppressed. Thus, both positively and negatively, the world's liberation movements challenge the Church to match their concern with a God and a Gospel of liberation.

In direct response to this challenge, liberation theologies draw their causes and constituencies from these freedom movements. Thereby, these theologies differ from earlier forms of social Christianity where advantaged groups sought to express their faith through bettering the lot of disadvantaged groups. Theologies of liberation are movements from *within* disadvantaged groups, and they variously proclaim a Gospel of Liberation directed to their own distinctive situation and need. Far from merely invoking claims of situational relevance, the theologies of liberation claim an "epistemological privilege for the oppressed"—that is, only the oppressed can see the world as it really is and as it ideally ought to be. This claim gives these theologies an unmistakably urgent and authentic tone. Liberation theologies are theologies *of* the oppressed, *by* the oppressed, and *for* the oppressed.

This intense militancy builds a certain divisiveness into the liberation theologies. Ordinarily, the liberation theologians do not address the problems of oppressed groups *en masse*. Rather, highly partisan theologies of liberation are written from and for distinctive groups. Ethnic, feminist, and Third World groups address the Church and the world primarily in terms of their own perceptions of oppression and programs for liberation. Even within these broad groups, there are further divisions.[5] Blacks, browns, and reds write their own theologies of racial liberation. Asians, Africans, and Latin Americans have their own theologies beyond class. The comparative absence of such natural divisions gives feminists a greater unity, but even here vocational and social differences are reflected in women's liberation theology. Internal differences sometimes put the liberation theologies in conflict with one another. Even when they address the problems of *all* the oppressed, as the best of them ultimately do, they see all oppression as an outgrowth of their own group's oppression. For black theologians, all oppression is racist; whereas for feminists it is sexist, and for those in the Third World, oppression is always colonialistic at base. These internal divisions remain unresolved though discussion has begun among liberation theologians over the ways in which the oppressions of race, sex, and class intersect.[6]

This theological partisanship draws an even sharper dividing line between the theologies of the oppressed and the theologies of the oppressors. As we shall soon see, the liberation theologies level their severest criticisms against those Christian beliefs, practices, and institutions that either actively or tacitly sanction oppression in the Church and in the world. For liberation theology, the enemy is not simply white, masculine, capitalist society. It is white theology, masculine religion, and Euroamerican ethics that must be overthrown. So strident have been the liberationist's internecine polemics that theological countercharges in kind have been evoked: Liberation theologies are charged with being racist, sexist, class theologies! Calmer heads have cautioned that the liberationist criticisms are justified no matter how one-sided they are and have begun to ask how these theologies for the oppressed can also become theologies for the oppressors.[7] They emphasize a recurrent liberationist claim that freeing the oppressed will also free the oppressor, since being an oppressor is as destructive to one's own humanity as is being oppressed. Thus, whatever else the liberation theologies might mean for their distinctive constituencies, they offer a unique opportunity for the liberation of all from the shackles of white, masculine, middle-class religion.

Quite apart from their leavening effect on other types of theology, theologies of liberation are destined to be a major force because they emerge from vast groups who have become aware of their own subordination and have begun to lay claim to power. As suggested already, liberation theologies are bound together by the shared interpretive category of somatic oppression. Identifying the oppressed and the oppressor, however, to say nothing of setting forth the goals and strategies of liberation, are matters of broad and sometimes sharp disagreement among liberationists. We shall explore this unity and variety more fully by examining the "Black Theology" of James Cone, the "Feminist Theology" of Mary Daly, and the "Latin American Theology" of Gustavo Gutiérrez. These three stand at the center of the discussion surrounding the particular mode of liberation theology that each represents.

Black Liberation Theology—James H. Cone

In the early sixties, the civil rights movement had become a matter of religious concern to whites and blacks alike. Martin Luther King, Jr., and other black ministers in the Southern Christian Leadership Conference were the spearheads of a passive-resistance strategy to bring down segregation in the South. Many of the white clergy and laity joined their struggle in a dramatic enactment of biracial solidarity. But as the decade passed, a new image of blackness began to emerge. Malcolm X was making converts to the Black Muslims. Stokely Carmichael was proclaiming Black Power. Rap Brown was extolling revolutionary violence. James Foreman was demanding reparations from the white Church for oppressed blacks. Rev. Albert

B. Cleage began to preach the Black Messiah. Out of this social, political, economic, and religious ferment came a new theology that jarred the theological establishment and stung the Christian churches. James H. Cone, a professor at Union Theological Seminary in New York City, published a book entitled *Black Theology and Black Power* in which he argued that Black Power even in its most radical expressions is not opposed to Christianity but is rather "Christ's central message to twentieth-century America."[8] Within five years, Black Theology had established itself as a theological movement of unquestioned importance and influence.

Cone's theology, worked out in systematic detail in *A Black Theology of Liberation* and put in historical perspective in *God of the Oppressed,* is an admittedly angry and passionate call for revolution.[9] Speaking to the black community but loudly enough for whites to overhear, Cone calls for the total commitment of Christian thought and action to the Black Revolution already under way. He leaves no question but that this commitment may include violence since liberation means "complete emancipation of black people from white oppression by whatever means black people deem necessary."[10] Moreover, against all false otherworldliness and spirituality, Cone makes it clear that the Black Revolution is a bodily revolution devoted to freeing the economically, socially, and politically enslaved black. "Black Theology is an earthly theology."[11]

Cone's revolutionary call rests on two fundamental assumptions—that Christianity has always been a religion of liberation and that theology must always interpret the Gospel in the light of the oppressed community's struggle for justice. A faith unconcerned with liberating the oppressed is not Christ's faith. A theology not centered in setting the captives free is no Christian theology. In the light of these assumptions, Christian faith and theology in North America have no choice but to become black because oppression and liberation are centered in the black community. For Cone, "Black Theology is Christian theology and possibly the only expression of Christian theology in America."[12]

Despite their common goal of liberation, Cone does not simply equate Black Theology and Black Revolution. Speaking to the revolutionary black radicals, he argues that Black Power and black religion are inseparable.[13] Again and again, he insists that the black Church has been the seedbed of the black struggle for self-identity and self-determination through the years. Even during the "white captivity" of the black clergy and black churches in the post-Civil War South, the black churches kept alive a spirit of black dignity and an ideal of black freedom. Moreover, Cone insists that the motive and moral power for thé Black Revolution can only come from the faith that black liberation is the work of a God who always sides with the oppressed and delivers them from their oppressors. On the other hand, speaking to the theological community, Cone argues that a theology of liberation cannot be "color-blind" in a revolutionary situation.[14] It will always be identified either with the oppressors or with the oppressed. Clearly the theology of white America is not on the side of the oppressed, no matter how fervently it exhorts white Americans to be "nice" to blacks. A Christian theology of liberation can only be a *black* theology of a *black* God freeing *black* people from oppression. Thus does Cone seek to make black religion the religion of Black Power and to make Black Power the politics of black religion by fashioning a Black Theology.

Cone is adamant that this Black Theology is centered in Christ and faithful to Scripture, as all proper Christian theology must be.[15] The normative biblical witness proclaims a God known and served in his liberating activity. The consistent theme of God's election of Israel and his incarnation in Christ is the liberation of God's people from social, political, and economic bondage. Israel prefigures the Christ who, as the Oppressed One, identifies from birth to death with those who suffer and empowers them to overcome through his life and resurrection.[16] But the biblical witness to the living Christ can come alive today only in the company of the oppressed, and in America that means the black community. Thus, Black Theology is subject to a single norm that has two aspects—"the liberation of black people and the revelation of Jesus Christ."[17] Jesus Christ is known and named today in the black ghetto and the Black Revolution. The Kingdom of God is a black kingdom, and the Messiah of God is a black Christ. Only the black can truly see and serve God in today's world.

Cone's repeated affirmation of blackness is matched by an equally unrelenting negation of whiteness. Not only are white theology and the white Church faulted for ignoring racist oppression. Not only are white values and institutions criticized for perpetuating racial injustice. But whiteness itself is condemned as the very essence of evil—as antihuman and anti-Christ. Nothing short of a "Black Copernican Revolution" can overthrow whiteness. Only an antiwhite Church and theology can bring about Christian love. Only antiwhite values and institutions can give proper form to human life. Daring the razor's edge of heresy and treason, Cone announces that white Christianity and white America must be destroyed before human life and divine love are possible on this earth.

Given his categorical distinction between black and white, Cone's theology is often seen as mere revolutionary rhetoric or as black racism masquerading as theology. Both assessments miss the subtlety and scope of thought that underlie his sledgehammer language and utopian vision. Cone's analysis of "blackness" and "whiteness" moves on two intersecting levels—each term has a literal and particular sense and a symbolic and universal meaning. When Cone speaks of Black Power, Black Theology, and Black Liberation, he generally has in mind the black-skinned people of America "whose children are bitten by rats, whose women are raped and whose men are robbed of their manhood."Similarly, when Cone excoriates white values, white theology, and white religion, he is usually condemning the white-skinned people of America who have enslaved, humiliated, and ignored black people for more than two hundred years. Cone's comments about black and white America are to be taken largely in their literal and particular sense. First and foremost, Cone is speaking of and for black people to and against white people.

But blackness and whiteness also have a symbolic and universal meaning in Cone's theology. These terms describe human attitudes and social structures that bear no essential connection to skin color or racial ancestry. In the early pages of his first book, Cone speaks slyly of reaching all his black brothers, "including black men in white skins." In the closing pages, he speaks more forthrightly:

> Being black in America has very little to do with skin color. To be black means that your heart, your soul, your mind, and your body are where the dispossessed are. We all know that a racist structure will reject and threaten a black man in white skin as quickly as a black man in black/skin. It accepts and rewards whites in black skins nearly as well as whites in white skins. Therefore being reconciled to God does not mean one's skin is physically black. It essentially depends on the color of your heart, soul, and mind.[18]

Cone reiterates the use of blackness and whiteness as symbols of oppression and liberation having universal applicability in *A Black Theology of Liberation,* though here he clearly soft-pedals this meaning for fear of "white people milking this idea for all its worth."[19] Being black means being "identified with the victims of humiliation in human society and a participant in the liberation of man."[20] By contrast, "whiteness symbolizes the activity of deranged men intrigued by their own image of themselves, and thus unable to see that they are what is wrong with the world."[21]

Having marked that blackness and whiteness are both "visible realities" and "ontological symbols" in Cone's theology, two cautions are in order. First, Cone has not worked out a clear statement on the relations between the literal and symbolic levels of discourse in his language of black and white. Though his dependence on Tillich's idea that symbols are visible realities with ontological depth is suggestive of a manner of their relationship, we are not furnished a hermeneutical principle for determining when Cone is speaking symbolically and when literally. This systematic ambiguity in Cone's usage implies a second and more important caution. Cone's literal and particular language must not be too quickly mythologized or too easily sold short. The priority for defining oppression and undertaking liberation clearly belongs with the community of black-skinned Americans. Hence Cone's ridicule of liberation nostrums by whites and his standard reply to white offers to help in the black cause: "leave us alone! give us room to do our own thing."[22] White-skinned Americans are too bound by the structures of white racism and too dependent on their rewards to understand racial bondage or to undertake racial liberation. Similarly, Cone makes clear that the initiative for liberating the oppressors along with the oppressed must come from the community of black-skinned Americans. White-skinned persons can become black—indeed, must become black—to enter God's kingdom of liberation and reconciliation. But white-skinned oppressors enslave and dehumanize themselves in their master's role. They can only be freed from such debasing behavior when the oppressed refuse to behave according to master's rules.[23] Thus, all who enter the kingdom enter "by means of their black brothers."

Considered as a whole, James Cone's Black Theology achieves an unsuspected blend of situational relevance and universal applicability. To the white and nonwhite communities of North America, he proclaims a highly concrete revolutionary Gospel calling for the economic, social, and political liberation of blacks, browns, and reds. But, by also universalizing "blackness" and "whiteness" as symbolic modes of existence, Cone offers a radically new conception of Christian community and mission. He calls the whole Christian community, black and white, back to the prophetic religion of ancient Israel and the iconoclastic faith of primitive Christianity. He calls the Church and every Christian to the life of *perpetual* revolution—breaking down all the walls that divide and building in their place one new humanity.

Women's Liberation Theology—Mary Daly

Revolutionary ferment in the sixties also had a sexual dimension. The most obvious and newsworthy form this revolution took was in the area of sexual relations per se. That "bodies in revolt" should storm the barricades of public prudery and private guilt was hardly surprising. But, though it had long been under way, no one was quite prepared for the "sexual revolution" to break into the open the way it did in the sixties. A new sexual candor in the media and the arts and a new sexual freedom in conversation and relationships profoundly altered sexual perceptions if not sexual practices. Sex came to be seen as a human good even by those who sought to put brakes on the new permissiveness.

At the same time, however, at a deeper level, a far more radical and far-reaching revolution in the relations between the sexes was also under way. Growing out of the same sociological and technological changes (urbanization and mobility, education and affluence, the pill and penicillin), this "women's revolt" was a very different kind of sexual revolution.[24] Betty Friedan's *The Feminine Mystique* demythologized the "happy housewife" stereotype of the American woman, calling it an economic and psychological trap maintained by and for the benefit of men.[25] Kate Millet's *Sexual Politics*[26] unmasked the covert power and domination of men over women in all their relationships through a critical study of the culture and literature of the sexual revolution. Simone de Beauvoir's massive *The Second Sex*[27] catalogued the causes and consequences of misogyny with a detailed study of the literature in history, anthropology, biology, psychology, philosophy, and theology. These women and their writings gave focus and slogans to a women's personal and social existence in the modern world, including religion. The Church was quickly drawn into the orbit of feminist criticism and activism. Mary Daly, a theology professor at Boston University, caught the public's attention in 1968 with a study of the sexist attitudes and practices of Christianity in her book *The Church and the Second Sex*. Since then she has remained at the center of women's liberation theology as one of its most articulate and radical advocates.[28]

The Church and the Second Sex is, compared to Daly's later works, a temperate call for reform of sexist thinking and behavior in the Roman Catholic Church. To be sure, she sharply criticizes the Church for perpetuating the subjugation of women in and beyond the Church through the sexist models of women's identity in its theology, through the sexist control of women's behavior in its ethics, and through the sexist denial of women's access to its heirarchy. But Daly still believed that the resources present in the tradition itself coupled with the new understanding and opportunity given women in the wider society could achieve a reform of the Church's androcentric theology, ethics, and polity. The creative ambiguity of a "personalist strain" in traditional theology and the inspiring example of women saints and leaders of religious orders point the way to reform. A creative ferment in contemporary theology and church life create the opportunity for reform. The time seemed right for women in the Church to pioneer a new level of cooperation between the sexes that could eventually undermine all hierarchical arrangements and class distinctions within the Church and in the world. Whether or not the institutional Church was ready to embrace this pioneering "democratization" of the sexes, Daly was convinced that the "seeds of transcendence" had been sown in the past and that a genuinely liberating, humanizing Church of the future was already springing up among women and men of courage and openness.

How different the substance and strategy of Daly's next book. *Beyond God the Father* rings of revolution rather than reform. For Daly, the five intervening years had been truly revolutionary because during that time the women's movement organized and radicalized.[29] Both developments are clearly evident in *Beyond God the Father*. Many of the same themes of the earlier book are repeated here—the religious roots of sexist oppression, the dehumanizing effects of sexual stereotyping, the liberation of men and women from sexual alienation. But all are radicalized in a strident manifesto for a feminist revolution in the Church and in the world, to be fought without the help or cooperation of men. The spirit and substance of Daly's radical shift is caught in Gail Murray's blunt declaration, "Brother, you cannot whore, perfume, and suppress me anymore. I have my own business in this skin and on this planet."[30]

Daly wields the logic and language of feminist revolution with consummate skill and stunning effect. The world is categorically divided into the oppressed (women) and the oppressors (men). Though ultimately men are to share in her envisioned human community "beyond sexual caste," Daly leaves no question but that men are to blame for the social arrangements and symbol systems that "have shortened and crushed the lives of women." As perpetrators and benefactors of a sexual caste system that determines the whole of individual identity and social reality, men are simply incapable of seeing or solving the problem. Liberation can begin only when women "bond together" in a sisterhood that is "Antichrist, Antichurch, and Antiworld." Liberation will be achieved only when human life and earth are freed once and for all from the "rape" of patriarchy.

Such liberation means far more than men sharing household chores and women gaining equal rights. Liberation from patriarchy means "castrating" God—"cutting away the Supreme Phallus!"[31] As long as God and God's surrogates are male, then male is God! A world "beyond the death of God the Father" will be a world without the priorities and privileges that belong to the "God-Fathers"— whether biological (the male parent), psychological (the sugar daddy), matrimonial (the head of the household), political (the city fathers), or ecclesiastical (the holy fathers). A world without fathers will be a world without hierarchy and without oppression, a world of equality and fulfillment for all.

Daly's fierce language is more than mere revolutionary rhetoric or empty demagogery. She understands what all great revolutionary leaders have known intuitively about language and what depth psychology, sociology of knowledge, and linguistic philosophy have recently made plain to all of us.[32] Human personalities and groups, attitudes, and actions are formed by a culture's words and images. Personal and social existence are constructed and maintained by a network of symbolic utterances, objects, and gestures. Though incredibly complex, these symbolic networks usually depend on certain key symbolic constructs—good and evil, mind and matter, church and state, God and world, male and female. Thus, Daly's concentration on such images and her language of sexual wounding and counterwounding (rape, castration) are deliberate strategies of linguistic confrontation.[33] She seeks thereby to force people into a situation requiring new perceptions and values by attacking the language that subliminally builds sexist stereotypes and sexist oppression into our very minds and muscles.

Moreover, Daly's "linguistic therapy" goes far beyond linguistic confrontation and attack. Beyond her strident "antitheology" lies the makings of a positive theology of women's liberation that promises a new humanity and a new earth for all. Daly models her feminist theology on the key concepts of classical Christian theology—God, Fall, Christ, Ethics, Church, and Eschatology. But each of these doctrines is wrenched out of the experiential context of patriarchy and placed into the experiential context of a new consciousness emerging among feminist "model-breakers" and "model-makers."[34] With masterful irony, Daly reverses the content of these doctrines by "selectively perceiving" new meanings within their primary images that are totally opposite to the traditional understanding of them. Beginning for obvious reasons with the image of God the Father,[35] Daly notes the move toward personalistic and processive thinking about God in a variety of contemporary theologies including liberation theologies. Yet none of these theologies breaks with the masculine God, and thus none successfully overthrows the patriarchal structures of oppression. Whether God is black or white, Marxist or capitalist, egalitarian or autocrat matters little if God remains male. Racial, economic, and political oppression cannot end until sexist oppression is overthrown. Sexual aggression is the "primordial aggression," and women are the "primordial aliens." As such, women serve as models for all other aggression and alienation. Only *women's* liberation theology goes to the heart of all oppression, because only women's liberation theology challenges the patriarchal God that symbolizes and makes legitimate a racially, economically, and politically repressive social order. Accordingly, Daly summons women to reach "outward and inward toward the God beyond and beneath the gods who have stolen our identity."[36]

Daly is not ready to call this God a person—even a female person. She does accept Johann Bachofen's theory that a universal matriarchal society and religion preceded patriarchy.[37] Indeed, Daly insists that the centrality of the Virgin Mary in the Christian tradition reflects this older religion of the Mother Goddess.[38] Despite all the official attempts of the Church to domesticate her, Mary remains a manifestation of transcendence that is more ancient and universal than Christianity or patriarchy. Still, Daly is reluctant to "resex" and "re-name" deity as the Mother Goddess because feminist experience suggests that "neither the Father, nor the Son, nor the Mother *is* God."[39] In their new-found self-awareness, feminists are moving toward "androgynous being" where all sexual separation and alienation is overcome. Their experience of this "mysticism of sorority" suggests an "unfolding God" beyond dichotomies and dogmas in which all things have *one* being and value. A name for this humanizing process will emerge in time from the feminist experience, but for now, according to Daly, this "Verb of verbs" best remains nameless.

In similar fashion, Daly reverses each of the other classical theological loci. The classical view of the Fall is "seen through" as a rationalization of male superiority and female inferiority. Feminists must exorcize the "original sin of sexism" by falling into a freedom beyond the goods and evils of patriarchy.[40] Christ as Savior and Lord is denied for the obvious reason that all male Lords are sexist and for the less obvious, though more important, reason that all Saviors are scapegoats.[41] Not only do symbolic scapegoats keep alive the practice of projecting suffering and evil on real scapegoats—on women and all their fellow oppressed in marginal races, classes, and religion. Scapegoat Saviors also deflect us from searching out the presence of the God in all, the God who gives freedom and courage to each to achieve "completeness of human being." The overthrow of all such "Christolatry" permits a new morality free of aggression and competition—a feminist ethics that says "no" to all victimization and violence.[42] Daly admits that the nonhierarchical and nonrepressive society envisioned in this benign ethics is nowhere in sight in the institutional Church, but it can be seen emerging in an "antichurch" of sisterhood.[43] Feminists bonding together are breaking down the psychic and social structures of sexist stereotype and oppression that still stand in the way of men and women becoming "integrated, androgynous personalities." These churchwomen are the harbingers of a "cosmic covenant" that will bring all persons into "living harmony with the self, the universe and God."[44]

But the time for this "diarchal society" has not yet come. Vast changes in sexist psyches and sexist societies must still take place before life beyond sexual caste is possible. These changes cannot happen apart from the breakup of all the symbols and roles of patriarchy, and those who mount a total attack on patriarchy must undergo a perilous journey into nonbeing and disvalue because they must challenge the very meaning that our culture gives to human being and value. Given the risk, only the oppressed who are excluded from full being and value will have the necessary outrage and courage to begin and complete the journey. For that reason, Daly warns against all premature cooperation with men. "It is a time for men to learn at last to listen and to hear, knowing that this is how to find their own promise, and to discover at last the way to adequate speech."[45] Women alone must make the breakthroughs that can alter the course of human evolution. Women alone must write the liberation theologies that will free us all.

Latin American Liberation Theology—Gustavo Gutiérrez

We have seen that the modern world is very much a product of political and economic revolution. Human thought and life as we know it today are unthinkable apart from the populist (American and French) and proletarian (Russian and Chinese) revolutions that broke up the old feudal empires and economies and established the modern world's nation-states and rational economies. These revolutions were not simultaneous or worldwide, and as late as mid-century vast populations and territories of the so-called underdeveloped countries remained essentially untouched by their modernizing influences. In the past two or three decades, however, political and economic revolution has been very much in the air within underdeveloped countries. Sometimes acting in concert, more often acting alone, countries of what has come to be called the "Third World" have become increasingly combative against the "First World" capitalist nations of Western Europe and North America—often with the encouragement of the "Second World" socialist bloc. This conflict has, in the last ten years, taken on the proportions of a global class war. Nowhere has revolutionary activity been more vigorous than in Latin America. The desperate plight of the Latin American poor, made all the more obvious by modernized and industralized capital cities, has galvanized enough popular support to mount a number of revolutionary uprisings and to make revolution an exportable "commodity."

Out of this ferment has come a new theology that clearly belongs to the liberation theology movement. Like black theology, it arises out of a specific context of oppression. Like feminist theology, it contends that the reversal of these oppressive conditions will require a significant revision of Christian belief and practice. Like both, it promises liberation to all the bodily oppressed through deliverance from one particular form of oppression. In this case, however, *class* oppression is viewed as the underlying source and model of all other forms of human bondage. Moreover, because it grows out of the struggle for economic and political liberation in Latin America, this theology is marked by the peculiar history and needs of that struggle. Nevertheless, this "Latin American liberation theology" has stirred up as much interest and controversy abroad as it has at home. In the eye of that storm is a Peruvian priest named Gustavo Gutiérrez. His book, A *Theology of Liberation,* is the most influential text of the Latin American liberation movement.[46]

Gutiérrez's theology, like most Latin American liberation theologies, breaks little new ground in matters of theological content. His biblical exegesis and theological formulations echo the latest European scholarship. But Gutiérrez does radically alter the *way* theology is done. He capsules this new way in the neologism "orthopraxis."[47] Theology as orthopraxis shifts the primary axis of faith from right knowledge (ortho-doxy) to right action (ortho-praxis). Gutiérrez believes that theology has been too long concerned with formulating truths and too long unconcerned with changing lives. Not that he collapses theology into anthropolgy or reduces dogma to ethics, but he does bend theology to "the historical praxis of liberation." This means providing specific theological sanctions and guidance for the political and economic revolution under way on the Latin American continent. It means addressing all forms of class oppression with a Word of faith *and* a work of revolution.

This concern to rebalance belief and action, worship and service is reflected in Gutiérrez's understanding of liberation. He distinguishes three interpenetrating levels of the process of liberation: political, historical, and spiritual.[48] On the political level, liberation expresses the aspiration and effort of oppressed peoples and social groups to escape the domination of wealthy nations and oppressive classes. At a deeper historical level, liberation means a conscious acceptance of humankind's responsibility for its own historical destiny. Historical liberation places political liberation in the broader horizons of the gradual unfolding of all of the dimensions of human life into the creation of a "new man and a qualitatively different society." Finally, at a still deeper level, liberation requires a transforming encounter with Jesus Christ that roots out the very basis of injustice and oppression in the human heart. This spiritual liberation is the ultimate context and *telos* of political and historical liberation. Though these three levels of liberation are not the same, one is not present without the others.

> Without liberating historical events, there would be no growth of the Kingdom. But the very process of liberation will not have conquered the very roots of oppression and exploitation of man by man without the coming of the Kingdom which is above all a gift. Moreover, we can say that the historical, political liberating event *is* the growth of the Kingdom, and *is* salvific event, but it is not *the* coming of the Kingdom, not *all* of salvation.[49]

Thus, political, historical, and spiritual liberation are inseparable parts of a single, all-encompassing salvific process.

These three levels of liberation not only structure Gutiérrez's thought, but they also roughly correspond to three levels of analysis that enter into his theology.[50] Political liberation must be guided by scientific understanding of the structures and functions of oppressive and nonoppressive societies. Gutiérrez draws heavily on Marxist- and Freudian-informed scientific accounts of the causes and consequences of class conflict and the strategies and benefits of class liberation.[51] But such scientific accounts do not establish the wider historical horizons and the deeper spiritual realities within which genuinely humanizing political liberation occurs. Historical understanding inspires and guides political revolution by furnishing a positive vision of a new kind of person and society that fulfulls "all men and the whole man." Such historical projection is not a work of empirical extrapolation but of "utopian imagination."[52] Utopian thinking postulates, enriches, and supplies new goals for political action beyond the "feasible" or the "attainable." Utopian thinking simultaneously legitimates and critiques all scientific knowledge and practical programs of political liberation. Utopian thinking is the internal dynamism of all "political" science and praxis since it continuously drives history forward and subverts the existing order.

But such historical projects of utopian liberation require the informing understanding of faith, the enabling efforts of love, and the sustaining courage of hope to be freed of shallow consumerism, evasive idealism, and narrow nationalism. Christian faith reveals to us the deep meaning of the history we fashion in our political action. Every human act that seeks to establish a more just society builds up "the communion of all men with God." Christian love humanizes economic, social, and political revolution and in this humanization reveals the God who requires and rewards love among people by his own loving presence. Christian hope opens the oppressed and the oppressors to a new future and prevents any confusion of the Kingdom with any one historical stage or revolutionary achievement of human community. Thus does Gutiérrez bring together scientific rationality, historical imagination, and religious perception in his liberation theology. Like the three levels of liberation, these levels of analysis are woven together "in unity, without confusion." They are profoundly linked, though none is reduced to the other. As we shall see, this way of doing theology redistributes and ultimately redefines the content of theology in surprising ways—especially in ecclesiology, ministry, and spirituality.

Addressing theology to the political and historical praxis of liberation means always starting with a concrete situation of human oppression and liberation. For Gutiérrez, that concrete situation is a continent dominated externally by the world's great capitalist countries and riven internally by ever-increasing class differences and disorder. Though Latin American social order has always been maintained by the few for their own benefit, the exploited lower classes are beginning to make their voices heard and to forge a radically different society. In this situation, the Christian has no choice but to identify with the marginalized who are "cheated of the fruits of their work, stripped of their being as men." Such identification means accomplishing more than simply raising the gross national product or extending social welfare services. It means pursuing the construction of a social order where workers are not subordinated to the owners of the means of production and where the governed are not tyrannized by their political leaders. The Christian's responsibility in Latin America is to participate in the revolutionary creation of that just and free society.

Commitment to this process of liberation, with all of its political demands, sets new requirements for the mission of the Church, the task of the ministry, and the practice of spirituality. The Church *as institution* must lend its social and ideological power to the cause of liberation.[53] Obviously, the Church's own complicity in creating and benefiting from Latin America's unjust and repressive social order must not stand in the way of joining liberty's cause.[54] To be sure, the Latin American Church's wealth and prestige is scandalous, considering that continent's harsh poverty and politics. But a beginning tranformation of ecclesiastical structures and clerical life-styles promises new credibility for the Church and the clergy among the oppressed.[55] Moreover, appeals to church unity must not be allowed to deter the Church from casting with the marginalized in their struggle for freedom. Fears that revolutionary involvement may discredit the Church by linking it to a future order or to an unsuccessful cause must not be heeded.

Gutiérrez acknowledges the risks but insists that the Church cannot remain neutral in a divided society and revolutionary situation. The Church's social influence and political power in Latin America are a fact. "Not to exercise this influence in favor of the oppressed of Latin America is really to exercise it against them."[56] Indeed, the only way the Church can be a "universal sacrament" of Christian love and unity is by taking the side of the poor and alienated. Christian love requires us to liberate oppressed and oppressors alike from the political, economic, and social circumstances that destroy the humanity of all. Christian unity requires us to tear down all the walls of class and race and culture that divide the human family and the empirical Church. Furthermore, neither love nor unity precludes conflict or even violence. In a world where conflict and violence are built into the structures of social order, those structures will not fall without conflict and violence. The Church cannot be *for* universal love and reconciliation without standing *against* all forms of injustice and alienation.

If the Church is to become this living sacrament of love and unity, then profound changes in its manner of preaching the Word and celebrating its faith must be made. The primary duty of evangelization for a Church committed to liberation is "conscienticizing" and "politicizing" the oppressed.[57] The liberation Church has a responsibility to educate the oppressed to the true nature of their own misery and bondage and to enlist them in the revolutionary struggle for justice and freedom. Evangelization by conscienticizing and politicizing has both a negative and positive thrust.[58] The Latin American Church must make a "prophetic *denunciation* of every dehumanizing situation, which is contrary to brotherhood, justice and liberty. At the same time it must criticize every sacralization of oppressive structures to which the Church itself might have contributed."[59] Such public criticism of the present order must go to the very causes of the situation and not merely attend to the consequences of an unjust and repressive order. This denunciation, however, must be matched by the *annunciation* of the love and forgiveness of God which is present "in the historical becoming of mankind." The Church must proclaim without any evasions that alienation from God is at the root of social injustice, that freedom in Christ is the ground of political liberation, and that even the just and free society only foreshadows a coming Kingdom beyond all oppression including death. Gutiérrez once again acknowledges the dangers of reducing the Gospel message to a "revolutionary ideology" by construing evangelization in this way.[60] But biblical faith demands that those risks be run. The God we know in the Bible is a liberating God "who intervenes in history in order to break down the structures of injustice and who raises up prophets in order to point the way to justice and mercy." Dangerous as it is, only this kind of evangelization can humanize and make divine the structures of society and the hearts of individuals.

Gutiérrez further insists that this kind of evangelization is made real only by proclaiming the Gospel from a position of personal solidarity with the oppressed. In today's world "only the oppressed person, only the oppressed class, only the oppressed peoples can denounce and announce."[61] Only by participating in the sorrows and struggles of the oppressed can we understand and preach the Gospel of liberation. This identification with the oppressed requires a new understanding and acceptance of the Christian vow of poverty.[62] Gutiérrez rejects as incomplete all mere materializing or idealizing of "poverty" as a Christian virtue. Material poverty as such is a scandalous condition. Spiritual poverty is at best a commendable attitude. But neither captures the full meaning of "Christian poverty" for today. A more authentic and radical Christian witness of poverty calls for total identification with the poor—"the oppressed one, the one marginated from society, the member of the proletariat struggling for his most basic rights . . . the exploited and plundered social class, the country struggling for its liberation."

This solidarity with the poor is chosen not as an end in itself but in order to protest against material poverty and to struggle to abolish it. Only by rejecting poverty through making ourselves poor to protest against it can our denunciation of injustice and our annunciation of liberation ring true.

Gutiérrez sees this solidarity with and protest against poverty as the highest expression of Christian spirituality, where spirituality is understood in the biblical sense of living freely and creatively "in the Spirit as sons of God and as brothers of man."[63] Such identification with the poor stands at the heart of the two nodal points of spirituality—conversion and worship. "Conversion means going out of oneself, being open to God and others; it implies a break, but above all it means following a new path. For that very reason, it is not an inward-looking, private attitude, but a process which occurs in the socio-economic, political and cultural medium in which life goes on and which is to be transformed."[64] No clearer occasion or expression of conversion can be found than conversion *to* the neighbor, the oppressed person, the exploited social class, the despised race, the dominated country. Thus breaking with our own privileged life-style and social class is at once an act of repentance and transformation. Moreover, it is an authentic encounter with and imitation of Christ who is specially present in the unsheltered, the unfed, the unclothed of the earth. Conversion is indeed the touchstone of all spirituality, but "conversion to the Lord implies this conversion to the neighbor."

Gutiérrez argues the same re-visioning of worship in his view of the Eucharist.[65] The same double motif of liberation from sin and liberation from poverty is present in all the biblical accounts of the Eucharist. As bread and wine, it signifies that sharing the goods of the earth is God's gift to us and our offering to God. As a meal, it establishes community and brotherhood for those who sit at table with one another. As a Passover feast, it recalls the Israelite deliverance from political and economic slavery. As a memorial to the death and resurrection of Jesus, it commemorates our liberation from all forms of sin's bondage. From the biblical perspective, celebration of the Eucharist is only genuine when communion with God is inseparably bound to brotherhood among persons. " 'To make a remembrance of Christ' is more than the performance of an act of worship; it is to accept living under the sign of the cross in the hope of the resurrection. It is to accept the meaning of a life that has been given over to death—at the hands of the powerful of this world—for love of others."[66] Our true worship, like our true conversion, is found in that "spirituality of liberation" which stands with the poor against all poverty.

Thus does Gutiérrez see theology growing organically out of the process of liberation in Latin America. He acknowledges that this Latin American liberation theology is still very much in the process of development. Fuller scientific analysis of the social order, more daring historical vision of the human future, and clearer religious understanding of Christian symbols in the Latin American context are needed. Even more important, the oppressed themselves must be heard in their own language for this theology to ring true to the Latin American situation.[67] But, for all of these limitations, Gutiérrez believes that Latin American liberation theology addresses the Church local and universal with the Word of truth. Latin America is a microcosm of a world and a Church being torn apart by social imbalance and revolutionary uprising. Therefore the question of the meaning of Christianity and the mission of the Church is the same for Latin America and for the world. But the courage to address that question, if not the right to answer, may be found only in a Church on a continent where misery and upheavel abound. For that reason, a liberation theology of and for Latin America is a liberation theology of and for the world.

LIBERATION THEOLOGIES IN QUESTION

Once again, we find both unity and variety. The differences among black, feminist, and Latin American theologies are truly monumental and may seem to preclude all agreements save their shared concern with bodily liberation. But careful study suggests some important agreements in matters of theological style and substance. These very different expressions of liberation theology exhibit almost identical patterns of logic and language. They all divide the world into the oppressed and the oppressors and grant to the oppressed alone the responsibliity to define oppression and to undertake liberation. They all use language as a weapon of confrontation and as a means of transformation. They all ground the transvaluation of Christian symbols in a new experiential consciousness born out of oppression. Finally, they all seek a new humanity and new society *for all* through the particular liberation movement that they champion.

Viewed from one angle, these similarities are unexceptional since they are the stock-in-trade of all revolutionary ideologies and messianic movements. But their weight taken together does tell on the very substance of theological reflection in important ways. Quite apart from the undeniable relevance and power of these liberation theologies for their distinctive constituencies, they have made a remarkable impact on Christian thought and life by addressing a different constituency in a different way for different ends. Unlike most new theologies, which address those alienated from the faith by their own powers of mind and body, liberation theologies speak to the powerless—to the marginalized that the world and the Church tend to ignore. Rather than seeking a new consensus with the world, as do most contemporary theologies, theologies of liberation set the Church against the world in the sense that conflict and contestation become the central demand of faith. Finally, liberation theologies are less concerned with intellectual challenges to belief than with practical obstacles to life. They are less concerned with understanding the world than with changing it. Consequently they all bend the substance of theology to the ends of praxis. Liberation theology is, in Robert McAfee Brown's words, truly a "theology in a new key." Little wonder that they have generated such interest and controversy beyond their own pales. Not the least important among these reactions is a variety of liberation theologies "for oppressors" and "beyond partisanship."[68]

Despite their positive impact, theologies of liberation are roundly criticized—often in as strident and categorical a voice as their own. As noted earlier, their more belligerent critics simply dismiss them as being as equally guilty of race, sex, or class bias as the bias they attack. But less defensive and sweeping critiques also find much to fault in these new theologies. Their tactics of confrontation and intemperate language are routinely questioned as are their preoccupations with social liberty and somatic life. Their overemphasis on certain unquestionably important themes is frequently criticized— the social source of sin, the political dimension of liberation, the contextual frame of reference, the utopian ideal of freedom, the ethical uses of dogma, the social relevance of worship, the moral justification of violence, the heuristic use of Scripture. But the key critical problem is their categorical division between the oppressed and the oppressor. Critics are almost unanimous in calling this dichotomy pernicious. Unless liberation theologies ground their critical and constructive concerns on more universal grounds than race, sex, or class oppression, they cannot hope to escape the same ideological taint and social narrowness that they so sternly criticize. Whether done from an ethnic, feminist, or Third World perspective, if their promises to free oppressors and oppressed are to be redeemed, liberation theologies must rise to a perspective that argues for liberation of a universal humanity.

Efforts to ground Christian theology in a universal humanity characterize all three types of theology remaining in our study. As we have seen, theologies of secularity, process, and liberation seek to find a new basis for faith in the very preoccupations of modern thought and life which undercut the more traditional forms of Christian thought and life. By contrast, we shall see that theologies of hope, play, and story claim to find a more inclusive basis for faith in the universal human gestures of hoping, playing, and storytelling. These gestures are seen to possess both an implicit dimension of religiousness and distinctive appropriateness to Christianity. For chronological reasons, we will begin our analyses of these more broadly based new theologies with the theologies of hope, which emerged in the early sixties as the European counterpart to theologies of secularity. As we shall see, they bear important similarities to process and, especially, liberation theologies since they variously reinterpret the Christian faith in terms of the pull of the future and the praxis of politics.

5
Hope as Ground and Goal

Jürgen Moltmann, Carl Braaten, Gabriel Vahanian

Living in a changing world where changes are in some measure under human control makes the future an unavoidable problem. Life is no longer primarily a matter of remembrance as it once was. In primitive cultures, situations of instability and uncertainty were handled by reestablishing the primordial foundations of reality through myth and ritual. Traditional cultures dealt with the unexpected and the unexplained by recollecting the essential patterns of reality through revelation and reason. Even to look ahead in primitive or traditional cultures was to look back to where the future would return or was disclosed. By contrast, life in the modern world is a thrust into a future whose sequence and shape are by no means clear. Half by accident and half by design, we have made ourselves the artisans of our own environment and our own humanity without sure patterns to guide and trustworthy powers to help us. We know not what to hope *for* in the future nor what to hope *in* for the future.

A clear sense of hope's quandary can be gained from sampling those two distinctively modern apocalypses spawned by our new-found power of world-construction and world-maintenance—science fiction and futurology. Once consigned to the category of pulp, escapist literature, science fiction has become a major literary and cinematic art form in the last twenty years.[1] A whole new wave of science-fiction scenarists are addressing the problem of the human future in a world where the boundaries of scientific discovery and technology are radically open. In highly imaginative ways, science fiction catapults us beyond the near future into a world of space travel, advanced cybernetics, galactic politics, and alternate realities. There, we are promised or warned, the human future will be decided. Whether or not that future will remain in human hands and redound to human good is an open question. Answers to the question of what to hope for and hope in run the gamut from the apotheosis to the disappearance of humankind. For example, Isaac Asimov's *Foundations* peers thousands of years ahead to the perfect society where "physical technology" and "mental science" maintain a perfect order.[2] But Arthur C. Clarke and Stanley Kubrick's collaboration on the film *2001: A Space Odyssey* offers a dreamy vision of man halfway between ape and angel being drawn into a vague "overmind" through the tools of death and the machinery of immortality. These themes—humankind succeeding and being superseded—are endlessly explored in a congeries of science fictional replies to the question of hope. Amid all these contrary scenarios of the future, however, the hope persists that somehow and somewhere some kind of life will continue.

Hope's same ambivalent message rings through the writings of futurology, the social scientific counterpart to science fiction.[3] Futurology, of course, does not deal with long-range futures or speculate about barely conceivable technology. Futurology deals with the science and the society that can be extrapolated from present-day knowledge, technique, and circumstance. Indeed, given the almost canonical status of Herman Kahn and Anthony Weiner's *The Year 2000*, futurologists have concentrated on forecasting the arrival of the third millennium by using the best available techniques, computer data, and interdisciplinary findings of social analysis.[4] Despite their more modest projections, the futurologists in their high-level think-tanks also send out sharply conflicting signals about the human prospect.

Most futurologists start from a shared sense of the potentially disastrous future that lies ahead—the control of human beings through surveillance, mind, and drug technologies; the destruction of earth by resource depletion, environmental pollution, or thermonuclear holocaust; the disappearance of human life through runaway population, worldwide starvation, or doomsday weaponry. These nightmare possibilities are annotated and supported with enough hard data to show that they are the *possible* future. Whether and how these frightening prospects can be avoided remains a matter of disagreement. For example, John R. Platt in *The Step to Man* predicts that by the year 2000 a newly discovered sense of being "one society, indivisible, for life or death" will enable us to bring scientific technology and social engineering to the point of creating a new humanity and a new earth.[5] In *An Inquiry into the Human Prospect*, Robert Heilbroner sees much less hope for life in the future.[6] He believes the problems of population growth, environmental destruction, and military conflict can be solved only by very costly trade-offs; catastrophe will be avoided only by the rise of totalitarian governments that manage populations and resources without regard for individual rights and freedoms. Nevertheless, even the most dismal scenarios of futurology also hold out some measure of hope for life's continuance beyond Armageddon.

Science fiction and futurology are but illustrious expressions of a culturewide epidemic of future-consciousness. Interest in the second coming of Christ flourishes among fundamentalist Christians. Utopian vision is extolled by philosophers and political scientists alike. Life "after death" is being investigated by serious scholars as well as by spiritualist adepts. Many people search for the key to health, wealth, and wisdom in astrology, fortune telling, and pop-parapsychology. Most commentators on the contemporary scene see this upsurge of interest in the future as a predictable reaction to the time's apocalyptic perils. But a growing number of social scientists, philosophers, and theologians see these cultural preoccupations with the future as symptomatic of a deeply felt universal and fundamental need for human hope. Granted that hope rises to the level of heroism or illusion in situations that seem to threaten utter defeat, but hope is no less present in times of plenty. Among those thus concerned with hope are contemporary "theologians of hope" who see Christian faith reflecting and fulfilling this universal human need.

THE PERSISTENCE OF HOPE

In his *Critique of Pure Reason*, Immanuel Kant argued that human life turns on three questions: What can I know? What ought I to do? What may I hope? Modern philosophy and theology have, for the most part, concentrated on the epistemological question, giving much less attention to the ethical question and hardly any attention at all to the third question of hope. That theology since Kant's time should have increasingly less to say about hope may seem strange. Does not the Christian faith hinge on "the blessed hope" of life everlasting? Certainly traditional Christianity made much of the hope for immortality. But, as we have seen, modern life and thought have increasingly turned away from otherworlds and afterlives in deference to concern for this world and this life. The centuries-long association of Christian hope with a future beyond death is precisely why Kant's third question has gone begging. Modern philosophers have simply rejected the question as meaningless. Modern theologians have taken longer to fumble away belief in life after death, but in the twentieth century they have largely demythologized the eschatological symbols into existential and ethical categories. They have translated the "resurrection faith" into an affirmation of radical freedom or of body-soul unity. The question of hope *in the future* has, for all practical purposes, been set aside by contemporary theologians and philosophers alike.

Meanwhile, questions about what we can hope for *in this world* have become increasingly urgent as the limitations of earth's resources and human resourcefulness have dimmed the human prospect. Whole new technological sciences have arisen to fashion a usable future, and entirely new healing sciences have been established to rescue the victims of a useless future. Moreover, secular and occult eschatologies have reestablished the fantasies and faiths of immortality that always seem to give hope to the masses. In other words, the question "What may I hope?" has been taken up in this century by the sciences and the arts, by the visionaries and the fanatics. Hope has proven more persistent a phenomenon than modern philosophy and theology had thought it to be.

Lately there has been a modest revival of the question of hope in philosophy that, in turn, has served as a catalyst for a theological recovery as well. One of the first people to draw attention to hope as a defining feature of humanness was the Christian existentialist Gabriel Marcel. His book *Homo Viator* builds a metaphysics on man as a "traveller" who lives by hope.[7] Humanistic psychologists such as Karl Menninger and Erich Fromm have called for a recovery of hope as an intrinsic ingredient in human wholeness.[8] Sociologists such as Peter Berger and Clifford Geertz have made hope a structural feature of social order.[9] Literary critics such as William Lynch and Frank Kermode have shown that hope is a primary theme in all artistic activity.[10] But no one has contributed more toward a theological recovery of hope than Ernst Bloch, a Central European revisionary Marxist philosopher. His massive *Das Prinzip Hoffnung (The Principle of Hope)*, written in the early forties, has made an immense impact on the postwar religious thinkers of Europe.

Bloch argues that living in hope and expectation should be the basic posture of human existence at all times and not simply in the situations of extremity.[11] Humankind *is* the hoping creature who dreams about the future and struggles to attain it. To be human is always to be on the way to something else. Bloch sums up his philosophy of existence in the formula "S is not yet P." This aphorism means that human persons are their development into the future rather than out of their past. As a Marxist, Bloch argues that human freedom and historical progress begin with "the criticism of religion." Echoing the early Marx, he sees Christianity as hope's protest against all human misery and privation. But, unlike Marx, Bloch sees a positive power in the symbols and stories of the Christian religion when they are understood as human projections. Christianity's great contribution to the world is "the principle of hope," though this gift has often been obscured by the literal beliefs in an otherworldly deity and destiny. Rightly interpreted, however, Christianity's vision of a new humanity *not yet come* is the essence of true religion and authentic existence because it keeps life open to "the pull of the future."[12]

This new thinking among philosophers, psychologists, and sociologists permits us to sketch a phenomenology of hope.[13] Such a description of hope as a persistent structure and process of all human existence will serve three purposes in the present discussion. First, it will clarify further the idea that human hoping is a basic posture rather than an episodic occurrence of life. Second, a phenomenology of the linguistic expressions and experiential dimensions of hope will enable us to distinguish theologies of hope from the very similar positions of process and liberation theologies. Finally, an analysis of hope that brackets the concrete objects and consequences of hope will help illumine the very different kinds of answers that specific communities and individuals give to the question of hope.

What then is hope? What does it mean to speak of hope and of hoping? Hope is related to expectancy, but ordinarily we only hope for something that is good for us—whether it be good health, good fortune, or good conscience. Similarly we may long for what is remote and unlikely, but we do not actively hope for the unthinkable or the impossible. Many hopes turn out to be vain, but while we are hoping we cling to the possibility, if not probability, of attaining our hope's desire. By the same token, we ordinarily do not hope for those things that will inevitably happen or that are easily obtainable. We speak of hope only when some human good does not already lie within reach and may still be denied to us. This means that whatever we hope for is not completely at our disposal. Whatever we might contribute, hope's realization depends upon circumstances and contributions finally beyond our control. Genuine hopes are always directed toward something not completely dependent upon ourselves.

These commonsensical, linguistic understandings of hope point to a deep distinction between two kinds of hope. Perhaps the best way of getting at this distinction is through analyzing hope's negation. Some hopes that are negated only bring disappointment, others bring despair. Some hopes can be dismissed without threat to our being, while the loss of other hopes would leave us "without hope" in this world. We can mark this distinction positively by speaking of hopes (the "thousand things" hoped for that give life pleasure) and of hope (the "one thing" hoped in to give life meaning). The former "everyday hopes" (plural) are directed toward future objects and states that belong to the ordinary world. "Fundamental hope" (singular) is ordinarily not directed to existing objects in the world. Fundamental hope is directed toward something that can endure the negation as well as include the realization of our everyday hopes. Indeed, fundamental hope often becomes visible only when we are deeply shaken by the loss of worldly hopes. In other words, both everyday hopes and fundamental hope are universal structures and processes of life. Persons who hope *for* the thousand things also hope *in* some one thing for life's summed up meaning and value.

Seen in this light, the often-noted connection between hope and religion becomes obvious. Human hope is not exhausted by the reach into the future for the goods of embodied life. Such everyday hopes—whether realized or frustrated—are only meaningful when wrapped about by hope in life's transcending depth and destiny. Whether that depth and destiny is otherworldly or this-worldly, supernatural or natural, personal or impersonal, singular or plural, real or imaginary is a matter of difference between religions and philosophies, groups and individuals. But all find the ground and the goal of life in hope. Little wonder that this new understanding of hope should call forth "theologies of hope." Hope is at once a cultural preoccupation, a universal experience, a religious gesture, and, as we shall see, a biblical outlook. What could be a better basis for an apologetic theology both contemporary and Christian?

THEOLOGIES OF HOPE

The theologies of hope are in part a reflection of the current interest in the human future. Christian theologies of late have proven marvelously sensitive and responsive to such shifts in cultural mood. Indeed, the potpourri of postwar theologies we are reviewing reflects in part contemporary theology's penchant for cultural monitoring and marketing. Nothing is to be gained by denying that theologies of hope are part of a growing, worldwide preoccupation with the future. The fact that the problem of the future reaches from the highest mandarins to the humblest victims of society establishes a new common currency for exchanges between the Church and the world.

While admitting that the cultural times are right for talk of hope, theologians of hope insist that their theological work does not simply pander to cultural fears and fantasies about the future. They are convinced that the theology of hope is *the* theology for all occasions, and that for two reasons. First, they point to the accumulating evidence in scientific, philosophical, and literary circles that hope is a universal structure and process of human existence. The very fact that Marxist philosophers following Bloch have rehabilitated the utopian tradition in Marxism is seen as especially telling evidence for the persistence of hope.[14] But theologians of hope point to a second and far more important reason for choosing hope as the ground and goal of all theological reflection—hope is the central category of biblical faith. Except for the hiatus of eighteenth-century Rationalism and nineteenth-century Liberalism, most theologies have acknowledged the importance of the "last things" in the New Testament. But theologians of hope argue that Orthodoxy's otherworldly and Neoorthodoxy's this-worldly interpretations of biblical eschatology have obscured the true meaning of Christian hope. Only recently—thanks in part to new historical studies of biblical eschatology—has the importance of the real future within eschatological faith been recognized.[15] In reclaiming that dimension of the real future, the theology of hope claims to recover the primitive faith of both the Jewish and the Christian communities.

This means that all the theologies of hope seek to reconstitute biblical eschatology in the modern context. Their different programs share certain broad similarities. They all seek to "dehellenize" the faith by divesting Christian life and thought of static and otherworldly sensibilities. To that end, they all work with horizontal patterns that recognize change and development as normative for all things. They are all aware that this shift to horizontal thinking builds a revolutionary principle into the fabric of life and faith. Since hope and the future are always shared with others, this revolutionary transformation of life always has a political dimension. So dominant are the horizontal, revolutionary, and political motifs that theology of hope is sometimes also called "theology of the future," "theology of revolution," or "political theology." Despite these thematic similarities, there are also important differences, and these similarities and differences will become clear through an examination of the hope theologies of Jürgen Moltmann, Carl Braaten, and Gabriel Vahanian.

Eschatological Hope as Promise—Jürgen Moltmann

Theology of hope probably owes its impetus to the struggles for a new beginning by a person and a people who were defeated and discredited in war. In a candid autobiographical note, Jürgen Moltmann acknowledges that his theological work is deeply rooted in personal and national experience.[16] As a young prisoner of war held in an English camp, he discovered that human beings "cannot live—often, cannot even survive—without hope." Back home at war's end, while studying theology at the University of Göttingen, he perceived that a humane Germany and a liberated Church could only be born of hope in a new future beyond the suffering and shame of their past. Hope rubbed raw and made real by barbed wire and national humiliation opened the way to a new personal and historical context for theological reflection. Only hope grounded in a Christocentric faith can withstand the crucifying experiences of life. Only hope inspired by an eschatological faith can understand the resurrecting experiences of life. Thus did Moltmann find in hope an axis for joining Christology and eschatology in a way both distinctively modern and decidedly biblical. His major statements—*Theology of Hope* (a "Christological eschatology") and *The Crucified God* (an "eschatological Christology")—launched a new theological movement and perhaps initiated a new theological era.[17]

Of course, Moltmann's theology of hope has a wider horizon than the renewal of personal and national existence. He expressly designs his theology to meet three great threats of modern atheism to Christian faith—the interlocking challenges of secularism, reductionism, and utopianism. The most fundamental challenge comes from the modern world's secular dissolution of classical Christianity's "hierarchical transcendence." Christianity's absolute God may no longer be claimed as the necessary and evident ground of all things. The world can be explained, controlled, and changed in terms of its own immanent structures and inherent powers. A second and related challenge is the modern world's humanistic reduction of hierarchical transcendence. Christianity's absolute God need no longer be thought of as the sole basis for personal identity and social order. Personal and social life centered in God can be reduced to idealized projections of human need and human value. Still a third challenge to the Christian faith comes from the modern world's utopian critiques of hierarchical transcendence. The call to overcome human suffering and inequity need no longer be referred or deferred to Christianity's absolute God. The opportunities and responsibilities for creating a new person and a new society must be vested in human hands. In short, for modern secularism, reductionism, and utopianism, Christianity's hierarchical God is intellectually superfluous, morally dispensable, and politically dangerous.

Moltmann believes that these interlocking challenges to Christian faith cannot be met so long as *any* hierarchical conception of God and world is retained. It matters not if the language of "vertical" transcendence is changed from height (the "God above us" of orthodox Christianity) to depth (the "God in us" of liberal or neoorthodox Christianity).[18] All notions of absolute dependence on an absolute God have been dissolved by our discovery of the world's autonomous order and creativity. Moreover, Moltmann is convinced that such vertical patterns of God and world not only have been, but should have been, dissolved. He agrees with the Feuerbachian-Marxist charge that Christianity's hierarchical God has been the source and sanction for a hierarchical world that protects the privileges of the powerful and perpetuates the miseries of the weak.[19] Thus Moltmann argues that the older "transcendence theologies" and the newer "immanence theologies" both fall before the intellectual and moral challenges of modern atheism.

Moltmann does, however, see a way around this discredited "God beyond us" and "God within us." A return to the eschatological outlook of the Bible opens a way for appropriating what truth there is in modern secularism, reductionism, and utopianism without surrendering belief in God or responsibility for the world.[20] That return can only come if we can free ourselves from the mistaken approaches to the use and meaning of biblical eschatology that have dominated Christian thinking since the "hellenizing" of early Christianity. So deeply engrained are the vertical and substance patterns of Greek thought—even in those contemporary theologies that profess to eschew their influence—that Moltmann develops his own position in continuous critical discussion with these other positions. Like an artistic image framed in negative space, Moltmann's thinking emerges largely in contrast to the spectrum of alternative positions that he examines and finds wanting. This style of theological exposition and argumentation compounds the difficulty of grasping his exceedingly complicated theological system, but the subtlety and originality of that system might well be lost without it.[21]

At the very outset, Moltmann sets himself apart from all theologies past and present that have treated eschatology as only a portion of

Christian faith and theological reflection. Moltmann sees eschatology
as the center and circumference of faith and doctrine.

> From first to last, and not merely in the epilogue, Christianity
> is eschatology, is hope, forward looking and forward moving,
> and therefore also revolutionizing and transforming the pres-
> ent. The eschatological is not one element of Christianity, but
> it is the medium of Christian faith as such, the key in which
> everything is set, the glow that suffuses everything here in the
> dawn of an expected new day. For Christian faith lives from
> the raising of the crucified Christ, and strains after the
> promises of the universal future of Christ.... Hence eschatol-
> ogy cannot really be only a part of Christian doctrine. Rather,
> the eschatological outlook is characteristic of all Christian proc-
> lamation, of every Christian existence and of the whole
> Church. There is therefore only one real problem in Christian
> theology, which its own object forces upon it and which it in
> turn forces on mankind and on human thought: the problem of
> the future.[22]

Eschatological theology offers a new exegetical and systematic approach to all the problems of theology—God and world, revelation
and reason, salvation and ethics.

Moltmann not only sets his view of the central place of eschatology in Christianity against all the major theological traditions, but he
also avers a horizontal scheme radically different from the two prevailing patterns of interpretation. The older "God above us" theologies typically limit eschatology to the "end of the world." For them
the coming of the Kingdom of God is an end-time happening that
does not touch everyday life and historical events here and now. By
contrast, the newer "God within us" theologies variously translate
the Bible's eschatological symbols into present experience. The
"coming kingdom" symbolizes each concrete moment's eternity and
God's universal availability. Moltmann argues that the former "futurist eschatologies" do not do justice to God's present judging and
redeeming work in history. Yet he believes that the latter "presenta-
tive eschatologies" err as grievously in the opposite direction by ob-
scuring the future judgment and redemption of God.

Moltmann traces both distortions of biblical eschatology to a common problem—the hierarchical or vertical understanding of God that
has persisted in theologies as varied in their philosophical orientation
as Augustine's Neoplatonism and Bultmann's existentialism. Against
both schematic perspectives, Moltmann offers a horizontal or "historical eschatology" that holds present and future together without separating or identifying them. Indeed, he maintains that in the
experience of hope the present and the future are always related as

"contradiction in identity." The future hoped for can only come to be in the present (identity), but the hoped-for future is always something other than the present (contradiction). Historical eschatology's power lies in this contradiction in identity.

Armed with this horizontal understanding of eschatology, Moltmann shows how eschatological hope grounded in the historical promises of God deals with the three great challenges to the Christian faith noted earlier. He contests secularism with a new theological model of divine transcendence, reductionism with a new theological analysis of historical imagination, and utopianism with a new theological basis for revolutionary politics.

The need for a new model of divine transcendence is patent to everyone who is aware of the secular challenge to all hierarchical conceptions of God. Moltmann, however, believes that this challenge does not really touch the biblical God. The God of the Bible is no hierarchical God, whether "above us" or "within us." The God of the Bible is "ahead of us in the horizons of the future opened up to us in his promises."[23] In other words, for an eschatological outlook, the future is the primary mode of the being of God.

Moltmann claims full biblical warrants for this crucial "paradigm shift," to use Thomas Kuhn's term for a fundamental change in metaphysical presuppositions. Unlike the spatial paradigms of all hierarchical ontologies of God, the language about God in ancient Israel and early Christianity is unmistakably temporal. "Here one speaks of God always only in connection with historical activity and thus of the deity of God only in connection with his coming kingdom. . . . God is not the ground of this world and not the ground of existence, but the God of the coming kingdom which transforms this world and our existence radically."[24] This means that, since God comes to the present from the future, his action in no way contradicts or duplicates the causal influences emanating from the past. Yet God is causally active in the present as that future trajectory which beckons the present to follow one among the several courses of action that are open to the present. In this way, Moltmann distinguishes without separating scientific causality (the causality of the past) and divine causality (the causality of the future). He thereby concludes that the science-versus-religion debate and all extensions of that quarrel concerning orders of being and causality are misconceived. The eschatological God transcends all arguments that say "God is" or "God is not" by raising both into a higher synthesis of truth which says that "God is not yet."[25]

Moltmann's "Coming God" has obvious affinities with process views of God—God guides the present from the future. But, unlike process thinkers such as Cobb or Teilhard, Moltmann offers no philosophical explanation of how God acts from the future. Rather, he depends on the biblical category of "promise" as the way to explain how the present is determined by the future. Indeed, as we shall see, the language of promise is the "essential key" to unlocking the whole meaning of Moltmann's theological eschatology.[26] God's promise is what breaks open hope to the contradiction in identity of experience and time. God's promise divides reality into the anticipated and the unknown, lays down conditions and gives assurance, evokes dissatisfaction and gives gratification. This "overspill of promise" is God's way of influencing while transcending the present from a future that is coming but not yet here. It is God's way of giving order and direction to history through creating an interval that evokes human freedom and invites human obedience. In other words, God's promise is not a predictive word, which history will make true in the future, but a dynamic word, which truly makes history in the present.

The Bible is the record and witness of God's promises to humankind. We see there a deepening and broadening of God's eschatological promises. The promise of the Hebraic covenant is universalized and radicalized in the Christ Event. God's resurrection of the crucified Jesus is a *novum ultimum* that opens up an utterly new future to the world.[27] The Christ Event is the prolepsis that illumines a dialectical process running through all of human history. God will bring life out of death. God does identify with the full horror of the world's captivity to the powers of death in order to endow the world with the unspeakable blessings of life. Only hope based on the whole Christ Event—passion and resurrection—is saved from presumption and despair.[28] An eschatology without Christology misses the suffering and death required of all hopeful faith in God's promised Kingdom. A Christology without eschatology loses the joy and confidence of all faithful hope in God's promised Kingdom. Thus the cross and the resurrection of Christ taken together constitute the prolepsis of God's promise and humanity's hope—God's promise finally to judge and redeem all, and each person's hope to live forever through dying daily.

As the dynamic ground for human hope, God's promise of the future is not fulfilled without human involvement because that promise imposes conditions as well as poses expectations. That God's promise will be fulfilled is assured by his dramatic triumph over great obstacles in the Christ Event. But when and how that promise will be fulfilled depends upon the response of individuals in hopeful faith and faithful hope. Such response is inseparable from historical imagination and revolutionary action. As noted earlier, the Christian faith has suffered serious challenge from reductionistic interpretations of religious beliefs as idealized projections of human wants and needs. While Moltmann certainly does not reduce beliefs in God and his Kingdom to human deception as do the "masters of suspicion" (Marx, Nietzsche, Freud), he does acknowledge that the language of religion is the language of projected dreams and imagined expectations. How could faith in a coming God and hope for a coming Kingdom speak in any other way? The God who is "still not yet" and the Kingdom that is "still on its way" can only be projected. Indeed, Moltmann argues that strictly speaking the term "eschato-logy" is wrong.[29] The Greek term *logos* denotes rational theory and descriptive language of a reality that is there now and always and, as such, can be accurately described and rationally analyzed. In this sense, there could be no *logos* of the future unless the future were the regular recurrence of the present. But the crucified and resurrected Christ shatters all interpretations of experience based on such historical possibility or probability. The Christ Event "does not mean a possibility within the world and its history, but a new possibility altogether for the world, for existence and for history."[30] Thus, Christian eschatology cannot speak of the future in "the form of the Greek *logos* or of doctrinal statements based on experience, but only in the form of statements of hope and of promises for the future."[31] The language of hope and promise is the language of wish and of dream, of poetic license and utopian imagination.[32]

Humankind's projected hopes and God's proleptic promises are for Moltmann by no means individualistic and otherworldly.[33] The Kingdom of God, coming "on earth as it is in heaven," must triumph over all "the threatening nothingness that surrounds us." That Christian vision of a new self and new community on the way certainly includes more than anything envisioned in the revolutionary utopianisms of our time, but it dare not include less. Eschatological hope constrains the Christian to join in the political struggles for economic, social, and racial justice now under way around the world.[34] There can be no human dignity or community without an end to poverty, subjugation, and humiliation. "An all-embracing vision of God must be linked with the economic liberation of man from hunger, with the political freeing of man from oppression by other men, and with the human emancipation of man from racial humiliation."[35]

Here then we have a rounded view of Moltmann's theology of hope. God's promise of the future and human hope for the future in Christ Jesus brook no sentimentality or escapism. The world is not the "heaven of self-realization" that the "immanence theologies" announce, nor is it the "hell of self-estrangement" that the "transcendence theologies" denounce. The world is neither because it is *"Das Noch-Nicht"*—the still-not-finished world. In that *prospective and pro*-mised world,[36] those who live by hope are stirred to revolutionary impatience with what is and are moved by revolutionary boldness to bring the Kingdom into the midst of life. But all easy identities between the coming Kingdom and our utopian dreams are shattered by the contradiction between present and future that is signaled by the cross and resurrection. Material abundance, government by the people, equality for all are not the last signs of the coming Kingdom.

> What is the abundance of life? The death of death. What is complete freedom? The elimination of every rule, every authority and power. What is God? The elimination of nothingness itself, which threatens and cajoles everything that exists and insults everything that wants to live but must die.[37]

Eschatological hope grounded in that promised future will not rest satisfied until God is all in all. In the meantime, "hope against hope" is a limitless resource for inventive imagination and an inexhaustible power for historical transformation.

Eschatological Hope as Revolution—Carl E. Braaten

The American counterpart to European theology of hope has been spearheaded by Carl E. Braaten. Growing out of his earlier concerns with history and revelation, Braaten's turn to eschatological categories is heavily indebted to the influence of Jürgen Moltmann and, especially, Wolfhart Pannenberg, who along with Moltmann pioneered the new future-oriented theologies in the early sixties. Like their theologies, Braaten's articulates a new context for the experience of transcendence and a new relation between theory and practice in our pluralistic situation. He too seeks to reverse the decline of Christian faith and the rise of secular consciousness through a reappropriation of biblical eschatology. But, reflecting the greater pragmatism and activism of the American scene, Braaten has highlighted the practical implications of this eschatological orientation. His major theological statement, *The Future of God,* concludes with a call for an "ethic of revolution" that links revolutionary action with eschatological hope. His subsequent *Christ and Counter-Christ* and *Eschatology and Ethics* further delineate the functional implications of eschatological hope for the Church's ministry and mission and for the Christian's social and political responsibility.[38] Indeed, all of his writings are an exercise in what he has called "eschatopraxis"—"doing the future now ahead of time."[39] All are explorations in "the revolutionary dynamics of hope."

Braaten sees eschatological hope as the only way to bridge the ever-widening gap between the thought-worlds of the Bible and of modern culture.[40] That bridge cannot be laid, however, without fundamental alterations to both sides. Although both worlds are preoccupied with the question of hope, their answers are by no means commensurate. The biblical hope for a coming Kingdom and the secular hope for a better world suggest very different "horizons"—very different defining boundaries of thought and life. The central task for theology today is to find a way to bring those two horizons together.

How then can the eschatological fervor of early Christianity and the revolutionary futurism of contemporary life be merged? Braaten believes that the biblical message can be correlated with the present age if both can be shown to share the horizon of a common future that links the past to the present without sacrificing what is particular and valuable in each. That overarching and integrating future cannot be furnished by the prevailing secular models of progress which see the future as an extension of the present. Whether that extension is conceived in mechanistic or evolutionary terms, a future implicitly contained in the present excludes the radical newness of the coming Kingdom of God. Nor can that overarching future be modeled on prevailing theological accounts of the Kingdom of God which see the future as an eternity beyond time. Whether that eternity is conceived as another world or an existential moment, a future explicitly severed from the present negates the importance of the ongoing history of mankind.[41] In other words, prevailing secular models of the future exclude the eschatological future from concrete history, while prevailing theological motifs divorce concrete history from the eschatological future. The only future that can establish a common horizon for the biblical message and the modern mind is the *future of God.* Only the God "ahead of us" whose Kingdom is coming on earth can bring biblical hope and secular hope together.

For Braaten, the meeting point for the coming God of biblical eschatology and the becoming world of secular futurology is none other than Jesus Christ.[42] To be sure, the question of God can arise independently of Jesus Christ since the question of God is the quest for hope common to all humankind. The question of God is "the question about the possibility of man's becoming truly fulfilled beyond the deformities of his past and present, and especially beyond the inevitability of his having to die."[43] But this quest for ultimate fulfillment which is the quest for God is realized only in Jesus Christ because he is where human hope in God and God's hope in humanity are perfectly joined. "Jesus is the representative in whom God and man exchange hope for each other. Because of Jesus' cross God has a reason to hope for man; on account of Jesus' resurrection man has a reason to hope in God. For Jesus' sake we do not give up on God and he does not give up on us."[44] Because God raised Jesus from the dead, persons have hope in God as the power for a revolutionary future over every "deadliness" that threatens to destroy life. Because Jesus was faithful unto death, God has hope in human beings as the partisans of a revolutionary future despite all the suffering that inevitably comes with life. In short, Jesus opens up the future for both God and humankind.

A theology of hope built on the paradigm of crucifixion and resurrection can be nothing other than a theology of revolution.[45] The historical movement of God and humankind toward the future can be no straight-line development or gradual ascent if it must pass through the dying and rising of Jesus Christ. That future can be reached only through the total revolutionary reversal of the old (crucifixion) and the total revolutionary establishment of the new (resurrection) in history. This historical revolution is total in two ways. First, it is an unbounded revolution. The "Christian revolutionary" undertakes to transform "everything in religion, morality and culture; anything from politics, to economics, to technology."[46] In the process, the Christian revolutionary draws no boundaries between the friend and the foe of the revolution. All are comrades in the revolutionary struggle to join persons and earth in a Kingdom of unity and love. Second, this is an unending revolution. The Christian revolutionary can never rest satisfied with any historical approximation of the Kingdom. There are no "postrevolutionary situations" where the Christian can end the struggle. "The Christian always looks forward in hope for the kingdom that is still to come, and by exercising this hope he is critical of everything that already is."[47] In short, the paradigm of Christ's crucifixion and resurrection imposes a logic of radically inclusive and unending revolution on the believer and the Church.

Braaten sees this same logic as the underlying meaning of late Jewish and early Christian apocalypticism. Eschatological hope in the Scriptures is couched in the language of a total juxtaposition of this present evil age and the blessed age to come. In the New Testament, this juxtaposition is also described as a cosmic contest between the Christ and the "Counter-Christ."[48] This apocalyptic "dualization" of reality has been one of the reasons why modern Christians have found biblical eschatology unintelligible. But Braaten sees through the bizarre dualistic imagery of biblical apocalypticism to its revolutionary logic. The logic of apocalypticism is transformational rather than developmental. It anticipates an *adventus* (the appearance of something new not yet within things) rather than a *futurum* (the actualization of potentialities already within things).[49] Jewish apocalypticism pictured this coming Kingdom in totally futuristic terms, but this splitting of reality into the present "here and now" and the future "then and there" was the seedbed for our modern-day sense of freedom and history. Jesus built on this apocalyptic tradition and in the process transformed it proleptically by bringing the future into the present. Like Jewish apocalypticism, he too saw God's coming from the future into the present as a negation of existing reality, but Jesus understood that apocalyptic negation means permanent transformation rather than total annihilation of the past. Jesus thus transformed the older apocalyptic dualism from the bad news of sheer earthly destruction to the good news of vital earthly fulfillment.[50]

Braaten translates the revolutionary logic of continuity/discontinuity and already/not yet into a revolutionary ecclesiology and ethics of hope. As an eschatological community, the Church's primary function is "to proclaim and pioneer the future of the world in God's coming kingdom."[51] The Church must always exist "ahead of the world" as the place where the world can become conscious of its future destiny in the freedom and love of God. As such, the Church is not the Kingdom of God but only the sacramental sign of the Kingdom that is emerging in, with, and under the conditions of the present world. The Church "signs" this coming Kingdom through a ministry and mission that seeks to embrace the world's pluralities within a universalism of hope.

The ministry of the word in the revolutionary Church opens up the distance and difference between the present world and its future in God's Kingdom. "As law the word attacks everything in the present that refuses to inherit the future; as gospel the word brings samples of the ultimate future into the pain of the present."[52] The preached word is the driving wedge that breaks with the past and brings in the future. Similarly, the ministry of sacrament in the revolutionary Church takes up life's division and destruction into a new context. Holy Communion portends the messianic banquet when the many will eat and drink together at one table. Holy Baptism marks the beginning of a daily struggle against the old for the sake of the new. This revolutionary ministry can in turn only be carried out in a revolutionary mission that awakens the world to the universal Kingdom dawning in the midst of all its cultures and all its religions.[53]

This revolutionary ecclesiology cannot be separated from an equally revolutionary ethics.[54] Ethics in service to the coming Kingdom of God is goal directed. The fact that the Kingdom is future reveals the imperfections and incompleteness of every social and political form of the coming Kingdom. But the prolepsis of the Kingdom releases God's presence and power in the present social and political order. Moreover, this proleptic presence and power of God has been revealed through Jesus Christ as transforming love. As the norm of ethics, love takes the form of law and grace. Love limits the misuse of freedom and attacks the structures of oppression. This means that Christian love compels the believer to support the given structures of a society so long as they are fluid enough to serve the ends of love. But that same love requires the believer to change those structures if they stand in the way of a more loving society—"even to overthrow them with force when the controlling powers have become insane and demonic."[55] This "messianic license" to act beyond the law does not exclude violence, but force must always be subservient to grace. There is no room in Christian ethics for revenge and retaliation. Finally, every act of the Christian must hasten the arrival of a Kingdom of peace and reconciliation among persons and nations. For Christian love, law is always the imperfect instrument of a perfecting grace of selves and of God at work in the world.

Thus does Braaten recast the whole of Christian thought and life in the mold of eschatological hope. Central to that recasting is a new conception of transcendence that Braaten approaches in two different ways. He subverts the older spatial images by temporal ones—God is not above us but ahead of us as the power of the absolute future. Braaten alternatively subordinates the older supernatural language to what he calls "contranatural" imagery—God is not the archetype of a static world but the advent of a becoming world. Neither of these models is developed into a full-blown ontology by Braaten. He rather delineates them by implication in his descriptions of how persons experience transcendence as the power of the future or as the power of contradiction. Eschatological hope is revolutionary not so much because it gives us a new idea of God, but because it draws us into the world as God's revolutionary messengers of faith and mediators of love.

Eschatological Hope as Utopia—Gabriel Vahanian

Seeing Gabriel Vahanian placed within the theology of hope may seem strange to some. Vahanian is vaguely associated in the minds of many with the death-of-God movement of the sixties, though what he contributed other than the slogan remains unclear to them since he roundly criticized the movement.[56] Even those who are more familiar with Vahanian's writings of that period may not see a connection between his theological iconoclasm and the hope movement. But the connection is there. Vahanian's protest against absolutizing any finite achievement or relationship keeps life perpetually open to the future. Moreover, a number of his recent publications have made the relationship between his iconoclasm and eschatology increasingly clear—the one is presupposition and consequence of the other.

> The essence of Christianity, a religion based on incarnation and hence on the time of the end, is an eschatological conception of the world, of man as well as of God. . . . Because it is essentially eschatological, Christianity is necessarily iconoclastic. To the extent that it is iconoclastic, Christianity is likewise eschatological.[57]

As we shall see, Vahanian's reconstitution of biblical eschatology in the modern context goes its own way in divesting faith of all static and hierarchical proclivities. Indeed, his thinking is sharply critical of the hope movement stemming from Moltmann precisely at the point of its conceptions of the futurity of humankind and of God.[58] But Vahanian does unfold an eschatology that connects with a universal structure of human hope and that builds a revolutionary principle and a political dimension into the whole of Christian faith. He thereby does offer to the contemporary discussion a distinctive kind of theology of hope.

Vahanian has been thinking and writing for years about the way to do theology in the present age. He has always placed an uncommon demand on his readers at the point of both substance and style. His dense originality and condensed vocabulary can be penetrated only by the most attentive and reflective reading. Those who follow his daring constructions and subtle distinctions, however, have always found him breaking radically new ground in cultural and theological studies of religion. Like any trailblazer, he scouts and stakes out the frontiers and leaves the consolidation of those advances to a later time and perhaps other thinkers. This gives his thought a certain schematic form, but that form is required of necessity by the character of the times. Vahanian believes that we are now living through the dawning of a "technological civilization" that will radically alter both humanity and world and thus decisively change culture and religion.[59] Since the character of that new age is still emerging, theology can only be preparatory for the new humanism and faith to come.

Vahanian first wrote of this epochal transition in *The Death of God* as a collapse of radical monotheism into radical immanentism in Western culture. There he admits the finality of this collapse of the cultural framework in which God's otherness had been articulated for centuries, but he laments the resulting reduction of God to "a cultural accessory or a human ideal." This reduction deprives life of iconoclastic symbols—those "imageless images" which alone keep human life human by continually breaking human life open to novelty and change.

Vahanian continued this protest in *Wait Without Idols* where he argues that the skepticism of modern literature serves as a kind of "negative" iconoclasm by destroying an idolatrous sense of human power and worth.[60] Indeed, Vahanian maintains that modern literature has taken over the iconoclastic function that a proper theology ordinarily fulfills. In *No Other God,* he sounds the call for a "post-Christian" theology that would allow both human beings and God to survive the death of Christendom.[61] Vahanian sketches out that theology in his latest book, *God and Utopia.* Here he shuts the door on all forms of theology that see self and God in the context of either nature or history. Neither of these is the real locus of human existence in our time. Rather, it is technology that sets the problems and holds the prospects today for any revitalized understanding of persons and God. Indeed, as we shall see, Vahanian contends that technology opens the way to a new theology by conjoining "the utopian dimension of human existence" and "the eschatological dimension of biblical faith."

Vahanian sees human existence for believers and unbelievers alike as essentially utopian.[62] Human beings are bound to go beyond themselves in becoming human. "Man is man only insofar as he is new man."[63] Humanization as distinguished from mere hominization is always "ahead of itself" in utopian imagination and construction. This "utopianism of the human reality" functions both as a limit and as a horizon of existence. As horizon, the human reality confronts persons as a dare without prototype. As limit, the human reality contests every present expression of the "new man" as less than a final achievement. The utopian is always a dialectic of the *novum* (the latest, new thing) and the *eschaton* (the last, ultimate thing). In other words, the "utopian reality of man" means that human life is always a life of advent (life coming from the future) and of dissent (life becoming something different). Both valences of the utopian dimension are caught etymologically in the word "utopia," which comes from the Greek *ouk topos,* meaning "nowhere." Thus, human life happens where, strictly speaking, "it has no place."[64]

This "utopian beyondness" of human life makes clear why, for Vahanian, every culture has a religiosity, why every humanism is paired with a faith.[65] The utopian always transcends the given. Transcendence is affirmed not as something alien to human beings but as something that belongs to persons and to which persons belong *when they are fully human*. This transcendence is, of course, what religions speak of symbolically as "God." As we shall see, there are very different ways of conceiving the relation between "God" and persons, between the way "God" fronts persons and persons confront "God." But whatever the conceptuality of a given culture and its religiosity, "God" is that "nowhere" where human life becomes human. God is God and human beings are human only if they remain "other" to one another. If they merge into one or diverge into two, both divinity and humanity die. Thus, for Vahanian, "transcendence is affirmed and, accordingly, grasped as the utopianism inherent in the human reality in its integrity."[66]

The utopian reality of humanity and divinity is always expressed through language.[67] More is implied by this claim than the commonsensical acknowledgement that we can only communicate about persons and God in words and gestures, in images and rituals. For Vahanian, symbolic language is the very medium of the life of persons and of God. Symbolic language is the advent of "the human" because language "enables man to conceive his being as a project but prevents him ultimately from identifying it with the realization of this project. ... The word provides man with a home and a city, and tells him at the same time that here is no abiding city."[68] Utopian language is equally the event of the divine. "In order for God to exist, humans must hope and be able to speak. Through language, God bursts forth in the human reality."[69] Through language, the human is the event of God and God is the advent of the human.

There can be no doubt that Vahanian sees biblical faith as the perfect match for this linguistically mediated utopian process of humanization.[70] The eschatological orientation of the Bible portrays human beings as "futurable" and God as "iconoclastic." More important, the Bible sees "coming God" and "man becoming" meeting in Christ—the "utopian metaphor" *par excellence* where God and humankind are joined together without separation or confusion, without division or change.[71] Indeed, the utopian character of authentic humanism and the "eschatic" nature of biblical faith are structurally identical. But this formal identity must not be misunderstood. Vahanian brooks no reduction of utopian humanism and eschatic faith to some universal experience equally enjoyed by all. As already noted, both the human and the divine come to appearance in language. But that language is always culturally and religiously particular. The utopian reality of God and persons is always expressed in a culture's own religiosity, and every religiosity is always articulated in a specific cultural framework.[72] This means that any given symbol system may either express or repress true humanity and true divinity. Indeed, any given symbol system can spell death or life to humankind and God.

Vahanian calls each such symbol system a "technique of the human" and notes that each technique is borne by a distinctive "vector of culture."[73] The heart of his theological program centers in sorting out the ways these techniques differ and why their vectors change with the passage of time.[74] He begins by making a crucial distinction between "soteriological" and "eschatological" techniques of the human.[75] Soteriological techniques—religions of the salvation of humankind—envision God as the condition of human existence. In soteriological religiosity, God's transcendence is conceived as exterior to human life and the world. Human existence is thereby defined as "scarcity" and "heteronomy," and humankind's utopian destiny is projected into another world that can only be anticipated through "spiritual" evasion of this world. By contrast, eschatological techniques—religions of the reign of God—see humanity as the condition of God. Eschatic religiosity sees God's transcendence as anterior to human life and the world. Human existence is marked by "abundance" and "autonomy," and humankind's utopian destiny is realized in this world becoming "other" through "bodily" engagement with it.

Vahanian further divides soteriological techniques into two broad categories according to whether the process of humanization is seen as a liberation from nature or from history. A soteriological religiosity vectored on nature centers in a "supernatural" conception of transcendence.[76] Whether expressed in the concrete language of myth or the abstract language of metaphysics, God's supernatural reality is seen as the necessary origin of everything that is. Only a return to the supernatural world above can make up for the mysteries and miseries of life in the natural world. But that "paradise" can be recollected now in the soul's flight from this world in ascetic piety. By contrast, a soteriological religiosity vectored on history turns on an "apocalyptic" conception of transcendence. Whether expressed in the vivid language of myth or the visionary language of "ideology," this apocalyptic God is seen as the necessary completion of everything that is. Only the arrival of the apocalyptic world ahead can resolve the vicissitudes and injustices of historical existence. But that "kingdom" can be envisioned now through the spirit's negation of this world in ascetic action. To complicate matters even further, Vahanian sometimes subsumes the supernatural and apocalyptic expressions of soteriological religiosity under the inclusive vector of a "mythic" conception of transcendence, which envisions a "counter-world" above nature and beyond history. But, whether speaking broadly of mythic frameworks or more precisely of supernatural and apocalyptic matrices, soteriological "techniques of the human" always distinguish selves and God, world and Kingdom by separating them spatially and temporally.

Given these distinctions, Vahanian argues that Christianity has been a "salvation religion" throughout most of its history. To be sure, there was no way historically that Christianity could have avoided taking the cultural form of a soteriological faith because the only cultural vectors available in the Greco-Roman world were mythic. But, for reasons that should be obvious, these mythic carriers were never adequate to the essentially eschatological religiosity of a true humanism and the biblical faith. They always consigned the utopian reality of persons and God to some paradisal past or apocalyptic future. "Their utopianism has consisted largely in changing worlds rather than in changing the world."[77]

Nevertheless, Vahanian does not view this "Constantinian Christianity" as one dark age of unrelieved spiritual apostasy and moral bankruptcy, and that for three intriguing reasons. First, as already noted, the dominant mythological framework of Western civilization permitted nothing other than a soteriological form of religiosity. The biblical faith had to be adapted to this cultural framework or simply disappear. Second, even though relegated to a world above nature or beyond history, the utopian reality of persons and God were negatively present in this religiosity. These negative, otherworldly forms of utopia at least stood watch iconoclastically against every temptation to deify nature or society. Finally, something of the positive power of eschatological faith was present even in these supernatural and apocalyptic faiths because of the reality of the Church. As long as the christological understanding of persons and God was "bodied forth" in the Church, Christianity could never be at ease with temptations to retreat from the present world into a past paradise or a future apocalypse. Without the Church—that most maligned of all institutions—"Christianity would have only been a 'salvation' religion completely cut loose and disengaged from every concern for the world, fixed instead on the *other world*."[78]

Having admitted that eschatological faith survived in ambiguous fashion in the supernatural and historical theisms of the classical past, Vahanian contends that now all such forms of salvation religion have come to grief in the modern world.[79] These "misshapen" utopianisms have lost their power to bring humanity or divinity to appearance. An axial shift in the sensibilities of Western civilization has "dishabilitated" the entire Christian tradition by undermining the mythic framework in which its theologies have been articulated. God is no longer the necessary precondition of human existence. The God of salvation religion who explains life from above nature and who completes life from beyond history is no more! This cultural vehicle of God has been dissolved by humankind's progressive and irreversible "technological triumph" over human scarcity and impotence.[80] Vahanian, of course, speaks of this complex cultural and religious phenomenon as "the death of God." The death of God is the final passing of the mythological framework that has formed and informed religion and culture from the dawn of Western civilization. For that reason, the death of God is an unprecedented crisis for both religion and culture.

Vahanian sees in this crisis great danger and great opportunity. The danger is two-fold—that religion and culture will surrender to atheism and simply reassign the attributes of God to persons (secular humanism, the death-of-God theologies), or that they will return to a pristine theism by simply remodeling human dependence on God (the new theologies, the new religions). Down either road lies disaster for humanity. Neither atheism nor theism can furnish a technique of the human reality and its utopianism in a technological civilization.[81] Both will "swallow men up in godlessness"—in the idolatry of persons deifying themselves or depending upon God. The gravity of this two-fold danger is the very obverse of the grandeur of a two-fold opportunity—that religion and culture will face anew the living God of the Bible and that they will pioneer a "pleromatic" ecclesiology that will embrace humankind and earth in a communion at once pluralistic and universalistic. Vahanian believes that these dangers can be avoided and the opportunities redeemed if, and only if, technology is recognized as the vector of a new religiosity and as the technique of a new humanism.

Whether we like it or not, we have opted for a technological civilization that is radically altering both life and world.[82] Technology for Vahanian means more than tools. Technology is a method. There was an "artisan" stage of technological development stretching all the way back to the very dawn of human evolution when the tool merely extended human power and alleviated human work. But implicit in

that primitive stage was the method that has finally emerged with the
"scientific" stage of technological development—a method that is
transforming existence and eliminating work. As a technique of the
human, that method makes people producers of nature and history
rather than their product. That method delivers people from the
mythic world of scarcity and heteronomy into the technological world
of abundance and autonomy. "In technological terms, every problem
is by definition soluble."[83]

Seen in this light, technology is anything but the threat to humanism and faith so widely announced and deeply feared. Without a
doubt, technology has dissolved utopias of deferral and dependence.
But such utopias have never been fully adequate to that utopian reality of God and persons required of an authentic humanism and eschatological faith. The heart of technology for Vahanian is its power to
transform. Technology liberates individuals from an impersonal nature and history and empowers them to humanize both. What then is
technology if not the continuation of utopian humanism and eschatological faith? Vahanian does indeed see an intimate bond between
technology and the biblical understanding of divine transcendence
and human destiny. "From the points of view of both technology and
the Christian tradition, man cannot make his proper place unless
there is a place for man which is neither residue of nature nor after-
glow of history. Man remains to be realized. Thus, both technology
and Christian utopianism inaugurate an ethic of the coming man."[84]
In other words, technology is both the fulfillment and the denial of
the Christian tradition. In negating Christianity's mythological conception of religion, whether in its supernatural or apocalyptic version, technology prepares the way for a fruition of eschatological faith
that endows human beings and God with new dimensions.

Vahanian is under no illusions that technology's great promise
will happen automatically. Technology will foster the utopianism
proper to human existence only if it gets "the religion it deserves."
That new religiosity requires a new language and a new ecclesiology.
Here Vahanian is still feeling his way and his writings at this point
reach an unparalleled density and difficulty. But the essential shape
of this requisite linguistic and ecclesial revolution is clear enough to
be grasped.

Linguistically, an eschatological faith can speak of God and his
Kingdom only by speaking of persons and their world. The person is
the event of God, though God is the ever-present other by which persons become what they are not. The world is the event of God's Kingdom, though the Kingdom is the never-present *eschaton* that calls

forth the world as a *novum*. But language about persons and world in a technological civilization must be "bodily" and "fictile." The shift from mythology to technology is a "shift from a civilization of the soul to a civilization of the body."[85] Technological civilization gives humankind an earthly dimension heretofore neglected in favor of the soul and its heavenly aspirations. Body language brings the utopian reality of persons and God into the realizable present and thereby makes the human body and the social structure the instruments of the Kingdom, the incarnation of God. But body language that does not sink into factualism or soar into fantasy must be fictile—it must shape the present by joining the real and the imaginary.[86] Indeed, every human body and social structure is a "bridge" between the imaginary and the real precisely because language is the "artificer" of the human.[87] "Language nudges the body into the word as well as anchoring the word in the body, even as the imaginary is anchored in the real. Indeed there is no utopia except in terms of the realizable, and the imaginary is nothing other than a utopianism of real."[88] Eschatological artifice does not overwhelm the imaginary with the real, nor does it sublimate the real in the imaginary. It emanicaptes humankind from both, "thereby bringing hope within reach."[89]

Ecclesiologically, an eschatological faith is not identical with or separate from the customs and structures of society. The Church is, rather, "the eschatological principle of political and social organization of the human order."[90] The utopian Church in a technological civilization faces a challenge of coming to terms with the twin threats of the "technocratic" systematization and privatization of life. The often-voiced fear that technology brings dehumanization and faithlessness centers in technology's admitted breakup of distinctive customs, roles, and communities. Bureaucratic rationalization and multinational corporations are making geographic and sociological boundaries obsolete. Considered politically and racially, this technological leveling could be seen as the latter-day beginnings of a "city of earth" where there is neither East nor West, black nor white, male nor female. But what of the individual, who seems lost in this "gigantism" and "interchangeability"? Will the individual and the interpersonal simply disappear in the extraordinary artificiality of the technological environment and persona? While acknowledging the dangers of such a loss, Vahanian contends that artificiality need not oppose humanness. After all, linguistic artifice creates the utopian "nowhere" where human life happens. "Far from being a robot, artificial man is the man who makes himself."[91] Artificial man can be authentic man if he makes himself "in the image of an imageless God."

The Church cannot contribute to this artistic process of humanization by establishing havens of seclusion or ghettos of particularity. The Church must go beyond all such confessional and geographical boundaries.[92] Neither liturgy nor polity should separate the Church from the community of persons. Yet the Church will lose its iconoclastic function and its eschatological anchorage if it is nothing but the world. The utopian Church is an *other* world in the present world precisely because it is "pleromatic"—bringing all things everywhere into fullness by naming the One God who is everywhere because he is nowhere, and who is for everyone because he is for no one.[93] The utopian Church is anywhere anyone makes a new world.

Here in bold strokes is the sum of two thousand years of Christianity. Vahanian paints a remarkable portrait of humankind and world in transition from a mythic to a technological civilization. That transition need not be ruinous to culture or religion if a new technological utopianism can be articulated in word and communion. Happily, that utopianism is fully compatible with the eschatological utopianism of biblical faith and true humanism. "Technological utopianism is focused neither on the past nor on the future, but on the present, on the time of the human, the only time with which God could be contemporary, the only time attuned to the fullness of time, pleroma of the God who comes."[94]

THEOLOGIES OF HOPE IN QUESTION

The theologies of hope present a compelling medley on the relevance of eschatology to the Christian faith and modern world. Their variations on this theme are keyed to hope as the primary concern of modern culture, as the distinguishing feature of human life, and as the central thrust of biblical faith. There are similar-sounding passages in all the theologies that work with this root metaphor of hope—transcendence as horizontal, change as normative, life as corporate. But, as we have seen, there are also striking differences in the ways God and persons, future and present, Kingdom and world are correlated in these theologies. For this reason, theologies of hope are more a confederation of theological proposals than a distinctive school of thought.

Taken broadly as a movement, theology of hope has had considerable influence though it has not sustained the level of interest that it first generated in the late sixties. Its luminaries still command a fair share of younger followers and loyal critics—one sure indication of the lasting importance of a new theological orientation. Quite apart from such questions of lineal succession and survival, theology of hope has permeated the entire contemporary discussion with the themes of hope and the future and with the language of image and the imagination. Moreover, it has widened the range of serious theological dialogue with the major intellectual challenges and practical problems facing the Christian today. Theological efforts to take into account the Feuerbachian, Marxist, and Freudian critiques of Christianity and to meet the problems of secularization, revolution, and technology head on are models of candor and openness in current theological discussion. Challenging all privatism and parochialism, the theology of hope summons the believer and the Church to come to terms with a restive and changing world.

Critics have, of course, had much to say about the weaknesses and failures of the theology of hope. Apart from their detailed criticism that is the stock-in-trade of all theological exchange, two major questions dominate the critical discussion. One is the problem of the way the past, present, and future are related in theology of hope. This problem is multifaceted since temporality figures large in all talk about God and human existence. Quite apart from a certain one-sidedness of emphasis on the future, serious questions have been raised about God and the future and about Christ and the past. Saying that God is open to the future is something very different from claiming that God is *in* the future and comes *from* the future. Theology of hope gives no adequate account of how this futuristic conception of God avoids turning God back into a supernatural being or construing God as a humanistic idealization. Questions about time come from another direction from those who find difficulties in seeing how the future can truly be open if that future is somehow decisively revealed in the past event of Jesus Christ. Conceiving the Christ Event as paradigm of a universal process of history or as preview of a coming consummation of history does not resolve the inherent problem in looking to a normative past in order to understand an open future. None of the historical dialectics and linguistic contrivances of the theology of hope seem to have put these theoretical problems about past, present, and future to rest.

A second major line of questioning concerns matters of practical application. If the future cannot be extrapolated from the past, how then is the future to be purposefully shaped? Theology of hope is clear that doing the future "ahead of time" requires utopian vision and revolutionary action. But theology of hope is finally less daring and demanding than its theory suggests. For all the talk of a new world and a revolutionary Church, theology of hope remains remarkably uncritical of repressive structures and vested interests within the Church and the world. For the most part, it does not dare the future by playing or politicking beyond the far edge of today's prevailing ideals and orders of reality. In short, theology of hope does not seem to set in motion the visionary fantasy and revolutionary fervor that hope for an unimaginable future in an unbearable present demands.[95]

This reluctance to gamble the future in revolution or to gambol it in play has been redressed by other contemporary theologies. As we have seen already, liberation theology presses all theological talk of revolution into militant praxis. Though learning much from theology of hope, liberation theology is quite critical of the former's failure to "materialize" the Kingdom and to "radicalize" the Church in the cause of revolution. In the next chapter, we will discover similar criticisms that come from a very different direction. Theology of play finds theology of hope too unrelenting in its critique of the present and too unimaginative in its vision of the future. Theology of hope underestimates the revolutionary power of festive joy and adventurous play. When put to the service of faith, the power of play to "suspend" reality can create new men and women and a new world.

6
Play as Clue and Catalyst

Hugo Rahner, Harvey Cox, Robert Neale

North America seems bent on becoming one gigantic playground. Play in all its forms constitutes the primary lived world of the majority of North Americans. How else can we explain the spectacle of Super Bowls, the fervor of contract bridge, and the wealth of movie stars? How else can we explain the energy and enthusiasm, the resources and ingenuity devoted to the leisure-time activities of sports, games, and entertainment?

As a people, we have an insatiable appetite for professional and amateur sports—not just for the dominant ones of football, baseball, basketball, and hockey but for tennis, bowling, skiing, skating, golf, track, racing, soccer, boxing, gymnastics, swimming, weight lifting, billiards, mountain climbing, hang gliding, frisbee, and seemingly any other competitive activity involving skill and chance that people are willing to call a sport. Game playing commands something of the same devoted following as does sports. Among the game players are the gamblers, who "play" everything from the horses to the mean temperature of the day, and the television viewers, who thrill to the game shows that fill so many hours of the broadcast day. But most people actually play games "just for the fun of it"—table games, card games, party games, yard games, electronic games, word games, and any other rule-governed activity that affords suspense and satisfaction to those who take part. Still, after all of this, we have the need and the means to be entertained—radio and television, theater and cinema, concerts and spectaculars, books and magazines, cassettes and records, and any other means of filling our lives with pleasure and distraction from daily rounds.

Moreover, all this playfulness is not merely an interlude of escape from the workaday world of politics and business, of education and industry, of citizenship and friendship. Play spills over into these other areas of life by providing the fundamental metaphors and guiding paradigms of understanding and behavior. Politicians devise "game plans" and financiers "play the market." Scholars "play with ideas" and workers "belong to the team." Citizens must "play by the rules" but friends can "play around with each other." Every area of life and thought seems touched by play. As Michael Novak has suggested, we are "one nation under play, with sports and games and entertainment for all!"[1]

Commentators on the North American scene are divided over what to make of this preoccupation with play. Among those holding a strictly utilitarian view of the place of play in human life, the assessments range from guarded approval to outright disapproval. Some see our unrelenting pursuit of play as a necessary "safety valve" for handling the drudgery and boredom of living in a superindustrialized and superurbanized society. Like the "bread and circuses" of Imperial Rome, our special opportunities for play mitigate the regimented labor and life that precede and follow them. Others see our nonstop playfulness as an integral part of our economy. The tellingly named "leisure and entertainment industry" is the perfect answer to a capitalist system's need for continuously expanding markets of desirable and consumable products. Since these products make use of the energy and ability of the players, this industry has the added advantage of an inexhaustible supply of its most important raw material. Still other pundits see today's culture at play as the decisive sign of our moral and spiritual decay. For them, the old ideals of thrift and work have disappeared from a land grown fat with abundance and permissiveness. The crass commercialism of the merchants of play and the equally crass enthusiasms of the consumers of play answer one another perfectly and together reflect the decadence of our land.

There are, however, other commentators who take a very different view of our culture's playful bent because they see human play in nonutilitarian terms. They are quite prepared to acknowledge that all is not well as things stand in our "nation under play." They too criticize our overly escapist, commercialized, and compulsive playing. They lament the way many people refuse to let play *be* play by always "working" to become more effective players or only "playing" to become more productive workers. But these utilitarian corruptions of play do not reduce play to an optional activity made necessary by our increasingly automated and affluent society. Rather, the play of children and of adults is seen as having an indispensable place in the life of each individual and every society. Play has its own place alongside of work in the life rightly ordered. Our culture's frantic playfulness is an overdue reaction to the suppression and suspicion of play that has long prevailed in our work-oriented culture. Whatever *over*reaction there is in this recovery must not be allowed to subvert play again to work. Among those commentators thus disposed toward play are certain "theologians of play" who see in this activity a clue and catalyst for Christian renewal in our time. For them, play and faith have a very similar place in human life.

THE PLACE OF PLAY

Regardless of how widespread the popular pursuit of play, a "theology of play" may seem woefully out of touch with our culture's thought world. How can play and faith be brought together in a culture, nurtured by puritanism and capitalism, that weds faith and work? As improbable as it might seem to some, there is a growing trend among scholars to explore the positive relationships between play and all other human activities including religion.[2] Scholarly studies in a variety of fields have shown that the play experiences of children and adults must be taken seriously because these experiences have a vital place in personal and cultural life. Not only have these scholars studied play itself, but they have heuristically applied the insights derived from studying play to other areas of thought and life with impressive results. Everything from the stock market to funeral rites is seen in a new way when viewed from the standpoint of play. Such play studies have been developed by anthropologists and ethnologists, psychologists and sociologists, economists and mathematicians, philosophers and political scientists. Indeed, the increasing use of "game" and "play" metaphors by a variety of original thinkers suggests that a whole new understanding of human beings may be emerging. In the final analysis, we may be neither *Homo sapiens* ("man the thinker") nor *Homo faber* ("man the maker") but *Homo ludens* ("man the player").

Of course, sages and poets, theologians and philosophers have drawn on metaphors of play to talk about serious things for at least three thousand years. But the serious and systematic study of play as

a human and cultural phenomenon began less than fifty years ago
with the Dutch cultural historian, Johan Huizinga. His epochal book
Homo Ludens, which was published in 1938, was the first systematic
attempt to show that the "play-element" is the *basis* of culture.[3] He
defines play as "a voluntary activity or occupation executed within
certain fixed limits of time and place, according to rules freely accepted but absolutely binding, having its aim in itself and accompanied by a feeling of tension, joy and the consciousness that it is
'different' from 'ordinary life.' "[4] Huizinga observes that the play of
primitive people always had a sacral and communal character. Indeed, "play-contests" were the primary means by which civilizations
were established and maintained. Through the centuries, these sacral
and communal games have undergone extensive development and in
the process have seemingly lost all touch with play. But Huizinga argues that such familiar cultural activities as law, war, education, poetry, art, myth-making, and philosophy still reflect the "eternal play-
element" of their origins. Further, he warns that we must return to
"the rules of noble play" in the pursuit of these activities or we will
fall into "barbarism and chaos." The heart of those rules and the point
of play are the same—the limitation and mastery of the self through
fair play. "Fair play is nothing less than good faith expressed in play
terms."[5] Play, like faith, channels competitive instincts into productive and peaceful activities.

Other scholars from a variety of disciplines have refined and modified Huizinga's thesis, variously arguing that his views on play are
too narrow or too broad. For example, Roger Caillois's anthropology
of play broadens Huizinga's analysis by recognizing improvisational
play as well as structured games and by bringing a broader range of
human instincts under the civilizing influence of play. Erving
Goffman's sociological role-theory uncovers the games and the per-
formances that underlie all face-to-face interaction among people in
social situations. Jean Piaget's studies of childhood correlate the
three stages of the child's growth to three stages of child's play, beginning with the assimilative somatic play of the infant and culminating in the socialized games of the preteen. Erik Erikson's
developmental psychology extends play into adult life, seeing in the
play of child and adult alike the human ability to deal with experience by creating model situations and to master reality by experiment
and reconstruction. Herbert Marcuse's revolutionary politics calls for
the complete subordination of work to play as the only way for our
society to overcome the repressive and exploitative traits of labor.
Ludwig Wittgenstein's linguistic philosophy uses games to clarify the

very different purposes that language serves and to analyze the very different logical rules that govern each distinctive "language game." In short, the play-element looms large in all human experience, though how that element is analyzed and related to other human activities is variously conceived in the scholarship on play.

No encompassing "phenomenology of play" that could correct and correlate all these different analyses has yet been ventured. That task will not be easy because play studies are deeply divided over important theoretical and practical issues. These disagreements are partly due to the different questions and procedures that prevail in the different academic disciplines. More serious divisions come from different working definitions of play. Play scholars are sharply divided over how play relates to questions of utility, rationality, and reality. Many scholars define play in opposition to all three—play is an "economically useless" activity of "make-believe" that transports us from "ordinary" to an "extraordinary" reality. Other scholars take exception to one or all of these definitional characteristics by tying play more closely to work, problem-solving, or mimesis. No resolution of such differences among play scholars will be attempted here, but our purposes can be served by focusing attention on three *functions* of play that seem to emerge from their discussion. As a universal human phenomenon, play has a vital role in all human education, recreation, and invention.

Play and play-like activities "play" a fundamental role in the formation, restoration, and transformation of human life in all of its personal and social expressions. The educational power of play is beyond question.[6] Not only are children and citizens socialized through the games they play, but such playing is at the heart of all learning and discovery. Both formal and informal education relives the past, envisions the future, and, in that light, constructs the present by playfully creating and enacting model situations. The playing child and the thinking adult are doing essentially the same thing. As William Blake puts it, "The child's toys and the old man's reasons are the fruits of the two seasons."[7]

Given play's educational abilitiy to step sideways or forward into a new situation or even into another reality, the remaining two functions of play are easily describable. Play "recreates" an existing situation by relieving old burdens and releasing new energies. Nothing is to be gained by denying or castigating play's retreat from the drudgeries and tragedies of daily life. "Going on holiday" for a month, a day, an hour, or even a moment does enable us to do our work and handle our problems with greater efficiency and satisfaction. "Getting away from it all" does bring us back to it all strengthened and stabilized. And such withdrawal is not mere escapism; the very change of pace in play's retreat opens up a new perspective and creates a new situation. Finally, play educates and provides recreation only because of its surplus powers of invention. By suspending the rules and responsibilities of the day, play opens the horizons to a new tomorrow. The omnipotence in play of individual will and imagination gives leverage against all fixed structures and habits of life. Human play is a principle of transformation written deeply into life— a principle that only dies when people are too old to play. Thus described, the three central functions or characteristics of human play are inseparable. Pulling them apart for purposes of scholarly study is as destructive as separating them in actual times of play, thereby causing play to lose its power to open up life to creative freedom and alternative realities.

Viewed from this angle, the relation between play and faith is not as farfetched as it might have seemed at first. Important formal similarities are immediately obvious. Both play and faith tutor persons and groups in the skills and arts of human life. Both rehabilitate persons and groups by relieving old burdens and releasing new energies. Both revolutionize persons and groups through envisioning and enacting "counter-environments." There are material similarities as well—the concrete attitudes and actions, images and implications of play can be applied *mutatis mutandis* to the life of faith. At least that is the claim of the new theologies of play. These theologies believe that faith must look to play to find again its appropriate language and logic. Indeed, they contend that the Christian faith has waned in our time primarily because we have lost the spirit of play and the play of the spirit in our religious beliefs and practices.

THEOLOGIES OF PLAY

The original relationship between play and religion for primitive persons and groups has become something of a commonplace among historians of religion and culture. Sports, games, and drama all had their roots in ancient myth and ritual. These early connections have, of course, been dissolved over the centuries, and such play no longer has an explicit religious function and content. Admitting that dissolution, a number of contemporary religious thinkers are nevertheless convinced that play retains an implicit religious structure and meaning. Players always step out of one world into another. Not only is that play world free in principle from life's ordinary rules and roles.

The very limits of space and time can also be suspended. Implicit in all such play is the experience of a "transcendent universe" not unlike the one described and experienced by the religious. Whether that world experienced in play *is*, in some sense, the religious world or is only *like* the religious world is a matter of considerable disagreement among the religious thinkers exploring this line of thought. Some are prepared to argue that play as such is a religious experience of transcendence that differs from traditional piety only in degree.[8] Others are somewhat more restrained in their theological claims for play. They argue that play offers both new possibilities and new models for the Christian experience of transcendence, though ordinary play and authentic faith remain distinctive domains of life and thought. Christian "theologies of play" like those dealt with in this chapter generally take this latter approach.

Christian theologies of play are bound together by a common strategy. They all reinterpret the Christian faith in the light of the phenomenon of play.[9] They all apply the insights drawn from the familiar structures and dynamics of play to an ailing and obscure theology. They, of course, differ considerably in the way they execute this project. For one thing, they differ in how far they go in developing a coherent theological statement modeled on play. Much of the work is tentative and sketchy, only laying the groundwork for a projected theology of play. Further differences result from whether theoretical or practical concerns predominate. Some play theologians are primarily concerned with faith's play in words—that is, they explore the theoretical advantages of adopting the language and logic of play in theological discourse. They search out how images of "the player" applied to God and man playfully open up new ways of believing. Other play theologians are more interested in faith's play in action— that is, they test the practical consequences of applying the meaning and motives of play to Christian life. They show how experiences of play applied to liturgy and life point to new ways of behaving as a Christian in the modern world. Still others, mindful of play's origins in both religious myth and ritual, seek to show how faith's "word play" and "body play" can be held together. A good sense of these similarities and differences among the theologies of play can be drawn by comparing the thought of Hugo Rahner, Harvey Cox, and Robert Neale.

Faith as Humor—Hugo Rahner

That a theology of play should come from the hand of a Roman Catholic priest is hardly surprising. We have seen that Roman Catholic theologians have produced some of the most radical and innovative of the new theologies. What is surprising about the theology that Hugo Rahner sketches out in *Man at Play* is the kind of play theology that it is.[10] For one thing, it is entirely orthodox. Rahner nowhere questions the supernatural worldview of classical Christianity with all of its claims to a miraculous origin and destiny for humankind, church, and world. But he gives this supernaturalism a compelling winsomeness and even plausibility by viewing it under the aspect of play. The old faith appears in a remarkable new light in his spare description of "the playing God, the playing man and the playing Church."

The second surprising thing about this intriguing little book is the evidence that he marshals to make its case. Nodding but once to Johan Huizinga, Rahner drives home his point with a wealth of comment on play drawn from the poets and philosophers of ancient Greece and the saints and theologians of the early and medieval Church. Exercising that finely tuned Roman Catholic sense of tradition and universalism, Rahner methodically annotates his theology of play from the writings of the late pagan and early Christian *ludimagistri*—masters and schoolmasters of play! This is not to say that Rahner adds nothing of his own or to deny that he often turns his sources to his own vision of play and faith. But a theology of play that is as orthodox and as traditional as Rahner's clearly says something about the power and the universality of the metaphor of play for theological reflection.

Rahner's objective in drawing on these forgotten riches of antiquity and the early Church is to show the consequences of the modern world's loss of the faculty of true play.[11] This loss has twisted the modern world into "a hideous edifice of unrelieved utility" and "idiotic earnestness." This dreary workaday world not only deprives persons of the natural "rest and relaxation" that play affords, but it also cuts them off from the "sacral secret at the root and in the flower of all play."[12] Play is an experience that always points beyond itself because play never fully realizes what it seeks to achieve. Play is ultimately humankind's deep-seated longing for an unfettered harmony between body and soul.

> And so we talk of play whenever the mastery of the spirit over the possibilities presented by the body has in some way attained its perfection, a perfection that shows itself in the easy agility, the shimmering elegance of some acquired skill; when word, sound or gesture has been made pliable to the spirit; when the physically visible has become the expression of an inner fullness that is sufficient to itself.[13]

Of course, none of our ordinary playing achieves quite that relation between body and soul. At best our play is a kind of rehearsal, "fashioned into gesture, sound or word, of that Godward directed harmony of body and soul that we call heaven."[14] But even misshapen play is a schoolmaster of that life of faith that is the earthly fulfillment of play and the playful anticipation of heaven.

As we shall see, the life of faith to which all human play points is itself a playing out of life. This play of faith, like all play, is a delicate balancing act between two worlds. Faith seeks to balance the body and the soul in subtle union, making "the body so subservient to the soul that every word, gesture and tone of voice become a true expression of the spirit."[15] But faith never achieves that perfect union in this life, so faith must also balance the successes and the failures, the mirth and the sorrow that come with a life where souls do not always play into the body and where bodies always play out at death. Faith then, for Rahner, is that special "humor" that brings together the invisible and visible as well as the comic and tragic in one game, drama, or dance of life.[16] He explicates this understanding of faith in terms of the "playing of God, the playing of man and the playing of the Church."

Rahner believes we must first understand God as *Deus ludens* before we can understand man as *Homo ludens*.[17] He finds numerous allusions to God creating the world as a kind of game in the classical literature. Often these are couched in the form of philosophical or theological speculations, but they receive their most powerful expression in the imagery of myth, allegory, and art. There is the rich mythology of God as the Child King who omnipotently creates at will all the bright playthings of which the world is made. There is the fanciful allegory of Divine Wisdom in Scripture as the "little child" of God "making play before him" in creating the world, filling God with joy like any proud parent. There are the marvelous medieval paintings of the infant Jesus clutching the ball of the world in his hands like a treasured nursery toy. Behind all these images lies a profound metaphysical truth about the creation of the world.

> Everywhere we find in such myths an intuitive feeling that the world was not created under some kind of constraint, that it did not unfold itself out of the divine in obedience to some inexorable cosmic law; rather, it was felt, was it born of a wise liberty, of the gay spontaneity of God's mind; in a word, it came from the hand of a child.[18]

In other words, the world and everything in it including ourselves are, like all playthings, "meaningful but not necessary."[19]

Rahner sees in this paradoxical insight born of play a timely affirmation of the sovereignty of God and the dignity of the world. Treating the world and others as the strange playthings that they are means that they are given neither more nor less seriousness than they deserve. Nothing in the world can claim equality or superiority to God. The whole cosmic game from the round of the stars and the atoms to the life of the individual and the cell is played before God at God's pleasure. The world is no closed cosmic system obeying its own inexorable laws, but an order directed after the manner of a game. The Creator is free to make of the game what he wills. But in his free sovereignty, God creates this world; out of the vast multiplicity of possible games he could play he plays this one. Moreover, he finds his joy and expresses his love through just these bright, fragile playthings of which the world is made. The dignity of the world lies in this realization that the world is the product of neither accident nor necessity but of God's gratuitous love and joy. In short, both the sovereignty of God and the dignity of the world are affirmed in that "serious detachment" of God which is the spirit and constraint of all true play.

Because God is a *Deus vere ludens*—a God who truly plays—human beings too must be creatures who play.[20] The person who plays after the fashion of God knows two things and holds them both together. "The first is that existence is a joyful thing, because it is secure in God; the second, that it is also a tragic thing, because freedom must always involve peril."[21] Rahner describes this "man at play" who fuses these two contradictory elements into a spiritual unity as a "grave-merry man."[22] Such a man is always "two men in one"—a man of easy gaiety who feels himself living in invincible security and a man of sober gravity who knows the unavoidable hurts of life. The "grave-merry man" has mastered the art, almost superhuman in its difficulty, of taking life seriously while playing and of playing while taking life seriously. He has learned to kick the world away with the airy grace of a dancer while at the same time holding it as close as a favorite bedtime toy.

But how does the "grave-merry" person attain this happy mean—this kind of "Mozartian suspension between laughter and tears, between merriment and patience"? This is obviously the most important religious question for Rahner. Only the person who knows just where to find the middle in every situation is the person who plays rightly. Rahner finds that balance in what both Aristotle and Aquinas called *eutrapelia*—a nimble humor that sees true play in everything that happens and for that reason truly sees God.[23] *Eutrapelia* literally means "well-turning" and suggests a person who stands between two extremes. The person of true wit *(eutrapelos)* strikes the happy mean between the inveterate buffoon *(bomolochos)* and the humorousless boor *(agroikos).* The *bomolochos* never comes down to earth and the *agroikos* never rises above it. Only the *eutrapelos* has the fluidity of spirit to live between heaven and earth.[24] But that agile humor comes from being ultimately serious about God alone. Seriousness about God frees persons from the perversion of play (buffoonery) and the destruction of play (moroseness). Thus, humor and faith come together in that "vision of God" which is the ground and goal of all true play.

Implied in Rahner's discussion of *Deus vere ludens* and *Homo vere ludens* is his view of the Church as the place where the true playing of God and persons come together bodily.[25] The Church—as the continuing incarnation of the very fact of God having become human in Jesus Christ—is the "bodily gesture" and "complete sacrament" of the unceasing game being played by God in the whole visible creation. Indeed, the Church is where God and selves become "playmates" with one another. Drawing on the mystical theology of the Church, Rahner pictures this playing in the vivid imagery of a husband love-playing with his wife and of children playing in the street in the messianic age. The Church is where that final unity of soul and body, of God and humankind toward which all true playing moves has already begun. The Church dramatically stages that coming final harmony in the "colourful play-acting" of her liturgy.[26] What could be more fitting for God and persons at play than to clothe this deepest mystery in the dress-up game of beautiful gesture, measured step, and noble raiment. Here, then, in the Church is the earthly prelude to that "final harmonization of body and soul which we call heaven." Through word and sacrament, the Church anticipates that heavenly city where the streets will be full of "eternal children" and where the Ancient of Days will never cease saying: *"Ite et ludite!"* — Go and play!

Closing his reverie on this high note, Rahner recapitulates his entire meditation in the play-image of "the heavenly dance."[27] Not surprisingly, given his view of play as the blending of opposites, he sees dance as the root form of all play. The ultimate mystery of the dance is the harmony of the dancer's body and soul. This mystery reflects the larger mystery of the cosmic dance with all its measured harmonies of swirling cosmic movement. It parodies the even higher mystery of the dance steps of the Leader of the dance.

The Logos leapt from heaven into the womb of the Virgin, he leapt from the womb of his mother on to the cross, from the cross into Hades and from Hades once more back on to the earth—O the new resurrection! And he leapt from the earth into heaven where he sits on the right hand of the Father. And he will again leap on to the earth with glory to bring judgment.[28]

And finally the mystery of the dance anticipates that final Easter Ball when we will dance our way through the labyrinth of the world and into "the dance of everlasting life."[29] Thus do Rahner's images flow together into a dance of play that reflects and evokes the nimble humor of faith itself.

Faith as Celebration—Harvey Cox

The surprise and excitement that Harvey Cox's book *The Feast of Fools* generated when it first appeared is difficult to recapture today.[30] For one thing, the reading public has come to expect dramatic innovations and reversals of contemporary theologians. More important, as noted earlier, Cox has exemplified the mobile mind of contemporary theology by serially engaging each particular issue currently vexing the communities of faith.[31] We have come to expect Cox to marshal the relevant scholarship and assay the crucial issues for us in each late-breaking theological trend that comes along. But *The Feast of Fools* was genuinely surprising and exciting when it appeared because it was a dramatic departure from, if not reversal of, the secular theology that Cox had christened five years earlier in *The Secular City*. Here was a theologian, whose earlier call for a demystified faith of Christian social action had exercised enormous influence, now extolling Christian mysticism and liturgy, daydreaming and mythmaking. Cox personally downplayed the shift by offering *The Feast of Fools* "as a companion piece to an earlier work, not as a recantation."[32] And, as we shall see, there is more truth to his characterization than his critics have allowed because the "bottom line" of *The Feast of Fools* is still Christian social action. As Cox himself admits, however, there is a dramatic shift between the two books in the spirit and the means of political action—a shift as it were from work to play.

Cox's theology of play can be symbolized by the medieval holiday from which his book takes its title. The Feast of Fools was an annual festival where the ribald reversal of all things sacred and royal was permitted.[33] No custom or convention, prelate or politician was spared parody and mockery. Never popular with the dignitaries of

Church and crown, the Feast of Fools survived until the sixteenth century when it died out. Its demise, Cox contends, signaled a significant change in the Western cultural mood which will, unless reversed, be absolutely ruinous to culture and religion. That change of mood marked the loss of our civilization's capacity for play—especially for the play of festivity and fantasy. Unless something of the celebrative power and social criticism of the old Feast of Fools can be recaptured in today's culture and Church, our civilization is doomed to die the death of mental and moral sclerosis. Detecting certain signs of their recovery in the underground church and the counterculture, Cox lays the foundations for a wider recovery through a phenomenological analysis of the personal, social, and religious functions of festivity and fantasy.

Though recognizing the difficulty of talking about an activity that demands a kind of unselfconscious participation, Cox analyzes the ingredients and implications of festivity for human experience in general and for religious experience in particular.[34] Learning from a number of scholarly studies of festivity, he singles out three distinguishing characteristics. A festive occasion is always marked by "conscious excess," that is, by a purposeful departure from conventional mores and ordinary behavior. Festivity also always entails "celebrative affirmation" of something that has happened in the past or that is hoped for in the future. A third element, implied in the other two, is festivity's marked contrast to the everyday schedule of work, convention, and moderation. Festivity then is a time of celebration that "provides us with a short vacation from the daily round, an alteration without which life would be unbearable." As such, festivity is more than sheer escapism or mere frivolity. Festivity is that feeling-filled way individuals and groups retain the meaningful past and reach for a meaningful future.

Festivity's role in binding the times together can be better understood when we realize that past, present, and future can only become a meaningful whole if this historical horizon is surrounded by a "larger environment."[35] The larger environment gives history meaning by setting it off like a well-framed picture against a counter-environment. Religions have traditionally provided the means for symbolically linking history and this "cosmic circle." But the modern breakdown of religious symbols, which some have called the "death of God," has dissolved this vital "point of intersection" between cosmos and history.[36] Thus deprived of a cosmic framework, history becomes our total environment. But this "over-heats" history—makes all our failures and hopes, our indecisions and decisions *too* crucial.

When history is perceived as the whole of human reality, it becomes an unmanageable and terrifying burden. Not surprisingly, many flee the risks and the responsibilities of history-making in archaism, presentism, or futurism. But breaking time apart in this manner deeply distorts individual and social existence. Fleeing the past denies earth and body and our continuity with them. Denying the future destroys hope and change and our dependence on them. Evading the present erases joy as well as pain and our living experience of them. These distortions have left modern men and women desperately needing some way of restoring that vision of a wider reality that would enable them once again "to toast all the daughters of time."

Cox sees festivity playing an indispensable role in this restoration. Festivity allows us to "cool" history without fleeing it by placing the burden of history-making in a wider context of meaningful order. Festivity has the power, by its very nature and quite apart from what is actually celebrated, to affirm and transcend history at the same time. Every festive act celebrates something that has an important place in human history, past or future. But the "legitimated excess" of that festive celebration takes us out of history-making for a time, with all of its necessary working and planning and recording. Celebration, in short, is a paradoxical reminder that history is not the exclusive and final horizon of life.

> As both an affirmation of history-making and a temporary respite from it, festivity reminds us of the link between two levels of our being—the instrumental, calculating side, and the expressive, playful side. Festivity periodically restores us to our proper relationship to history and history-making. It reminds us that we are fully within history but that history also is within something else.[37]

Festivity, then, opens a way to transcend the "death of God" and thereby to make history a meaningful whole again.

A second and companion way of recovering the vital link between human history and the mystery from which it arises and toward which it flows is through fantasy.[38] Fantasy, like festivity, enables persons to go beyond the empirical world, but fantasy has far greater powers for transcending the world than does festivity. In fantasy, "man not only relives and anticipates, he remakes the past and creates wholly new futures."[39] Indeed, fantasy's creative reach distinguishes it not only from festivity but from mere imagination as well. Imagination opens doors of social convention or conventional wisdom that are normally closed to us. But fantasy is that "advanced imagining" that suspends not only the conventional rules but the perceived structures of reality itself. In fantasy, "we abolish the limits of our powers and our perceptions. We soar. We give reign not only to the socially discouraged impulses but to physically impossible exploits and even to logically contradictory events."[40] That peril attends this extraordinary power is obvious. Less obvious to many is the positive role that fantasy plays in life.

Fantasy's role is by no means limited to the little-understood but necessary place of night-dreaming in human life. Daydreaming fantasy is perhaps even more important. Long recognized as the source of all artistic endeavor, fantasy's contribution to research breakthroughs in science and technology is increasingly recognized by philosophers and practitioners in these fields. New techniques of "guided fantasy" in therapy and education suggest that fantasy has a central and determinative role in all psychic activity. Finally, more and more scholars in religion see fantasy as providing the human bridge between the empirical world and that larger reality that includes the being and value of all things. That bridge not only organizes and sanctions cultural arrangements but sometimes breaks apart those patterns and pioneers wholly new ones. In short, fantasy plays a decisive role in every reach for the world of fact and the world of faith as well as in all efforts to keep these two environments in proper tandem.

Ever concerned with practical matters, Cox concentrates his attention on the social enactment of fantasy in both cultural and religious ritual.[41] "Ritual provides both the form and the occasion of the expression of fantasy."[42] As shared or social fantasy, ritual comes very close to festive celebration. Ritual is a way of keeping in touch with the past and passing things on to the future. Likewise ritual feeds back into history, shaping the present in the light of such remembrance and anticipation. Finally ritual also gives a person access to a wealth of different ways to feel and act. But enacted fantasy differs from festive celebration in both form and content. Ritual remembrance and anticipation is more intentional than is festivity—in ritual, the imagination is guided toward the enactment of certain images of reality and responsibility. In content, rituals transcend the factual world more radically than do festive occasions. The pull toward a "counter-reality," which is only implicit in festive celebration, is always explicit in ritual celebration.

This counter-reality is by no means lacking in political significance.[43] Even when another world is only envisioned, that world exerts leverage on the style of life and shape of institutions in this world. Moreover, there are shared religious and cultural fantasies that envision a new age of the earth in which the relations between selves and with nature are fundamentally transformed. In Christianity, this vision of the coming Kingdom of God has often been neutralized by postponing the Kingdom to an epoch beyond history, by reducing it to emergent possibilities already within reach, or by spiritualizing the Kingdom as the individual's relation to eternity.[44] But at other times, this vision has acted as a catalyst for the culture to transcend itself and its current values.

This impact has been especially telling when the vision of the coming Kingdom has become an *"embodied* political fantasy" as it often has in the past in a variety of monastic and messianic communities. These communities, despite their frequent excesses, served as the "seedplots and models" for new life patterns and symbols for the Church and the world. Cox seriously doubts that such small-scale communities can have a comparable influence today. The Church no longer enjoys a hegemony over the other institutions of society such that what changes the Church changes the world. But some kind of symbolic and structural context for dreaming up and acting out political fantasies is required for human survival. Cox envisions this as some kind of meta-institution—"an institution that has the form of an ordinary institution, but that differs because it exists not for itself but to link the two worlds of fact and fantasy."[45] Today's Church is surely no such institution, but, freed from self-interest and self-importance, it can contribute to that coming meta-institution of festivity and fantasy so desperately needed today.

On the basis of this broad analysis of festive celebration and celebrative fantasy, Cox speculates on how the power to bind the times and to link heaven and earth can be reclaimed in Christian liturgy and theology. The liturgies and theologies presently available only mirror the culture's one-sided views of time and eternity. Some are historical and only emphasize faith's dependence on the past. Others are incarnational and look only to the present. Still others are eschatological and look only toward the future. Rather than paper over these differences or fashion yet another idiosyncratic liturgy or theology of his own, Cox suggests that the differences be methodically celebrated. He proposes a style of liturgical and theological existence that he calls a "method of juxtaposition."[46] This method purposely plays off the discontinuities between past, present, and future orientations that are so much a part of contemporary religion and culture. Focusing on just those discomfiting points where memory, hope, and experience contradict each other will break open this divided and divisive situation to new perceptions of reality. Cox believes this method of juxtaposition embodies the critical and creative power of festivity and fantasy and thereby opens the way for recapturing both in the liturgy and theology of the Church.

Cox further elaborates this way of living through our present impasse in theology and liturgy with the striking image of "Christ the Harlequin."[47] Noting that Christ has come to previous generations in various guises, Cox suggests that Christ can become most real and relevant to our time as a clown. He notes the appearance of this way of representing Christ in modern art, literature, and drama and even detects elements in the biblical portrait of Christ that suggest the clown motif. But, precedents aside, Cox is convinced that a "clown Christ" is imminently right for a century of tension and terror such as our own. The many-sided image of the clown (jester, fool, troubador, trickster, minstrel, mime) embodies what is most needed for faith in our time. "The clown refuses to live inside this present reality. He senses another one. He defies the law of gravity, taunts the policeman, ridicules the other performers. Through him we catch a glimpse of another world impinging on this one, upsetting its rules and practices."[48] In other words, the clown Christ incarnates a comic sense of life.

The comic perspective always occurs in a situation that is open to disparate meanings.[49] The elegantly dressed man who slips on a banana peel, the jester who ridicules the king, the punster who toys with language—all trade on disparity. The heart of the comic perspective is the experience and perception of disparate worlds. "A situation is invariably comic if it belongs simultaneously to two independent series of events and is capable of being interpreted in two entirely different meanings at the same time."[50] Cox believes this comic orientation can give faith precisely the leverage it needs to gain perspective on our pluralistic and secularistic situation. A comic faith can go beyond the tangle of today's liturgies and theologies by juxtaposing them. A comic faith can break through the preoccupations of today's materialistic and rationalistic society by transcending it. The comic perspective furnishes faith a fulcrum for opening up wholly new worlds of meaning and responsibility *without leaving this world*. The comic perspective opens the way to be genuinely in the world but not of the world.

Some, of course, will object that this "coming of Christ the Harlequin" is a denial of the sobriety that life demands and faith embodies. Cox counters by pointing out that neither sadness nor seriousness are absent from comedy. The mien of the clown always speaks of both. The opposite of comedy is not sobriety but tragedy. The tragic perspective on life, which has played such an influential role in Christian thought and life, deals with seriousness and sadness in a way very different from the comic. In tragedy, the hero defies life's limitations and losses as long as possible only to bow finally to their inevitability in stoic courage and dignity. The comic perspective acknowledges these same human flaws and failures but transcends them in laughter and hope. None escapes the comic's negation, but none is excluded from the comic's affirmation. In comedy, the proud and the powerful of the earth are humbled but not destroyed. The timid and the weak are unmasked but not debased. In comedy all persons fall prey to the vanities and disasters of life, but they always manage through the strange alchemy of laughter and hope to turn these painful and humiliating pratfalls into unexpected triumph.

The comic perspective cuts everyone down to size but at the same time opens up new worlds of possibility to everyone. Seen in this light, the crucifixion-and-resurrection logic of the Christian faith clearly belongs to the comic rather than the tragic sense of life. What then, Cox would ask, could be a more appropriate image of Christ than the harlequin? What could be a more uplifting calling for the Christian than to be a fool for Christ's sake? Thus, Cox avers

> that our whole relation to Christ, to any faith at all, and to the whole of existence for that matter, is one of conscious play and comic equivocation. Only by assuming a playful attitude toward our religious tradition can we possibly make any sense of it. Only by learning to laugh at the hopelessness around us can we touch the hem of hope. Christ the clown signifies our playful appreciation of the past and our comic refusal to accept the specter of inevitability in the future. He is the incarnation of festivity and fantasy.[51]

Faith as Adventure—Robert E. Neale

The theory of play and religion offered by Robert E. Neale is theological only in an anticipatory way. Like the natural theologies of yesteryear, his *In Praise of Play* merely lays the foundations for a fully developed Christian theology by establishing a universal capacity and need of God.[52] But Neale's search for solid experiential and logical grounds for faith differs from the natural theologies of the past in two very important ways. First and foremost, he locates the essence of all religion in the human experience of "full play." He contends that an adequate analysis of play discloses not only the defining category of human existence but also the characteristic ways people respond to the inescapable presence and power of the sacred in their lives. Neale singles out three such responses to the sacred dimension of experience—profane, magical, and religious. The "profane" response seeks to deny and the "magical" response to control those sacral dimensions of experience that lie beyond human control. Both these responses to the sacred are "work" responses. They both seek to manipulate life's meaning through laborious acts of reason and will. Only the "religious" response lets life happen as the adventure that it is by engaging the sacred in the spirit of play.

A second way Neale differs from the natural theologies of the past is in his concentration on the psychological dynamics of play and religion. Indeed, he characterizes his work as a "psychology of play and religion." This characterization will be misleading to those who believe that psychological theories must be limited to value-free descriptions of the structures and processes of mental, volitional, or emotional life. Neale certainly does not work within these limits, and for this reason his thought may be more accurately characterized as a *philosophical* psychology of play and religion. It is psychological in the sense that he defines and explores play and religion in terms of the inner dynamics of the psyche; it is philosophical in the double sense that he argues a normative view of psychological wholeness as full play, and he contends that full play is nothing other than a proper relation to the sacred dimension of reality. Neale would not deny that the more theological and cultural approaches to play and religion exemplified in Rahner and Cox are plausible and valuable for purposes of revitalizing Christian faith in our time. But, he is convinced that unless the inner experience of faith can be reawakened, all such theological and cultural apologetics are doomed to fail. Neale finds that inner reawakening of faith in the adventurous play of adult men and women.

Neale launches his new theory of play with a complicated analysis of the inner purpose and power of play. Only such a "psychological" definition of play can help us sort through the rival theories of play and the rampant counterfeits of playing that abound in the modern world. Neale begins quite simply by defining "play as play"—by focusing on the inner activity of play itself rather than on any of the social or cultural consequences of play.[53] He thereby clearly differentiates his approach to play from all those theories that see play as a necessary preparation for or diversion from work.[54]

His basic premise is that each person has a "dualistic nature" that is always experienced at some level or another as inner conflict or inner harmony. "The two poles of the duality are *the need to dis-*

charge energy and the need to design experience."[55] The effort to discharge psychic energy relates the individual to concrete moments in time and concrete objects in space. The striving to organize psychic experience relates the individual to abstract patterns of permanency and universality. The former establishes our sense of individuality and change while the latter gives birth to our awareness of identity and relationality. Both "full discharge" and "full design" are required for human fulfillment, and both basic needs are met to some degree in all human behavior. Ideally both needs are met at the same time, each limiting and exciting the other, as the need for design is energized and the need for discharge is organized. But this harmony is rare. More often, conflict between discharge and design prevails, where one need ignores its own limits and overrides the other. When discharge rules the inner life, the individual is enslaved by particulars and the inner life is chaotic. When the need for design rules, the individual is enslaved by abstractions and the inner life is lethargic. Most of life is a haphazard contest back and forth between attempts to satisfy one or the other of these two needs.

Building on this premise about the inner life, Neale identifies the life of continued conflict as the "work self" and the life of continued harmony as the "play self." The person who is constantly at work in the world is expressing a state of inner conflict. "From the psychological perspective, *work is the attempt to resolve inner conflict.*"[56] But the phychic energy spent on the conflict reduces the energy available for its creative surpassing or orderly containment, and so the conflict and the work of trying to resolve it continue. By contrast, the person at play in the world is expressing a state of inner harmony. There is little psychological work to be done when the needs for discharge and design both accept their limits and excite each other. "Play is psychologically defined as *any activity not motivated by the need to resolve inner conflict.*"[57] The play self is neither wild nor lethargic, neither chaotic nor rigid, but experiences a fullness of power *and* order. The play self has no need to be an "achiever" because its own sense of inner well-being is secure.

Neale immediately draws out two crucial implications of this approach to play. First, any given activity can be either work or play. Conventionally ideas of work and play are beside the point. The psychological source of the activity is what counts—whether conflict or harmony is expressed through the action. Second, Neale insists that states of "total conflict" and "total harmony" are theoretical abstractions and never occur as such in personal experience. "The conflicted or work self differs only in degree from the harmonious or play self."[58] But, as we shall see, the quantitative difference between work and play orientations has a qualitative significance of immense importance.

Having broadly defined play as play, Neale explains play itself as adventure.[59] As adventure, play is always suffused with chance, risk, and discovery. This spontaneity, surprise, and novelty are precisely why play is so threatening to the work self struggling along for mastery and control. Only an inner state of harmony can embolden the player to overcome the "shock of chance, fear of danger and suspicion of novelty" that lurks in every playful act. This inner state of harmony is expressed through four "elements" and two "modes" of adventuresome play.

The four elements of adventure are peace, freedom, delight, and illusion.[60] Peace is the most obvious result of the harmony of the basic needs for discharge and design. This peace is no cessation of activity—the player is no shiftless idler—but the absence of conflicted activity. The peace of the player frees him to embrace wholeheartedly the complications of existence and to address unselfishly the conflicts in others. Only the adventurer can tackle the world's conflict and complexity without internalizing that turmoil. Such experienced peace is closely bound up with an experienced freedom at once bodily, temporal, social, emotional, intellectual. "It is freedom *from* the conflicting demands of the basic needs and freedom *for* new discharge and new design."[61]

Such peaceful and freewheeling adventure always brings delight that can be mere fun or reach sheer rapture. Whatever the level of intensity, this joy is something other than the pleasure so laboriously sought by the "pleasure-seekers" of our culture. There is delight in the very danger, fear, and awe that those who *work at playing* are seeking to avoid. Finally, play's peace, freedom, and delight are so different and separate from ordinary life that every adventure contains the element of illusion. Neale softens the usual negative connotations this word carries by noting that it comes from a Latin term (*illudere*) that originally meant "to be in play." But he readily admits that the suspicions and accusations surrounding this term in a work-oriented world are fully understandable. Play does awaken feelings, thoughts, and behavior in the adventurer that are so different and separate as to be called another world. That illusive world experienced in adventurous play cannot help but be shocking to those who fear losing ground in their hard-earned battle with inner conflict as well as to those who have lost all awareness of actually overcoming psychic conflict. Adventurous play is always illusive "because it occurs *in this world but is not of this world.*"[62] What else could the experience of genuine peace, freedom, and delight be but an experience of a strange and wonderful world that totally contradicts our familiar and factual world!

These four elements of play are reflected in and through two modes of play—story and game.[63] More precisely, in adventurous play, stories harmonize time and games harmonize space. The play of stories puts the player in a different time from the work world. The world of work is either swamped by time (when the need for discharge prevails) or stifled by timelessness (when the need for design commands). The story time of an adventure reconciles the awareness of change and of permanence by transforming both "into a single awareness of powerful and meaningful time." Similarly, the play of games puts the player in a different place from the work world. The work world is either preoccupied with separate things (when the need for discharge rules) or with typical relationships (when the need for design predominates). The game space of adventure creates a field of action where the awareness of uniqueness and relatedness are held together in graceful movement. Underlying this highly refined analysis of the way play harmonizes the psychological experiences of time and space is the more easily grasped idea that the plot of a playfully enacted story and the rules of a playfully enacted game are the means by which the self's basic needs for discharge and design are harmonized in an ongoing life of peace, freedom, delight, and illusion. The plotless and unruled life of the worker is precisely why the work self is a seesaw between frenzied activity and stultifying routine. Only the adventure of playing out a life story and a game life eliminates the chaos and boredom of the worker's life.

Neale is under no illusion about the frequence of such experiences of play. Psychological conflict and the anxiety-ridden work of trying to overcome that conflict are the common lot of all for most of life. Even when playful adventure does break into our lives, the harmony experienced is usually mingled with conflict. Neale marks this experiential ambiguity by drawing a distinction between "partial play" and "full play."[64] Full play uses all the potentials offered at any given stage of an individual's physical, psychological, and social growth. Moreover, full play always involves other human beings and cultural pursuits since all the player's activities and relationships become an expression of play. Seen in this light, most of what passes for play among adults is only partial play. It does not engage the whole person or the whole of the person's activities and relationships. Even that children's play which fully engages their potential has a far smaller range than play of mature adults and, accordingly, from the latter's standpoint must be seen as partial play. But, though acknowledging its rarity, Neale contends that full play does occur, and when it does it creates a new self and a new world for the player.

Having thus defined and described play, Neale proceeds to establish the essential identity between play and religion. The first step is to make clear the religious character of the "other" world that breaks in on the playing self. Rather than using the categories of the Christian religion, Neale appropriates terminology from the history of religions and speaks of this world in terms of the "sacred" and the "profane."[65] He chooses this language because these theologically neutral terms are in keeping with the generally philosophical character of his analysis, but more importantly, this language enables him to reclaim a vivid sense of the fundamental ambivalence of all religious phenomena and all religious experience. The sacred (that which is holy) and the profane (that which is common) are always ambivalently related. The sacred is always experienced as a force or energy beyond the ordinary power of human beings and outside the common processes of nature. But this extraordinary power is always mediated through some ordinary object, person, or event. The sacred only shows itself through the profane, yet always shows itself as something other than the profane. Thereby the sacred and the profane always stand in a relationship that is both "antagonistic and complementary." This same ambivalence, in turn, is reflected in personal responses to sacred power. Every encounter with the sacred evokes a mixed reaction of "fascination" and "awe." The intrigue of experiencing the sacred attracts us, but the fear of losing the profane repels us. Finally, all religious experiences of sacred power provide an ambivalent response of attraction and repulsion.

Against this understanding of the sacred and the profane, Neale's account of the ambivalent relationship between play and work becomes more understandable. The sacred is the power that promises and provides the "otherworldly" peace, freedom, and delight that full play affords. But paralleling the ambivalent fascination and awe of all religious experiences of the sacred is the equally ambivalent partial play and full play of play's experience of the sacred. Full play carried to utter completion threatens the loss of the profane world just as full work carried to its extreme means the loss of the sacred world. The experience of power and the reaction of ambivalence are common to religion and to play because the dynamics underlying both are identical. So long as human life lasts, the sacred and the profane must somehow be held in balance.

Neale sees three predominant ways of maintaining this balance in actual experience—secular, magic, and religious.[66] The secular response to the tension between the sacred and the profane seeks to dissolve the tension by retreating into the profane world by means of daily work. This secular response occurs when awe overcomes fascination in the experience of the sacred. Seen in this way, the secular response is by no means limited to modern humanity. Primitive people were secular most of the time because they guarded themselves against the power of the sacred through an elaborate system of taboos and atonements. Women and men today, however, seem even more adept at walling out the sacred through their desacralized worldviews and life-styles. But Neale insists that the sacred cannot finally be so easily limited or safely ignored. Not only does the sacred periodically break through the secular individual's protections in surprising joy or sorrow.[67] Secular persons are also drawn despite themselves into minor and camouflaged forms of worship. The whole round of partial play that preoccupies our culture—sports, games, and entertainment—is a partial religious response to the sacred. "Fascination for the sacred is intrinsic to man and cannot be abolished."[68]

This ambivalence toward the sacred is more obviously manifest in the magic response to life. Magic is the most common solution to the tension between the sacred and the profane and most often passes for what is commonly thought to be religion. "Magic is the attempt to achieve the impossible—the mingling of the sacred and the profane."[69] This mingling is at bottom the attempt to *control the sacred as a means of controlling the profane.* For this reason, magic is generally found whenever individuals come to an unbridgeable gap in their knowledge of the world and powers of control. For the same reason, the magic response is the perennial temptation if not seduction of conventional piety. The religion most of us know is no religion at all but the magical attempt to dominate and manipulate divine powers for human ends.

No doubt the magic response is so common and widespread because it is a spurious form of religion. It strives to balance the sacred and the profane, the fascination and awe by choosing neither one. But, in point of fact, magic is a disguised form of secularity because it always strives to make profane use of the sacred. It uses magical charms and rites to try to get what cannot be gotten by everyday work. That such ploys are not the mystifications of the primitive alone is obvious to anyone acquainted with the "feel good, do right, stay strong" Christianity of our time. But all such effort to work out the play of psychic harmony are bound to fail. This mingling of the

sacred and the profane always leads to the disappearance of one or
the other. Either the sacred is swallowed up in pragmatic materialism
or the profane disappears in psychotic spirituality.

The true religious response to the sacred stands in bold contrast to
the secular and the magic responses. The religious response seeks
neither to ignore nor to seize the power of the sacred, but simply and
completely to accept it. Put another way, the religious response attempts neither to flee from awe into the world of work nor to balance
fascination and awe by working at play, but to subordinate awe to
fascination for the sacred through play. This religious response to the
power and fascination of the sacred is identical with the experience
of full play that Neale earlier described as adventure. Here the religious depths and dynamics of adventurous play can be seen for what
they are. The sacred calls us forth into the adventure that is full play
by bestowing the peace, freedom, and delight of living in two radically different worlds at the same time. To be sure, the experienced
adventure of that harmony never lasts, but the memory and hope of
that harmony enables the religious person to alternate "between play
for its own sake and work for the sake of his fellow man." That memory and hope enable the religious person to acknowledge both the
sacred and the profane worlds without dissolving their antagonism or
complementarity.The special grace of the person who is genuinely
religious is to play at play when that surprising experience comes and
to play at work in the meantime.

Neale further tests his parallel between play and religion by comparing the expression of play's adventure in story and game to the
religious adventure's embodiment in myth and ritual.[70] Not surprisingly, he finds that "all that was concluded about the nature of stories
and games applies to the nature of myth and ritual."[71] In a subtle and
extended discussion, he shows that myth and ritual, like game and
story, are neither separable nor identical. The religious response to
the sacred in and through myth bestows a new kind of time beyond
the secular avoidance of time and the magical extension of time. The
mythic time of the religious person is that adventurous moment
where anxiety about yesterday, today, and tomorrow is simply impossible. Similarly, the religious response to the sacred in and through
ritual creates a new kind of space beyond the compulsive obedience
to rules and structures that characterize the secular and magic life.
The ritual space of the religious person is that adventurous movement where the traditional rules and structures are merely the
rhythms within which life is playfully danced. In short, religious
myths and rituals are the stories and games of playing adults.

As such, myths and rituals are to be believed and practiced in the spirit of play. The religious person neither disbelieves the myths because they have nothing to do with life in the profane world (the "secularist") nor believes the myths in order to harness their power for life in the profane world (the "magician"). The religious person transcends the conflict between disbelieving and believing by *make-believing*. "The story is neither doubted nor buttressed by belief."[72] The religious story is simply enacted in word and deed with all the single-mindedness and seriousness of play. Make-believing frees the religious person to gambol in "the humor and exaggeration of divine tales" and thereby to be transported into that illusive new self and new world that mythic play creates.

Similarly, the religious person does not avoid rituals of sacrifice because of the suffering they entail (the secularist) or perform rituals of sacrifice because that suffering will forestall future suffering or insure future blessing (the magician). The religious person makes the sacrifice demanded of an active faith without calculating regrets or rewards in the profane world because that person has given up the profane self and world to the sacred.[73] This surrender no more entails suffering than does giving up work for play. The religious person sacrifices without the inner suffering that always comes from fearing loss or currying favor in sacrificial deeds. This frees the religious person "to perceive and enter into the suffering of others." Venturing that kind of sacrifice only deepens the illusive peace, freedom, and delight that ritual play evokes.

As noted earlier, Neale barely indicates how this general theory of play and religion can be translated into a theological recovery of Christian myth and ritual. He makes his point by commenting briefly on one matter of theological substance and one of theological style. Substantively, any new theology must deal with the problem of death.[74] Life's final event is always important to the religious person but especially so in the modern world where death is so studiously ignored or luridly portrayed.[75] Only the adventurous play of the religious person actually transcends the sting of death by dying to the profane self and world. The essential identity of adventurous play and religion gives new meaning to the crucifixion and resurrection that stand at the center of Christian faith—the birth of a new self and a new world comes through playing out in story and game the death of the old self and the old world.

Stylistically, a new theology must deal with the fetish of relevance.[76] The Church's endless succession of new theologies, which has taken a quantum leap in our time, can be traced to the desperate attempt to be relevant to the latest truths and interests of the profane world. The spirit of play frees the religious person from being bound to any theory or practice of the profane world. Only the adventurous play of the religious person underwrites the splendid irrelevance of theology that frees the player to serve and suffer for any and all, whatever their beliefs and behavior. In brief, Neale believes that the substance and the style of a Christian theology of play can come out of that adventure of full play which is the adventure of true faith.

Neale concludes his foundational study of play and religion by admitting that actual experiences of play and religion are not easily identifiable. We cannot simply look at the conventional activities of play and religion as they appear to the observer and easily decide whether they are partial or full play, degenerate or authentic faith. Everything depends on whether conflict or harmony is expressed through the activities. Moreover, he reiterates the disquieting discovery that the secular response is more common than the religious response and that the magical response is more common than both taken together. But Neale insists that the full play which is true religion remains the pearl of great price that is worth all that we are and own. "High adventure, at any level of maturity, is a rare and surprising event. The gift of the new self with a new time and a new space that is beyond belief and suffering, is no commonplace occurrence. Rather, it is, as correctly perceived by religious man, a miracle."[77]

THEOLOGIES OF PLAY IN QUESTION

These theories of play and religion have opened up a theological option of immense promise. Play is a many-sided activity that can be found in every sector of human culture and at every stage of individual life. Play can be profoundly social and socializing or deeply solitary and meditative. That this universal experience bears at least similarities to religious experience is obvious to all on reflection. Play is a voluntary and exhilarating activity that is separated in time and space and in logic and value from other activities. Indeed, in playing we step out of one world and into another—a world that usually demands serious effort and often delivers unfettered joy. Play is thus a form of transcendence that all human beings can and do experience in the everyday world of ordinary life. As such, play closely resembles religious forms of transcendence at virtually all of these points. What more promising "signal of transcendence" or metaphor of faith could be found than the experience of play. Yet, as we have seen, Christian theologians have scarcely exploited this new opening for a revitalized faith. The work of Neale and Cox, though rich with insights and implications for Christian thought and life, are nevertheless preparatory and provisional. Even the more completely developed appropriation of play by Rahner is only an elaborate sketch for a full theology of play.[78]

Why theology of play, among all the new theologies we are exploring, has produced such modest achievements is something of a puzzle, especially in light of the intense and inventive work on play within other academic disciplines. Several possible explanations come to mind. Perhaps by accident, those Christian thinkers most interested in play and religion have often had more limited concerns than those of theology proper. Professional concerns with religion and culture (Huizinga), psychology of religion (Neale), or Christianity and society (Cox) have militated against the development of fullblown theologies of play. A second possible reason is that play studies have had a central role in a wide variety of nontheistic interpretations of the religious life. The comparison of play and religion has figured large in the social scientific study of religion (Roger Caillois, Adolf Jensen, Emile Benveniste) and in radical humanistic interpretations of religion (Eugen Fink, David Miller, Sam Keen). The ease with which religion can be made intelligible as a purely natural and human phenomenon by comparison to play may have discouraged some Christian theologians from pursuing this line. A third and perhaps more telling reason could simply be our deep and pervasive suspicion of play. Despite our fascination with sports, games, and entertainment, we are still a culture deeply wedded to the importance of work. Indeed, we fervently believe that only those who work are entitled to play and that the only reason people play is to rejuvenate themselves for work. Our culture's inescapable bias that somehow play is "not for real" is too widespread for a play theology to be taken seriously or playfully. A culture and a Church as thoroughly oriented toward work as ours cannot help but see play theology as incomprehensible and dangerous.

This kind of prejudice has by no means been absent from the formal criticisms leveled against play theology. In fact, play theology has for the most part been summarily dismissed in theological circles. It is often singled out as the prime example of the frivolous and vacuous low to which the new theologies have sunk. The barely disguised scorn of these dismissals suggests a deeper discomfort with play theologies than mere academic disagreement.

Other more temperate and detailed criticisms have, of course, been directed against theology of play. Most of these criticisms turn

on two key issues—the "play-work" and the "play-reality" questions.
Critics are troubled by the consistently negative view of all kinds of
work, even when work is seen to be inescapable. If everything authentically human and religious is seen as play, then nothing will be
play-like anymore. Work and play can be quite different without being as antagonistic to one another as most play theologians make
them out to be. Commentators are equally troubled by questions
about the reality of the "play world" and the truth of the "play like"
in play theology. While assimilating religion into play in this fashion
may free faith from the rough handling it has received at the hands of
factual scientists and skeptical philosophers, it may also deliver faith
into the clutches of childish magic and wishful fantasy. Play theology
too easily skates over the methodological problem of the relation between the real and the imaginary. While a playful religion may not be
lacking in seriousness, it may be lacking in reality and truth, and that,
for many theologians, would be no laughing matter.

Despite its apparent eclipse as a thriving theological movement,
play theology has not been without influence. Many of its themes
have been picked up and developed in the context of other theological orientations. Play theology's emphasis on celebration and imagination are certainly not lost on the widening discussion of these
themes in the contemporary theological guild. Interest in the play of
myth and ritual is found in a variety of theological programs aimed at
restoring myth and ritual to the Gospel. The recovery of the language
of irony and the perspective of comedy in play theology is appreci-
ated among theologians attentive to those styles of discourse and existence. Indeed, all these themes within play theology have left their
mark on those theologians especially concerned with the linguistic
forms of communication and communion between human beings and
God. This influence is especially evident in those new theologies
that are preoccupied with the narrative character of human experience and Christian faith. These "theologies of story" constitute still
another new type of theology, and they will be our subject in the next
chapter.

7
Story as Medium and Message
John Dunne, James McClendon, Sallie McFague

The significance of storytelling in primitive or preliterate cultures is widely recognized in the recent scientific and historical literature on these cultures. Their world received its intellectual, social, and religious shape from the tribal myths, tales, and legends that were passed down from one generation to another "from the beginning of time." These sacred stories of gods and heroes, underworlds and afterlives served a variety of ends. They handled the baffling mysteries of life by envisioning an unseen world of powers that explained the miraculous and controlled the chaotic. They uncovered the recurrent patterns in nature by explaining how the world and everything in it came to be. They established the social identity of the group by defining leadership roles, kinship systems, social levels, and behavioral norms. They shaped the personal identity of each individual by laying out a repertoire of typical responses to the crisis situations of life. In other words, these stories served the metaphysical function of linking the individual to the mystery of the universe as a whole, the cosmological function of furnishing an intelligible and heuristic image of nature, the sociological function of articulating and enforcing a specific social and moral order, and the psychological function of marking a pathway to guide the individual through the various stages of life.[1] Ritually enacted and socially imposed, these stories patterned the thinking and living of all members within a given tribe or culture.

Modern persons have drifted far from this primitive dependence upon stories. There clearly is no one set of sacred stories that centers the self within the concentric circles of a familiar cosmos, earth, and group. Not only is the modern world rife with different sets of sacred stories, but these rival systems no longer pattern thought and life on all levels of existence for their adherents. Over the centuries, the old unified and unifying stories of the traditional religions have gradually given way to the new specializing disciplines of modern scholarship. The psychological, sociological, cosmological, and metaphysical have been parceled out to the various disciplines, each of which proceeds by its own canons of research and produces its own kind of explanation. Even within these limited domains of inquiry there are multiple disciplinary specializations to say nothing of partisan interpretations that further fragment and divide these areas of life and thought. In this differentiating movement from primitive religion to modern rationality, the center has not held—" 'tis all in pieces, all coherence gone."[2]

Nevertheless, stories as such have scarcely disappeared from our midst. Granted that we absorb much of our usable information about ourselves, our societies, and our world from the specialized disciplines and that this information remains incomplete and unintegrated. Granted that no metaphysical or religious vision has succeeded in bringing this highly differentiated and rationalized knowledge into a coherent pattern. But neither of these eventualities has dispelled our interest in stories. Indeed, men and women today may be more addicted to stories than any other group in history. From all walks of life, we gather at the feet of an electronic storyteller for an amazing number of hours each day and night. Even the advertising that is sandwiched between the soaps, sit-coms, adventures, and dramas sells a product by drawing the prospective buyer into a story briefly told. Such endless storytelling is apparently not enough to satisfy our needs, and so we flock to the cinema, attend the theater, frequent the library, purchase books, and subscribe to magazines at record levels—all to be told a story.

Many attribute this passion for stories to pure escapism or shallow mentality. But more thoughtful commentators see a deeper dynamic at work even in the tasteless narrative fare that fills our screens and bookshelves. For them, this persistent appetite for stories reveals a need for stories that is deeply rooted in personal and social existence. Human beings surround their lives with stories because they live their lives *as* stories. Citizens of the modern world, no less than those of the primitive world, live out of a storehouse of personal and cultural stories that largely make up their sense of reality. These contemporary stories are clearly more diverse and fragmentary than those of the primitive, and thus the personal and social identities are more pluralistic and fragmentary than their primitive counterparts. Nevertheless, stories still give the fundamental shape to personal and social identity in the modern world. Among those exploring the role of stories in defining personal and social reality are a number of "theologians of story," who find a close relationship between the power of stories and the power of faith.

THE POWER OF STORIES

Storytellers and rhetoricians, philosophers and pedagogues have long recognized the power of stories. For every age group and on every cultural level, stories have a special power to convey and provoke ideas, to express and evoke feeling, and to portray and invoke actions. Little wonder that stories and the way they work have been intently studied for more than two thousand years. Their characteristic forms and functions have been endlessly analyzed and variously explained in order to better understand and wield that power.[3] The structure of stories has been broken down into plot, setting, characterization, and point of view. Further distinctions between stories have been made in terms of their tragic, comic, elegiac, or picaresque themes. Still other differences have been drawn between the narrative modes of myth, legend, folktale, epic, chronicle, romance, fable, allegory, satire, biography, autobiography, the novel, and the short story. But the careful articulation of these various narrative elements has only clarified what the unlettered folklorist and the growing child know—stories have power over human imagination and behavior because they ring true to life.

Stories that ring true are not limited to those that imitate life. As the earliest mode of storytelling, myths—with their casts of gods and heroes and their settings in underworlds and afterlives—hardly imitate life and yet, rightly understood, myths can ring true to life. To be sure, there have been those thinkers since Plato and Aristotle's time who have insisted that stories are true, good, and beautiful only when they imitate the given. But the long history of storytelling and of thinking critically about storytelling makes clear that such checks on the imagination of the storyteller cannot be enforced. Again and again, storytellers have broken out of the realistic constraints of imitation and created ordered worlds unlike anything we have known on earth and populated with characters unlike any we have met on earth.

Yet these tales often ring with greater truth than the most faithful mirror of ordinary life. Whether or not a story "rings true" to life is less a matter of imitation than of revelation. The power of stories over human imagination and behavior is their power to reveal ourselves, our societies, and our world to us in a memorable and moving way.

For centuries, the revelatory power of stories was thought to be simply a matter of the information they communicated. But as philosophers, social scientists, and literary artists have become more and more aware of the intimate relation between human language and life, a new perception of the formative power of the story form has emerged. The impact of a story is not limited to the life exemplified or the principle illustrated in the story. Stories have the power to shape life because they formally embody the shape of life. Stories have a beginning, an end, and an in-between time when a group of characters in a particular setting interact with one another and their environment in an understandable if not always laudable or predictable way. That interaction turns on critical or dramatic moments in an unfolding pattern of relationships and circumstances that illumine why people act as they do and how things happen as they do. Everything included in the story is woven together to enhance and advance this story line. The story ends, whether happily or unhappily, when all the tensions and themes in the story line have been teased out. Finally, both the beginning and the ending of every story imply other stories presupposed and yet to be told. Individual stories are but episodes within larger and longer stories which, if told, would deeply color those episodes in significant ways.

How like the forms of our stories are the forms of our lives! We are born and we die and in between we strive to make intelligible patterns of all the people we know and all the experiences we undergo. There are always certain givens of sex, age, education, health, ability, individual peculiarities, and social circumstances that set limits to what we can do with our lives. We cannot become what talent and circumstance do not allow, though neither talent nor circumstance alone dictates what we must become. We may put our materials together in the standard ways prescribed by others, or we may shatter the conventional patterns with daring arrangements all our own. The unfolding pattern of our lives can follow straight, curved, or jagged lines of development without losing a sense of coherence. But such coherence requires selectivity. We fashion our lives by continuously editing out the unessential and confusing details. What we cut out is as important as what we put into our lives. These crucial exclusions and inclusions can only be made in the light of some *feeling* within us for the forms of life that we are discovering and creating as we go along. For, though we seldom dictate when and how our life ends, we always live our lives toward a sense of ending. Life is always a movement toward completing the life forms we are living, and thus human life is always seen from ending rather than beginning.[4] But even the end, however and whenever it comes, is not the end. Finally, our individual lives have their meaning within the larger and longer lives of our family, society, culture, race, earth, cosmos, and whatever "other worlds" there might be.

These parallels between life forms and story forms are not accidental. They are not simply the result of cultural influence or individual choice. They reflect a narrative quality that suffuses all human experience. Both time and space are experienced in all their concrete expressions in an inherently narrative way.[5] The human experience of time would be impossible without memory and anticipation. Without memory, experience would lack all coherence. Without anticipation, experience would lose all direction. But memory and anticipation can be held together without dissolving the present into sheer succession only if the remembered past and anticipated future are taken up in stories. The very possibility of the experience of human temporality requires a narrative form that can join the chronicle of memory and the scenario of anticipation without effacing the difference between the two. Similarly, the human experience of space is impossible apart from placement and movement. Without a sense of place, experience would have no contextual diversity. But placement and movement can be brought together without destroying intimacy or distance only if subjectivity and activity are linked in stories. The very possibility of the experience of human spatiality requires a narrative form that joins self and environment in dramatic interaction. In short, at the most elemental level human time is connected and human space is divided in a storylike way. The original of all storytelling about life is the story-making of life.

This narrative structuring of human experience explains why storytelling is a universal form of cultural expression and a universal aspect of personal experience. The endless round of stories told to us and by us serves two broad purposes. In terms of content, these stories are a veritable storehouse of models by which to measure good and bad performance. Our cultural and personal stories illumine life far more clearly and memorably than do our metaphysical and scientific systems. They organize our understanding of past actions and future hopes. They help us to sort out priorities and set goals. They sensitize us to the subtle nuances of human behavior in concrete situations. Our cultural and personal stories are mirrors that bring out every side and shade of human behavior.

But, as we have seen, these stories also reveal the formal structures of human experience. Every story that we hear or tell trains us in the art of recognizing, appreciating, and creating vital form. Every story is a reminder and a reassurance that, no matter how disordered our lives may be at the moment, order and meaning are possible. The mere form of a story about even the most wretched and tangled lives is an "assurance of form"—a promise that everything can be fitted into some coherent scheme of things. Moreover, every story is an opportunity not only to recognize various exemplars of form but to create new forms. Stories teach us that there is no one right way to tell a story. As we develop the ability to follow the plot of a story on paper, we sharpen our ability to shape the stories of our lives. Like the painter who learns by first imitating the masters, we learn the stories of others to liberate ourselves from bondage to those very stories. Such stories finally can free us to fashion the materials of our own biological and cultural inheritance into a personal statement of reality. By implanting the very concept of form in us, stories endow us with the ability to make our own lives into distinctive works of narrative art.

Seen in this light, the fact that a growing number of Christian thinkers have been struck by the similarities between story and faith is hardly surprising. The material similarities are obvious on a moment's reflection. The Christian faith centers in the story of a people prepared and commissioned to share the full truth of God with the whole world. That truth, in turn, is no abstract principle or spiritual illumination but a story—the story of a life, death, and resurrection that shows us God and ourselves. How then can Christian faith be better conceived and communicated than through stories of this Story? Alongside these material similarities are formal ones that are perhaps less obvious but no less important. Christian faith is a distinctive way of giving form by binding events and agents together in a meaningful pattern. Christian faith means building our own story with God and with one another on the plot of the story of Jesus. These material and formal similarities suggest a theology where story is the medium and the message of faith.

THEOLOGIES OF STORY

Christian thinkers across a wide theological spectrum have made considerable theological use of literature. Taking their cue from the use of literature among existentialist philosophers, these commentators have found valuable allies and instructive foes of the faith among recent and contemporary novelists, playwrights, and poets. Their conversation with the literary arts generated a whole specialized field of "theology and literature." Work in this field has taken one of two directions. One move is to exploit modern literature as a negative witness to Christian faith. Here the literature of the world is seen as a sign of the times—as a disclosure of humankind's despair and as a quest for transcendence. The other move is to highlight that modern literature which is a positive embodiment of Christian faith. Here the literature of the Christian artist is mined for its theological insights— as a source for a new imagery and sensibility of transcendence for our time.

Both of these quests for a new theology *in* literature are very much alive today. But neither reflects the concerns of a wholly different approach to theology *as* literature. In the latter, the narrative character of theological discourse and existence, as such, has moved to the center of attention. Here again, two broadly different concerns are reflected in the literature.[6] On the one hand are the biblical scholars who are exploring the narrative character of Scripture. "Story" has become the primary category for rethinking a whole range of unresolved problems within biblical studies—the meaning of faith, the message of Jesus, the uniqueness of the Gospel, the content of preaching, the dating of the Gospels, the relation between the Testaments, the historicity of the text, the formation of the canon, the hermeneutics of exegesis. This many-sided discussion is, of course, a continuation of the whole problem over history and myth that launched modern historical-critical study of the Bible. The category of story has broken open that discussion in remarkably innovative ways.

On the other hand are the Christian theologians who are exploring the narrative character of theology. These scholars are convinced that theology has too long been modeled on philosophical or scientific methods of inquiry and expression. Over time, this dependence has emptied the Christian story of its content and its power by systematically reducing that story to what can be philosophically or scientifically expressed and established. Seeing the Gospel as a story that can only be articulated as a story refocuses all the theological issues between faith and science and philosophy.

There is, of course, a good deal of overlapping between the biblical and the theological literature based on story. Though creative work is being done in both areas, our purposes will best be served by concentrating on the theological parties to this burgeoning discussion. These "theologies of story," or "narrative" theologies as they are sometimes called, broadly agree that the way toward theological renewal lies in the reconception of theology as story. They sharply disagree, however, over what kind of story and what use of story a rejuvenated Christian theology requires. These similarities and differences can be readily seen in a comparison of the narrative theologies of John S. Dunne, James Wm. McClendon, Jr., and Sallie McFague.

Theology as Myth—John S. Dunne

Since the early sixties, John S. Dunne has been exploring a new way of doing theology centered on myth. His theology is mythic in the original sense of the word *mythos,* meaning a "tale" or a "story." Broadly speaking, his theology searches out "the story we are in" both as a culture and as individuals. At the heart of every culture and every self is a distinctive story of humankind that is also implicitly or explicitly a story of God, and theology's task is simply to tell the stories behind and within this story.[7] But Dunne's theology is also mythic in the more familiar sense of *mythologems,* that is, stories of gods and heroes. His theology not only explicitly draws on the mythic imagery of the ancient religions and their later literary adaptations, but also embodies the great patterns and themes of that mythic heritage. His stories of the human adventure with God are told as recurrent cycles of crisis-withdrawal-return or of childhood-youth-manhood and as ceaseless struggles between good and evil, peace and strife, release and suffering, chance and necessity, purity and guilt, life and death.

Coming out of the contemplative tradition of Roman Catholicism, Dunne's theology takes the form of a series of spiritual exercises that are intensive inner explorations of interpersonal relations and spiritual awareness. Rather than employing traditional disciplines of meditation and devotion, he follows a method of what he calls "passing over" into the stories of others and "coming back" into his own story.[8] Passing over is a shifting to a new standpoint of another culture, another way of life, even another religion. Coming back is a returning with a new insight into one's own culture, one's own way of life, and one's own religion. Though acknowledging its distinctiveness, Dunne insists that the method of passing over and coming back is no modern-day concession to religious pluralism and privatism nor is it simply a modern-day innovation for mediating between epistemological subjectivism and objectivism. Rather, this way of doing theology derives from the mythic heritage itself.

Implicit in the necessity of passing over and coming back is the mythic vision of the continuity between the microcosm (self), the mesocosm (society), and the macrocosm (God). Implicit in the necessity of passing over and coming back is the mythic journey through birth, death, and rebirth. Thus, Dunne not only finds precedents for this method in such seemingly different techniques as Socrates' "knowledge of ignorance" and Gandhi's "experiments with truth." He also sees passing over and coming back enacted in the lives of the "masters" of all the world's great religions and reenacted in the lives of all their true disciples. Read casually, Dunne's series of experiments in passing over and coming back may seem only to be variations on a common theme. In successive books, he explores the stories of cultures (*The City of the Gods*), of others (*A Search for God in Time and Memory*), of religions (*The Way of All Earth*), and of self (*Time and Myth* and *The Reasons of the Heart*).[9] Each of these writings can and does stand alone as a penetrating study of the making and meaning of myths. But, read consecutively and attentively, Dunne tells his readers a story that recapitulates both his own and our time's spiritual odyssey.[10]

Little justice can be done here to the wealth of insights into interpersonal and spiritual matters that this long story affords. Indeed, summarizing the "contents" of Dunne's work is impossible because each book separately and all taken together constitute a necessarily personal exploration that can only be recapitulated by reading the books themselves. But we can give away the "plot" and sketch out the main chapters of Dunne's story. In Dunne's telling, his own life and the lives of us all are a passing over into what humankind is and a coming back to discover who God is and a passing over into what God is and a coming back to discover who humankind is. That dialectical movement is brightly visible or darkly shadowed in the myths of all cultures, religions, and selves.

Dunne's first book is a study of the cultural myths by which people through the ages have dealt with the fact that they must die. *The City of the Gods* is more than an effort simply to see our modern mythology of living and dying in historical perspective. This study is an attempt to transform our modern understanding of death by passing over into the myths of earlier epochs and coming back to our own with the insights garnered in those successive forays. Dunne argues that every human society is built on a mythology which gives expression to a distinctive understanding of the problem of death and its solution. Indeed, he finds a close correlation between the political, social, and economic conditions within a society and the way that society conceives of and resolves the threat of death. Thus, as social conditions change so does the characteristic mythology of life and death. Common to all these mythologies, however, is the effort to prolong life or to overcome death *on earth*.[11] As we shall see, by seeking to perpetuate life on earth, these cultural mythologies differ from the solution to the problem of death offered by the great religions.

Dunne sees the problem of death and its solution passing through four distinctive cultural stages. In the most ancient civilized societies, the problem of the separation of the dead from the company of the living was remedied by establishing a lasting bond between the lands of the living and the dead through the king, who was the sacramental representative of the people.[12] Early Mesopotamian myth promised the dead a vicarious life with the gods through the king who went to the gods at death.[13] Egyptian myth of this period saw the dead living on vicariously in the life of the king, a role which was handed on from one royal generation to another.[14] The eventual downfall of such sacramental kingships broke this bond between the lands of the dead and the living.[15]

In the following classical age, the problem of the passing of life into oblivion was countered by the promise of an undying past.[16] The early Greek and Roman republics bestowed an immortal past of fame and glory on all their departed citizens. The later uniformity of city life and universality of citizenship in Roman imperial society gave rise to a new sense of an immortal past. Each individual who ran the gamut of experience during a normal lifetime was seen as having lived the equivalent of every life in every time and place. This notion that each life experiences the fullness of every life lasted until the Roman ideal of social universality and uniformity was undercut by the emerging hierarchical patterns of life in the feudal period.

The medieval period found a new answer to death in each person playing out a special role in society which was, in turn, passed on intact to family heirs.[17] This way of perpetuating earthly life through public roles lasted until the modern world began to separate the private person from all public roles. This break-up of the medieval hierarchical society where everything and everybody had a place left the modern individual "alienated" from all protections against death. But the modern age redressed this vulnerability by granting inalienable sovereignty over death to the people and by guaranteeing an inalienable right to life to the individual. Placing the pursuit of life and the power of death in the hands of autonomous individuals seemed to bring death under human control by making it a part of life. But this way of robbing death of its sovereignty over life has become less and less tenable as the individual's right to life clashes with the people's sovereignty over life. More and more, death is forestalled by imposing it on others. Thus, solving death by "becoming a killer" poses the problem of death in a new form and indicates that yet another new cultural myth may be on the way.

From this study, Dunne concludes that no cultural solution to the problem of death has proven satisfactory including our own myth of a death autonomously willed or accepted.[18] The very fact that there has been a succession of solutions, none of which has lasted, suggests that the problem of death cannot be solved by prolonging life on earth. Dunne notes that a variety of Eastern and Western "mysticisms" have long counseled that all efforts to continue life on earth be abandoned.[19] But he argues that mystical renunciation of the will to live, whether based on the extinction of desire or on the immortality of soul, is finally no more adequate an answer to the problem of death than the mythological perpetuation of life on earth, though there is truth in both of these responses. The truth of all cultural mythologies is their recognition of the goodness of earthly and social life. The truth of all counter-cultural mysticisms is their protest against every attempt to divinize life or immortalize society.

Both truths, Dunne believes, can be brought together in the Christian understanding of God as the one in whom the living and the dead are alive.[20] Coming alive to the living God enables us to abandon all our frantic efforts to satisfy the will to live without renouncing the will to live itself. For such a life, death ceases to be a problem calling for human solution and becomes a part of the entire mystery of our being in God since "whether we live or whether we die, we are the Lord's." Thus coming alive to the living God enables us to achieve what our cultural mythologies only promised—to share the experience of dying while living, to appreciate the contribution the dead have made to life, to do deeds that will never be forgotten, to run the gamut of experience, to attain a status that will outlive us, to live an autonomous life and die an autonomous death.

Though no human society has ever been successfully built on such experience of God, individual lives have. Not surprisingly, Dunne's next book is an exploration of the presence and the absence of the living God in the life stories of others. Once again, his inquiry takes the form of passing over into life stories very different from our own to discover some new dimension of life and experience of God and bringing those discoveries back into our own life stories.[21] In fact, *A Search for God in Time and Memory* concentrates on laying out the peculiar difficulties and possibilities for a genuinely modern understanding and experience of the living God.

Passing over into the lives of others is not unlike writing biography or autobiography.[22] Dunne observes that we must begin by plotting the way characters and circumstances unfold and interact through time. But we must do more than think our way backward to birth and forward to death. We must see that lifetime is part of a larger "time out of mind"—beginning with a lifetime's own times and stretching backward and forward to the outermost limits where time ends in either being or nothingness. Ultimately, every life story is a story of the world and a story of God. Of course, how the world is perceived and God conceived varies from story to story.[23] The world may be pictured as a realm of law or a theater of experience or a maze of self-discovery. God may be imagined as an overwhelming brightness or as an encompassing darkness. Needless to say, these ways of portraying the world and God profoundly affect the narrative form that the life story takes—whether it is a tragic, comic, or ironic story of outward action or inner discovery. But finally, Dunne argues, whatever the cultural and individual particularities of a given life story, we get at the "content of life" only by "seeing through the mythos, realizing that the story is a story."[24] Seeing through life stories, including our own, is the way we can come to see the unbroken unity of the divine and the human in others and in ourselves.

Dunne characterizes the modern life story as one of inner discovery rather than of outward action.[25] Unlike the classical life story of "deeds" (life as a tale of unique achievements) or the medieval life story of "experience" (life as a story of recurrent events), the modern life story is the story of "appropriation" (life as a story of self-discovery). The modern-day breakdown of medieval society's mediated spiritual and temporal existence deprives the individual of any secured place before God or among other people. The search for a way to handle this state of unmediated existence runs through all the great religious and political revolutions of modern times. Dunne traces out in life after life the parallel stories of these modern quests for religious assurance and secular autonomy. He portrays the religious quest as a move from the "hell" of despair through the "purgatory" of uncertainty toward the "heaven" of assurance.[26] He describes the secular quest as a growth from the "childhood" of innocence through the "youth" of experimentation toward the "manhood" of autonomy.[27] Though both quests enjoy a certain success, neither subjective assurance nor objective autonomy finally puts modern men and women at ease with the darkness that goes before and comes after their lifetimes. Indeed, the growing violence and suffering of the twentieth century have begun to darken the "luminous interval" of life between the darkness of birth and death. As the modern story of the hidden God and the singular self becomes less and less illuminating, Dunne sees a new story of God and humankind emerging. That story of our lives and times is the story of "the dark night of the soul."[28] The deepening darkness within and without is an invitation to learn anew the truth of all the great religions—that "man is what God is" and "God is what man is."

As Dunne makes clear in the title of his next book, *The Way of All Earth*, this one truth of religion is the same the world over. Yet each world religion possesses a distinctive "insight" into that one truth and expresses that insight in its own story. Exploring these stories of the religions offers a way of overcoming the alienation from others and God that characterizes contemporary life.[29] Passing over into the religions of others broadens our appreciation of the different ways of persons and God. Coming back equips us to discover those other dimensions of humanity and experiences of divinity in ourselves in ways that we have never known before. Passing over to the other religions cannot help but relativize our own since we discover thereby that our own standpoint is only one among many. But coming back to our own religion cannot help but universalize our own since we find in returning that all possible standpoints somehow exist within our own. In other words, passing over into the stories of the religions and coming back to our own religious story has the potential to extend our sympathies and deepen our care beyond the circle of all beings to the sphere of Being itself. Dunne's process for discovering the truth of religion and his discipline of doing that truth become one and the same.

Dunne approaches his "experiments with the truth of the religions" through the lives of their great exemplars—Gotama the Buddha, Jesus the Messiah, and Mohammed the Prophet. He explores their lives first as religious stories of "a God in disguise"[30] and then as religious stories of "a journey with God."[31] This broad division of the material reflects a characteristic pattern of "withdrawal" and "return" that Dunne finds in the lives of all these great teachers. Their lives and teachings embody a rhythmic balance of solitude and community, of doubt and certainty, of austerity and sufficiency, of suffering and release, of life and death. But this architectonic division of material between "a God in disguise" and "a journey with God" also mirrors the movement and meaning of our own religious discoveries when we follow in their footsteps.

Passing over into their stories somehow reveals the whole truth of death and coming back reveals somehow the whole truth of life.[32] Passing over into the unknown territory of other religions, we discover our essential solidarity with all persons in the hidden life of God. Coming back to the familiar ground of our own religion, we discover the indelible distinctiveness of each human life in personal companionship with God. Dunne believes this dialectical movement undercuts the popular contrasts between the impersonalism of Eastern religions and the personalism of Western religions. He sees both emphases held together in all the religions.[33] Passing over we get a sense of the "universal self" in which all distinctions disappear. We see that every person is a "disguise" of God. In coming back, we return to the "human circle" where sympathies and cares lay their claims upon us. But the insights we bring back extend that circle to an ever-widening companionship of selves on a "journey" with God. Dunne envisions this never-ending process like being on a road at night. Standing still, everything is unbounded when we look up at the night sky, while everything including the sky is bounded when we look at the horizon. But the two visions approach one another when we begin to move. The bounded vision becomes unbounded because the boundary is always moving. The unbounded vision becomes bounded because the movement is always bounded. Thus, the religious life is a continual passing over and coming back. In passing over, humankind comes back to God, and, in coming back, God passes over to humankind.

Dunne sees this passing over and coming back in the axial moments as well as in the overall movement of the story of selves and God.[34] These moments form a patterned series of turning points in the "time" of humankind—the beginning of time, the transition from prehistory, the rise of the world religions, the transition from history to world history, and the end of time. The beginning and the end of time are shrouded in darkness, but the other transitions can be clearly marked. The transition from prehistory to history came with the invention of writing and the establishment of cities. The appearance of the great religions furnished cohesive centers for the great civilizations of history. The transition beyond these separate histories to a world history where all peoples and places are engaged with one another is well under way in our own time, though what the shape of that world will be is far from clear.

These patterned moments in time are paralleled by the stages of birth, childhood, youth, manhood, and death in the "lifetimes" of individuals. Between the darkness of birth and death, the transition from childhood leaves behind the "immediate" realm of momentary preoccupations. Going beyond youth means leaving behind the "existential" realm of fixed priorities. The transition to manhood, or adulthood, requires entry into the "historic" realm of widening horizons. Viewed in one way, each turning point in time and in lifetime is a move away from simplicity and contentment. Each step forward is a giving up and a dying to the securities of a protected existence. Such a view sees life moving toward nothingness. But, viewed from another vantage point, each transition in time and lifetime is a move toward enrichment and understanding. Each step forward is a waking up and taking on of the risks of an expansive life. From this vantage point, life is a journey toward "Being." Dunne, of course, believes that time and lifetime inevitably move toward the fullness of Being. Individually or collectively, we can resist that movement or reenact it. But whether we "walk through upright" or are "dragged through," each human life cycle and the course of human events will be brought to that end. Thus, the story of all humankind and the story of each individual are the same because each is the one story behind the stories of the religions—humankind is becoming what God is, and God is becoming what humankind is.[35]

Having traversed the stories of cultures, lives, and religions, Dunne finally turns to telling his own story, which he believes is also the story of his readers. His fourth book, *Time and Myth*, retells the stories of the first three books as one story. Each chapter explores the central story of its corresponding book in a narrative journey that goes "from time to lifetime to the moment." Thus, Dunne's one story is made up of stories about time and death, about lifetime and life, and about the moment and God. Each of these "stories within the story" draws on still other stories—myths, epics, biographies, autobiographies, novels—that are woven together in near-poetic brevity and beauty to form a single "meditation on storytelling."

Dunne's meditation begins by exploring each age of time in search of an enduring life, "a life that could last through and beyond death."[36] He discovers down every turn and path of the adventure of time that man is mortal.[37] Seeing ever-deepening darkness ahead in the story of death, he turns back to retrace the journey of a lifetime with tempered hopes and opened eyes.[38] He goes back over each stage of life savoring childhood's innocence, youth's urgency, and manhood's pain. But these rites of passage propel him from the "timelessness" of the child through the "inexhaustible time" of the youth into the "great time" of manhood where, once again like the story of death, the story of life leads to ever-deepening darkness. Seeing both the story of death and the story of life merge in darkness, Dunne plunges into this unknown guided only by those like Gotama, Jesus, and Mohammed who have told of their wrestles with the darkness.[39] He discovers that he has met the unknown in all the great moments of disturbance, solitude, and reunion throughout his own life. The unknown is there wrestling with the child, the youth, and the man through the whole night until the light dawns when man and God meet face to face and learn each other's names.

In his latest book, *The Reasons of the Heart,* Dunne narrows the focus of his story about death, life, and God even more to a solitary man's journey into the human heart.[40] The pattern of the journey is the by now familiar one of withdrawal and return. In this spiritual odyssey, the withdrawal is a journey into "solitude" and the return is a journey back to the "human circle."[41] Starting in the loneliness of modern existence, Dunne tracks this loneliness to a universal yearning for God that neither human solitude nor human community can assuage. The split between the mind in solitude that says "I am" and the body in community that says "I will die" leaves the heart divided between life and death. Only a recovery of "soul" can rejoin the mind and body in God.[42] The soul is that "fire point" that kindles the body and illumines the mind with the very life of God. This recovery of the soul fulfills the heart's desire for God by finding God *in* mind and body, *in* solitude and community, *in* life and death. Finally Dunne's journey into the human heart brings together the certainties of human existence with the certainty of God, and he is able to say, "I am and I will die, yet shall I live!"[43]

Thus Dunne concludes his opus in five movements. Each movement is an intricate variation on the themes of death, life, and God. Reflecting the catholicity that his neo-Platonic spirituality allows, he finds one story in the stories of all cultures, all lives, and all religions. That one story is coming to ever clearer appearance as religions, cultures, and lives pass to and fro and in that passage discover their still center and unsurpassable circumference in God.

Theology as Biography—James Wm. McClendon, Jr.
The Church has long found inspiration in the life stories of the heroes of the faith. Such stories play a central role in the liturgical year of Roman Catholic and Eastern Orthodox worship and are a familiar part of Protestant preaching. But James Wm. McClendon, Jr. sees a theological use for these stories of "singular and striking lives" that goes beyond moral uplift or devotional inspiration. He sees such stories opening up a new way of doing theology that is uniquely ap-

propriate for the modern situation. A "biographical theology" promises to return theology and reawaken faith to those living convictions that are at the very heart of Christian thought and life. McClendon explains and explores that promise in his book *Biography as Theology*.[44]

McClendon begins this programmatic essay with a discussion of ethics as a way of uncovering the need for a biographical theology.[45] He begins with ethics because an axial shift in cultural sensibilities, which is destined to affect all thinking and living, is most visibly under way in the moral realm. This pervasive shift can be seen in the collapse of a "utilitarian" *Zeitgeist* that has dominated moral thinking since the beginning of the nineteenth century. The core of Utilitarianism proper is the moral calculus that determines good and bad by the intensity and distribution of pleasure and pain—the greatest pleasure for the greatest number equals the greatest good, and the greatest pain for the greatest number equals the greatest evil. Underlying this particular theory of morality is a conception of human nature that pervades all modern-day thinking, including rival moral theories. A whole culture has been built on the notion that human behavior is primarily a matter of conscious choices guided by abstract principles and theoretical beliefs. But recent theoretical criticisms and practical breakdowns of the moral life have exposed the inadequacies of this utilitarian conception of human experience. McClendon believes that these challenges open the way to reaffirming the priority of character over deliberation and reflection in human affairs.[46] This reaffirmation rightly judges that character is the unseen wellspring of all choice and the hidden agenda in every argument. The moral actions of a person are expressions of the being of that person. By being the person that we are, we are able to do what we do.

McClendon is quick to point out that character is not necessarily fixed or a private matter.[47] In fact, a person's character is formed by continuous interaction with a community or communities that have their own distinctive character. These communities impose their character on their members through a complex system of formal and informal structures and sanctions. But the current flows the other way as well because individuals wittingly or unwittingly impose their character on the communities in which they live. This two-way interaction becomes especially evident in times of communal upheaval and in lives of extraordinary influence. "Thus, character is paradoxically both the cause and the consequence of what we do."[48]

Furthermore, character is for McClendon basically a matter of convictions.[49] Indeed, individuals and communities are constituted by "those tenacious beliefs which when held give definiteness to the character of a person or a community, so that if they were surrendered the person or the community would be significantly changed."[50] Such convictions may be operative in personal and communal life in a direct way without being consciously formulated or invoked. They may be communicated between persons or communities in an indirect way through lived embodiment or imagined example. But convictions can and do become a matter of reflective cultivation and justification in those transitional situations of individual growth or communal conflict where convictions become confusing or unclear. Herein lies the failure of all the moralities of "decision" and of "principle" that have dominated the utilitarian era. By reducing morality to specific decisions or abstract principles, these moral theories have left the deeper sources of conviction—moral motivation and evaluation—uncriticized and unsupported. As a consequence, individual and communal morality have withered at the roots. What is needed today, McClendon avers, is an "ethics of character" that will reestablish those living convictions which inform and shape both the individual members and institutional structures of our various moral communities—political, vocational, social, and familial.

But for McClendon the call for an "ethics of character" is inseparable from the need for a "theology of character."[51] The various convictions by which individuals and communities understand and conduct themselves do not exist in logic-tight compartments. Moral convictions cannot be separated from the more encompassing vision of reality and humanity that is a given religion's concern. Religious convictions cannot be divorced from the everyday behavior that is a given morality's concern. But this means that theology and ethics share the same space and are obliged to come to terms with each other's concerns. Their reflective and pedagogical tasks are essentially the same—"the investigation of the convictions of a convictional community, discovering its convictions, interpreting them, criticizing them in the light of all we can know, and creatively transforming them into better ones if possible."[52] Character, then, is the meeting place of theology and ethics. Nevertheless, in this meeting, theological concerns have a certain priority over ethical concerns because the latter necessarily imply questions that require theological answers. Accordingly, McClendon concentrates his energies on developing a theology of character.

McClendon's originality lies in suggesting that the most promising way into this study is through biography.[53] In every convictional community there appear from time to time those rare persons who embody the convictions of the community in a singular and striking way. Christianity, as a distinctive convictional community, centers on the character of Christ. But that character must continually find fresh exemplification within the Christian community, lest it become nothing more than antiquarian lore and the community die. That is why in Christianity there has been a historical succession of "saints" and "heroes" of the faith who have, through the force of word and deed, stirred up the convictions of the community. Their convictions have served to disclose, correct, or enlarge anew the community's religious vision and moral vigor. The importance and occurrence of such figures is hardly surprising once we recognize that religious beliefs are not simply theoretical propositions but are living convictions which give shape to actual lives and actual communities. What better way, then, to do theology than to attend to the lives that embody and enact those living convictions? Thus McClendon concludes, "Theology must at least be biography. . . .Biography at its best will be theology."[54]

McClendon insists that a theology based on life stories offers no shortcuts around the tough problems facing Christian thinkers today. Questions from a variety of directions have been raised about the authority of biblical beliefs and the credibility of theological claims. McClendon implies that some contemporary religious thinkers have seized on the category of "story" as a way of circumventing one or both of these challenges. Their use of story buries the question of theological truth or biblical authority in the narrative language of metaphor or confession. But McClendon will have none of this. Biographies of the faithful are not to be offered as uninterpreted illustrations or as normative exemplifications of Christian convictions.[55] The point of a biographical theology is not to dissolve theology in life stories or to absolve theology of contemporary accountability. Rather, these life stories are to lead the way into a critical reevaluation and constructive reformulation of the biblical message for today's Christian and today's Church.

McClendon envisions this critical and constructive task as a correlation between the lived convictions of exemplary Christians and the doctrinal formulations that are adequate to lives such as these.[56] Such a correlation involves a double theological use of the lives of these "saints." A biographical examination of their lives allows us to grasp whole as it were the freshness and power of their embodiments of religious convictions. In this sense, their life stories constitute a continually emerging canon of living faith. A theological interpretation of their lives permits us to restate and reconfirm the community's central traditions. In this sense, their life stories constitute a living dialogue of theological inquiry. Such life stories, in other words, are to be studied both for the "lived vision" they convey and for the "theological harvest" they afford.

McClendon proposes to get at the lived vision of his biographical subjects by searching out the central images that inform and convey each person's convictions.[57] Far from being mere literary devices in the hands of a biographer, these images bear the content of faith and the weight of life itself. As such, these images are never purely private or idiosyncratic. They are for the most part drawn from the storehouse of images furnished by that individual's primary convictional community and hence come laden with all the associations and implications of that tradition. But exemplary individuals always extend such "canonical metaphors" in new directions and often supplement them with images drawn from other convictional communities and traditions, thereby enriching the community's convictions without breaking continuity with the past. As these particular images converge in the saint's life, they shape that life's vision and reshape the vision of others.

Lived visions thus delineated, their correlation with theological affirmations will be completed by bringing the doctrines implied in their core images to propositional expression. McClendon leaves no doubt that statements of real states of affairs—metaphysical, historical, and factual—are implied in the images by which persons and communities live. Such images inform minds as well as stir feeling and move wills, and this information is the concern and content of doctrinal statements.[58] The "canonical metaphors" that an individual draws from the community come steeped in the theological doctrines of the community. But these doctrines undergo a kind of critical review and constructive reformulation each time they are given fresh embodiment in the life of a saint. Thus, the lives of the saints tell us what must be stressed in the community's doctrine and what from their experience may be laid aside. Each exemplary life thereby becomes a living commentary on what we can believe and why we can believe it. Each such life becomes a living explanation of and living evidence for the Christian faith in a given age.

Having explained the enterprise of biographical theology, McClendon offers four such biographical-theological studies by way of testing the theory. He chooses four modern saints for study, two well known (Dag Hammarskjöld and Martin Luther King, Jr.)[59] and two lesser known (Clarence Jordan and Charles Ives).[60] In each biographical sketch he searches out the living convictions of the man as these are embodied in certain dominant images and expressed in personal actions. Each life story is told with enough detail and depth that both the public and the private man come alive as a compelling and distinctive instance of lived theology. Each lived theology in turn is suggestively compared to the doctrinal traditions of the Church, showing what elements from the past have been perpetuated and what new notes for the future have been sounded. All of this is written with discerning insight and engaging warmth. In McClendon's hands, each life biographically told and theologically interpreted is a living lesson in how faith endures and theology works since each life reintegrates the past into creative expression in the present.

These four life stories cannot be reconstructed here, even in digest form, with any hope of capturing their personal vocations and living faith. What can be usefully reported here is the "theological harvest" that McClendon reaps from their lives. This harvest is admittedly small since he only focuses attention on the one doctrine of the atonement as a way of illustrating how biography leads to theology. Acknowledging that the central biblical affirmation is the meeting between God and persons and that each of these lives sheds light on that affirmation, McClendon chooses instead to explore the doctrine of the atonement as a particularly revealing example of how biographical analysis can serve theological inquiry.

There are four elements of the doctrine of atonement that seem necessary for any Christian understanding of "at-one-ment"—our estrangement from God and thus from one another, the overcoming of the bars to oneness, the costliness of this reconciliation, and the respective roles of God, Christ, and ourselves in this process.[61] These elements have been differently combined in a variety of doctrinal expressions throughout the history of Christianity, each formulation varying with the times and circumstances of the community. But none of these formulations seems adequate for today's Church and Christian. What doctrine of atonement, then, do we find embodied in the lives of Hammarskjöld, King, Jordan, and Ives?

Reading McClendon's accounts, we are immediately struck by the fact that none furnishes a formal statement of the doctrine of atonement.[62] Each life is, however, organized around familiar atonement images—Hammarskjöld's sacrificial motifs, King's Exodus analogies, Jordan's *koinonic* themes, and Ives's revival hymns. But in each life these biblical images are supplemented with other images that give them an extension much broader that Christians have generally allowed. Those converging images imply a doctrine of the atonement that breaks down all the lines of creed and caste, of race and class that

Christians have so often proudly drawn or silently tolerated. Atoning faith must recognize that God's at-one-ment is at work in *all* convictional communities to create one new humanity in one new earth. Again, these lives bear witness that at-one-ment cannot be achieved without risk, sacrifice, and even untimely death on the part of Christians. They show that Christian faith can take the grim enmity of death into a joyous and creative life. Finally each affirms in his own way that Christ is the pattern and God is the power of the atoning life. They unfailingly point to the costly act of God restoring us to himself as the deepest element in every atoning deed.

Their affirmations of what must be included in today's theology of the atonement implicitly set aside certain beliefs that have long been thought central to the Gospel.[63] The most notable departure is their conviction that the atoning work of God is not limited to the Christian community or mediated solely through the life and death of Jesus Christ. Though all four men belong to the convictional community that finds *its* relationship to God centered in Jesus Christ, they do not see as absolute the Christian community's experience or expression of God's at-one-ment. Moreover, they all "sit loose" with the importance of the historical facts behind the Gospel of Jesus Christ. Not that they deny the historicity of the Christ of the Gospels. But they are much more concerned with incorporating and extending the life of Christ in the history of our lives. In these ways, the theology embodied in McClendon's modern-day saints simply sets aside issues that have been of great moment for centuries of theological debate.

Acknowledging the programmatic character of his essay, McClendon readily admits that he has presented nothing more than a sketch of the theoretical framework and practical execution of a biographical theology. In a concluding chapter, he singles out a number of issues requiring immediate attention. More thought must be given to the question of how the biographical subjects for theological study are chosen.[64] Only those lives that have a compelling quality in them are likely to be chosen. But how is that quality recognized, and how is the bias of choosing only those persons who mirror the theologian's own convictions overcome? At stake here is a crucial question about the logical priority of biographical over doctrinal statements of theology.

More attention needs to be given to the interconnections between images and convictions.[65] A deeper grasp of the relations among the affective, volitional, and cognitive functions of images and between the expression of convictions as images or as propositions is a top priority. The relation between biographical theology and autobiography (our own and others) is also worth careful consideration. Confessional writing has a time-honored place in the Christian movement. How should those writings be forthwith taken and undertaken in the light of biographical theology? An obvious problem for biographical theology is what use to make of the Gospel portraits of Jesus Christ.[66] Does biographical theology put new questions on the New Testament scholar's agenda? How do the stories of the saints "continue" the incarnation of God in Christ? Finally, McClendon raises the holy question of the relation of the saints and worship.[67] Hoping to avoid a "too-sterile Protestantism or a too-fecund Catholicism", in this regard, he explores ways that the saints old and new can serve as encouragement and guidance for our lives in the presence of God while restricting worship and directing prayer to God alone.

These problems and others notwithstanding, McClendon has great hope for biography as theology. He sees in the study of life stories a way not only to remake today's theology but to remake today's theologian as well.

> Theology as self-involving means that the quest for an ethics of character and a theology of character makes a demand upon the character of the theologian, and upon those who, reading, share his task. We are called thus to find our selves, our own true selves, in the meeting with God which Christian faith celebrates. And these selves are irremediably *varied* selves. In this sense, we return from the lives we have examined to our own lives; the examiners become the examined, and our claim on our "saints" become their many-sided claim upon us.[68]

Theology as Parable—Sallie McFague

Like the other theologians presented in this study, Sallie McFague believes that Christian theology faces an enormous task today. For growing numbers of people inside and outside the Church, the language of the Christian tradition is no longer authoritative or meaningful. Momentous changes in modern thought and life have undermined the credibility and utility of traditional formulations of the faith. Many of these formulations have become tired clichés, empty generalizations, sterile literalisms. The task of theology is to overcome this gap between the Gospel and contemporary society—"to make it possible for the gospel to be heard in our time."[69]

Unfortunately, the way in which theology has long been done is an obstacle to any successful completion of that task. Indeed, the classical forms of theological reflection are partly to blame for driving a wedge between the traditional words of faith and their contemporary embodiment in life. The overly abstract and conceptual character of systematic theology is too remote from the only kind of language that keeps belief and life together.[70] The revelatory language from which faith was born and in which faith endures is parabolic language. Only a theological return to the "parabolic tradition"—the parabolic language of Scripture and its extension in Christian poetry, narrative, and autobiography—can make the Gospel credible and possible for our day.

McFague offers a prolegomenon to that kind of theology in *Speaking in Parables.*[71] She calls this parabolic theology an "intermediary" theology by way of indicating that it falls between the "first order" language of living faith and the "second order" language of systematic theology.[72] Parabolic theology is, on the one hand, not itself parable nor, on the other hand, is it systematic theology. Rather, parabolic theology mediates between the two as a form of reflection that stays "close to the parables" in both form and content. This kind of theology is not new in Christian history though it is a sharp departure from the great discursive theologies of a Thomas, Calvin, Schleiermacher, Tillich, or Barth. McFague traces a tradition of parabolic theology through Paul's letters, Augustine's *Confessions,* John Woolman's *Journal,* Kierkegaard's writings, Bonhoeffer's prison letters, and Teilhard's occasional writings. Her hope is that such a theology will "surface as a major genre, for it attempts to serve the hearing of God's word for our time by keeping language, belief, and life together in solution."[73]

Speaking in Parables falls into two main parts, a foundational part and a constructive part. The foundational chapters establish that the language of metaphor is the heart of all human utterance and that parable is the primary form of Christian discourse. The constructive chapters explore how such literary traditions as Christian poems, stories, and autobiographies can be used as sources for an intermediary or parabolic theology. McFague believes that a theology based on these sources can capture something of their metaphoric power and parabolic form without taking the actual form of poetry, narrative, or autobiography. In the past, parabolic theology has taken the form of letters, confessions, journals, reminiscences. What precise literary forms it will take in our day remains to be seen but whatever, "the result will be more like a parable than a system."[74]

Underlying this whole question of the forms of Christian discourse is the now almost common assumption that human beings are "linguistic."[75] Human beings are possessed of speech and possesed by speech. We give order to our world and give ourselves to that ordered world through speech. At the bottom of all such world-ordering and self-involving language are metaphors—those multimeaning images that jolt us to a new insight by revealing "similarities in dissimilarities."[76] Living as we do in a world where language is steeped in rational abstraction and scientific precision, we easily lose sight of the metaphoric foundations of all speech and thought. Nevertheless, the ability to note similarities and differences is the heart of all thinking and all speaking.

As such distinctions are made, gradually the world within and the world without are precisely and complexly organized through a process of "naming." In naming, the human mind "moves" from the familiar to the unfamiliar through metaphors.[77] We use what we know to "grope" toward what we do not know. Metaphorical movement is the human method of investigating the universe as well as describing it. There is an almost inevitable tendency in this process to hypostatize ideas and words as permanent objects of attention. This tendency is carried farthest in abstract language, discursive reasoning, and scientific knowledge. As we shall see, there is a place for such systematized speech and thought, even in theology.[78] But, in all fields, such linguistic and conceptual reifications must periodically be broken through in order to revitalize language and refocus understanding. These "deformations" of speech and knowledge are always a return to the plastic inventiveness of metaphoric seeing and saying. Thus, all language and thought is originally and generatively metaphoric.

Metaphor's indispensable role is particularly obvious in the case of Christian discourse and discovery. Christianity offers no way to God through mystic encounter or philosophic abstraction.[79] The only way we have of naming and knowing the unfamiliar and nonsensuous reality of God is through the familiar and sensuous images of earth. Indeed, McFague sees no way "around" the metaphor in getting to know God or in talking about God.[80] From the human side, all language and knowledge about God is metaphoric because human beings are always "one term" of the relationship. As "bodies who think," we can only understand God through our experience. From the divine side, all knowledge and language about God is metaphoric because human beings are the primary "abode of the divine." As "incarnate deity," God stands under all of our experience. Thus, the revelatory power of metaphor works both ways. On the one hand, images from the world of everyday experience are used to "figure" that which transcends the world. On the other hand, the reality mediated through those images "transfigures" the world of everyday experience. Taken together, God and the world are mutually configured in and through the metaphoric imagination.

The primary form of metaphoric imagination for Christian thought and life is the parables of Jesus.[81] These parables have, in the past, most often been regarded as illustrations of a single moral or as allegories of a hidden truth. But, drawing on recent studies of the parables by biblical scholars,[82] McFague sees the parables of Jesus as "extended metaphors"—as stories with a metaphoric form and content. The language of the parables of Jesus is deeply metaphoric. Built into every parable is something out of the ordinary that breaks the surface realism of the story and "shocks" us into seeing just those familiar circumstances in a new way and at a new depth. The "crack" in the story does not open up to some arcane or occult "religious" world. Rather, it opens up the hearer of the story to a radically new way of perceiving and engaging the "secular" world. Similarly, the message of the parables of Jesus is doubly metaphoric because the parables of Jesus are the "inverbalization" of Jesus as the parable of God.[83] The parables no more directly describe Jesus than Jesus directly reveals God. The parables only indirectly give voice to the voice of Jesus who only indirectly brings God to appearance in human flesh. In both the linguistic and the living parables of Jesus, God appears in "soft focus." Assertions about God and encounters with God are mediated through ordinary language and ordinary life. "In other words parables, and Jesus as a parable, operate in the way metaphor does."[84]

If the metaphoric form and content of the parables of Jesus are normative for the Gospel, then theological reflection stands in need of radical correction. For most of its history, Christian theology has been discursive and conceptual, systematizing universal truths in abstract formulations. By contrast, a parabolic theology will be evocative and existential, calling persons to hear the word of God through imaginative participation in the stories told. This kind of theology has surfaced often enough in the past that its chief characteristics can be enumerated.[85] First, parabolic theologians use highly metaphoric language. Neither woodenly biblical nor abstractly philosophical, their language uses the metaphors and images of their culture to bring their readers to hear the word of God. Second, their writings in one way or another reflect the process of "coming to belief." They are aware of the narrative quality of believing and for that reason they concentrate on showing the possibility of a growing confidence in the goodness and power that rule the universe. Finally, these parabolic theologians are implicated personally and vocationally in their theologies. Employing a variety of literary forms, they give testimony to the extraordinary power and love of God made visible in the ordinary events and passions of their own lives. In short, what has come to focus through the study of parables and a review of theology's history is "a model for theological reflection that insists on the metaphoric quality of language, belief and life."[86]

But what are the resources for parabolic theology? McFague's models are certainly the parables and the life of Jesus, but her sources are considerably broader than the canon of Scripture or even of Christian literature. She draws on all those writings within Western letters that are intimately connected with parables as extended metaphors—especially poetry, novels, and autobiographies. In poetry is a treasure house of metaphoric transformations of language; in novels, of metaphoric movements toward belief; in autobiographies, of metaphoric unifications of life. While Christian writings hold the richest treasures, the whole of Western literature has been so deeply influenced by Christianity that any poem, novel, or autobiography is of some value to parabolic theology. Precisely how these literary forms serve as sources for a theology that is intermediary to biblical and discursive language is the burden of the constructive half of McFague's programmatic essay.

McFague is clear that using poetry as a resource does not mean writing intermediary theology *as* poetry. But theological reflection that stays close to the parabolic form can learn much from the poets about renewing language and evoking insight.[87] Poetry is always a "deformation" of language—a stretching of language into a fresh context that shocks the reader into a new insight. The poet has an uncommon ability to breathe new life into dead symbols by making them metaphors again. McFague illustrates this ability through selective and sensitive interpretations of serious Christian poetry and popular Christian verse. She concludes that theologians who "educate their sensibilities" through poetry will learn to write theology that is sensuous and suggestive, personal and participative. They will not be afraid of ambiguity, irreverence, or humor. Studying poetry will not write their theology for them, but it will awaken them to the difference between words that are dead and those that are alive. It will make them responsive to new and unnoticed associations and juxtapositions in ordinary language. "If the basic task of theology is to help locate new contexts in which the word of God can be encountered, then theologians have much to learn from the way Christian poets, both ancient and modern, have created such contexts."[88]

Having learned about the metaphoric use of language from the poets, the theologian can learn about the metaphoric process of coming to belief from the storytellers, especially the novelists who have mastered the narrative art of character development.[89] Novels do not portray disembodied beliefs or momentary experiences, but rather a style of belief and behavior formed and revealed through the repeated decisions and changing circumstances of a lifetime. For that reason, Christian novels reveal much about the process of coming to belief because they show human beings actually grappling with the transcendent through the complexities and limitations of ordinary existence.

In a cursory review of the history of Christian novels, McFague notes that the more didactic and allegorical novels of the past are giving way to more parabolic novels in the present.[90] In the former, character and context are bent to proclaim the "message" of the Gospel which is well in hand. Novels that are closer to the parabolic form are more sensitive to the persistence of evil, the hiddenness of God, and the riskiness of faith. But this latter kind of novel, which sees an orderly world only indirectly and intermittently, is the kind most pertinent to our needs. The theologian instructed by such stories will not downplay the complexity, skepticism, and irony inherent in the experience of coming to belief in our times.[91] Moreover, that theologian will deal with the perilous story of coming to belief in a "storied" way. That is, parabolic theology will use stories to confront people with their own possibilities of coming to belief.

Parabolic theology can learn most about telling theological stories from autobiography.[92] Successful autobiography is inescapably parabolic because autobiography is metaphoric story through and through. The story of the self can only be told indirectly and incarnationally since the mystery of the self only comes to appearance in and through concrete speech and action.[93] When we write autobiographically, we move from the known to the unknown, through the details of our lives to the mystery of our selves. Each speech remembered and incident reported is a metaphoric unfolding of the "master form" of the teller's life—a form that is not only communicated through but constituted by the story told.

McFague's brief review of a variety of autobiographical writings suggests that the most engaging and inspiring autobiographies are not self-absorbed but vocationally oriented.[94] "It is the vocationally-oriented autobiographies, those that point away from a direct, inward perception of the self to what drives the self, drives it concretely in the world, which are the most revealing of the self."[95] When that driving power is conceived as God, autobiographical stories bring religious belief and daily life together in profound and continous interaction. Thus, a theology tutored by autobiography will not be afraid of the personal. The theologian's own life story can become a part of the data of theology—a way to make the old story new once more.[96] "In autobiographies, finally, intermediary theology has a source for understanding how language and belief move into a life, how a life can itself be a parable, a deformation of ordinary existence by its placement in an extraordinary context."[97]

Having thus spelled out something of the general relations between poem, novel, autobiography, and parabolic theology, McFague remains unclear about what such a theology will actually be like.[98] The very character of parabolic theology with its indirection and idiosyncrasy militates against prescribing literary forms or dictating religious content. The required reconstruction of the tradition and the self-involvement of the theologian mean that parabolic theology will always remain "open, hesitant, and unfinished." McFague is equally unclear about how parabolic theology relates to systematic theology.[99] Though she clearly believes the times call for parabolic theology and though she roundly condemns the failures of systematic theology, she does acknowledge the importance of systematically relating Christian thought and life to other domains of human knowledge and experience. She even hints at one point that parabolic theology is liable to "aberrations or obscurity" without the balance that systematic theology affords, though how that balance will be struck remains unexplained.[100] McFague is undaunted by these problems, however, because she believes that Christian faith demands and sustains a parabolic theology.

> A theology that takes its cues from the parables has no other course than to accept what may appear to be severe limitations—limitations imposed by never leaving behind the ordinary, the physical, and the historical. But these limitations are the glory of parabolic, metaphoric movement, for they declare that human life in all its complex everydayness will not be discarded but that it is precisely the familiar world we love and despair of saving that is on the way to being redeemed. The central Christian affirmation, the belief that somehow or other God was in and with Jesus of Nazareth, is the ground of our hope that the ordinary is the way to the extraordinary, the unsurprising is the surprising place.[101]

THEOLOGIES OF STORY IN QUESTION

Few theological trends have made such immediate impact and gained such widespread influence as has theology's recent "narrative turn." The rubric of "narrative" or "story" has generated a wide-ranging discussion that covers questions from biblical authority to personal conversion and extends from biblical historians to systematic theologians. This discussion has produced a burgeoning literature that breeches the walls of disciplinary specializations and shows no signs of abatement. The impressive diversity of this work on narrative modes of religious communication and discernment, coupled with parallel interests in story in other fields of study, indicates that theologies of story are destined to play a key role in Christian studies for years to come.

Beyond their detailed theories and specific insights, theologies of story have sharpened the focus on a number of crucial issues that stand at the center of theological inquiry today. The whole question of the linguistic nature of human existence is further complicated by the attention to the different genres of narrative discourse. Narrative theologies throw new light on the "grammar of reality"—on the different ways the human world is structured by different modes of speech. They have also raised the question of the historicity of faith with new urgency. Their emphasis upon myth, parable, and metaphor restages the debate over the cognitive basis of religious claims and the fictional nature of biblical narrative. In this connection, theologies of story extend the hermeneutical discussion that has long been a vital concern among certain biblical scholars. They have shown that all theological reflection must deal with such hermeneutical questions as the relationship between biblical text and contemporary audience, between speaking and writing, and between narrator and auditor.

Theologies of story have obviously broadened the cultural sources on which theology can draw for constructive reflection. Long restricted to depending on philosophy and using the social sciences only negatively and the literary arts anecdotally, doctrinal theology has found new form and content in these other disciplines. Narrative theologies have reintroduced primary forms of religious discourse into theological reflection. They have shown that the language of confession and address can be used to articulate theology's doctrinal content and systematic interests. Finally, theologies of story keep the spotlight focused on the centrality of the imagination in religious experience and theological reflection. They offer little clarification of what the imagination is or how it functions. But, by joining the religious imagination to both the literary and the scientific imagination, they hasten the day when comprehensive phenomenologies of imagination will be undertaken.

Despite their positive impact and impressive following, narrative theologies are beginning to generate criticisms and questions. The persistently autobiographical character of most narrative theology troubles many critics. Our own study shows that the theological use of three very different kinds of story comes down in the final analysis to reflections of a very personal kind. Those troubled by this language of confession and address find no leverage in theologies of story against the excessive religious privatization and psychologism of our time. Related questions from both within and outside the movement have been raised about what truth is communicated through theological stories and how this truth is established. Granted that Christian convictions are not about isolated facts and cannot be separated from practical considerations. Are theological stories reports of belief, descriptions of reality, recollections of history, explanations of events, commitments to action? Narrative theologians claim to use stories in all these ways, but they have been less than clear or convincing in explaining how "story-shaped" worlds are related to historical, scientific, or philosophical descriptions of these same worlds.

Doubtlessly echoing these encompassing problems of authority and truth, questions are beginning to be raised about the entire enterprise of narrative theology. Some critics simply argue that a distinction must be made between religious expression and theological reflection. Stories are indeed the stock-in-trade of religious testimony and exhortation, but the vision of reality expressed in such stories cannot be preserved or warranted by the stories themselves. Whatever truths are mirrored in these stories can only be sustained through theological reflection that discursively reconstitutes and defends those truths. For critics who argue this line, theology cannot itself be story and therefore religion cannot ultimately rest on story. Finally, other commentators are raising even more radical questions about the necessity and desirability of matching life and faith to stories. For these critics, the death of the modern novel and the appearance of the theater of the absurd are signs that we are coming to the end of the time of viewing ourselves and our world *sub specie storia.* "Seeing life as a story" imposes an artificial necessity and repressive conformity on the inchoate flow and creative disorder of lived experience. The syntactical constraints of any life story, to say nothing of the standardized stories of our religious, cultural, and civic traditions, are regarded by some contemporaries as obstacles to a mature humanity and authentic religiosity.

As we reach the end of our survey of the major types of new theology that have appeared in the last quarter century, we can see that this period has been a turbulent time of theological reflection and innovation. Amid the turbulence, we have located certain streams of thought and have traced their sources to various cultural preoccupations (secularity, process, liberation) or universal human gestures (hope, play, storytelling). But the streams themselves surge and seethe with the same turbulence that surrounds them. Finally, all the currents of theological reflection flow swiftly and roughly together into a veritable Niagara of undecipherable sound and undisciplined energy. Carried along in that flood, any predictions about where this cascade is going and what it will sweep aside or along as it moves through the next twenty-five years is risky. But forewarned is forearmed to meet the strenuous demands on religious thought and life that surely lie ahead, so those sightings must be attempted in a final chapter.

8
Pentecost or Babel?

Our study began with the suggestion that an unprecedented pluralism of belief-systems and life-styles is available today under the
heading of "Christian faith." While diversity and conflict have always
been a part of the life and thought of the Church, past disagreements
usually fell within a clearly defined spectrum of theological options.
That liberal-conservative spectrum has been shattered, however, by
the turbulent developments in Protestant and Roman Catholic theology in the last half century. These developments have not been entirely chaotic and random. Some underlying order and connection
can be teased out by uncovering the root metaphors or hermeneutical
keys that animate contemporary reflection. Thus we have focused our
survey of contemporary theology on the thematics of secularity, process, liberation, hope, play, and storytelling. Yet this typological analysis scarcely reduces the rich variety of belief-systems and life-styles
available to contemporary Christians. If anything, such analysis underscores the variety by revealing the remarkable differences even
among the theologians who share a common thematic concern. The
distance between a Robinson and a van Buren, between a Moltmann
and a Vahanian, between a Dunne and a McFague can hardly be
missed. The theoretical and practical differences within a theological
type are as great or greater than the differences between theological
types. The new pluralism cuts across all confessional and conceptual
lines of theological reflection.

Some will doubtlessly argue that there is nothing qualitatively new about this pluralism. They will readily admit that the number of theological options has mutliplied, but will stress that these differences still fall within the mainstream of a single great religious tradition—the Judeo-Christian tradition. This tradition, at least in North America and Western Europe, has long tolerated differing theological expressions. To be sure, in earlier years that toleration was often born of expediency rather than principle. But more recently theological diversity has become a defining mark of this tradition. Thus, some see in the new pluralism nothing more or less than quantitative increase in the ways this one great tradition is theologically articulated. Today's theological diversity is seen as merely an intensification of a state of affairs that long has been a part of European and, especially, American life.

This line of argument would be more plausible if the new pluralism were contained within Judeo-Christian bounds. But an expanding theological pluralism within this tradition mirrors an exploding religious pluralism in the wider society, both on a national and a global scale. The breakup of the great colonial empires and the rise of the African and Asian nations have brought to light a world of religious pluralism where biblical theism is only one tradition among many others, some more venerable than itself. The countercultural movements and trends of the last generation have introduced many new religions and parareligions to the American and European scene.[1] A bewildering variety of Eastern and mystical religions, occult and esoteric cults, political and self-realization therapies have permeated these societies. Literally hundreds of movements counting their followers in the hundreds of thousands have spread across what were once essentially Judeo-Christian societies. To be sure, these new movements are unstable and their followers are unpredictable. There is a great deal of change within as well as migration among these movements. But however ephemeral a given movement or fickle a given disciple might be, this pluralization of religious consciousness is no passing fad or fancy. These new experimental and entrepreneurial religions have clearly outlasted and outreached their countercultural beginnings. Alternate and even esoteric beliefs and practices are as likely to be found in mainline as in marginal groups these days. Religious diversity has become an inescapable fact of world, national, communal, and even family life.

What then are we to make of the new pluralism? Can the religious diversity that has emerged ever again be contained or supplanted by a single, dominant tradition? What kinds of structural and ideological changes would be required for one tradition to gain and maintain such dominance? If religious diversity cannot be overcome, what does that portend for the shape of religion in the future? Are we witnessing the first signs of a new Pentecost—are we on the verge of discovering that the many religions with their diverse symbol systems are essentially voicing the same faith? Or are we hearing the first sounds of a new Babel—are we on the edge of discovering that the many religions echo a pluralism at the heart of reality and consciousness as such? Of course, these questions cannot be answered conclusively. The past is too far and the future too close to know their resolution. But bearings can and must be taken since the present is always a blending of the past remembered and the future anticipated.

PLURALISM IN RETROSPECT

The new pluralism is deeply symptomatic of far-reaching changes now under way in the very character of religion. As we shall see, the fundamental clue for understanding these changes lies in religious diversity itself. The emergence of radically different worldviews (including humanistic and antireligious ones) *within the same society* suggests that the new pluralism is not simply a by-product of media exposure or high affluence. Rather, the growing interest in alternative belief-systems and life-styles within and outside of the established religious traditions reflects certain profound shifts in the way human worlds are organized and understood in the modern context.

Viewed in historical perspective, these shifts are but the latest stage in a long series of interdependent changes in religion and culture. Sociologist Robert N. Bellah marks out five such stages of "religious evolution"—primitive, archaic, historic, early modern, and modern.[2] Bellah defines religion as "a set of symbolic forms and acts relating man to the ultimate conditions of his existence."[3] As such, religion mediates a particular sense of ultimate reality, personal identity, and social responsibility through its symbols. But this religious sensibility has differed sharply from place to place and changed dramatically from time to time. Eschewing any notion of progressive development or inevitable progress, Bellah ties his five stages to changing patterns of religious symbolization and sociocultural order. Not all of the stages have occurred everywhere; nor must they appear in sequential order. Indeed, primitive and archaic religious stages are still to be found among aboriginal peoples to this day, and the early modern and modern stages of religion have only clearly emerged and become institutionalized in the post-Reformation West. But the earlier stages are rapidly disappearing, and the later stages are rapidly spreading throughout today's world.

In Bellah's account, primitive religion envisions a mythic world inhabited by ancestral figures, some human and some animal, who are the progenitors of all significant natural occurrences and the exemplars of all fixed social roles. "Not only is every clan and local group defined in terms of the ancestral progenitors and the mythical events of settlement, but virtually every mountain, rock and tree is explained in terms of the actions of mythical beings."[4] Everyday existence and religious life are intimately and fluidly related. Primitive religious life is not focused on worshiping these ancestral figures so much as on ritually acting out their heroic deeds and lives. There are no priests and no spectators in primitive ritual enactment. All present are involved, and each participant becomes one with the mythic heroes or totems. In other words, in primitive cultures there are no special religious roles and organizations that are separated from ordinary social roles and organizations. Religious roles are fused with other roles, and religious institutions are coterminous with other institutions. As such, religion reinforces social solidarity and transmits social roles from one generation to the next. As a "one-possibility thing," primitive religion furnishes little opportunity or inclination to change the world.

Archaic religion elaborates primitive myths and rituals into a systematic complex of gods, priests, worship, sacrifice, and, in some cases, divine kingship. For the archaic mind, there is still only one world acted upon by mythical beings who dominate particular parts of it. But those beings are now conceived as actively and willfully controlling the natural and the human world. Moreover, relations among the gods are hierarchically arranged according to their relative prestige and power. Especially important are the "high gods," whose knowledge and power are thought to be vast. Because the division between gods and mortals is more sharply drawn in archaic religion than in primitive religion, a system of communication and interaction between them becomes necessary. Worship and especially sacrifice are the means of commerce whereby gods and morals interact and influence one another.

Archaic religious institutions are still largely merged with social structures. But the geographical multiplication of worshiping cults and the sociological monopolization of priestly functions signal the emergence of a "two-class system" that differentiates religious practice and status from ordinary life. Although archaic religion still grounds traditional social structures and roles in the cosmic order, the very notion of gods acting over against mortals and of priests mediating between them introduces an element of openness that is lacking at the primitive level. Struggles between rival cults, seen as struggles between rival deities, create new social alignments and call for new religious symbolizations. In other words, the problem of maintaining increasingly complex religious and social orders in some sort of balance tends to undermine the very patterns of archaic religion and culture.

Historic religion, which emerges in societies that are more or less literate, breaks through the "cosmological monism" of the earlier stages by affirming a transcendental realm of universal reality and ultimate concern. Though articulated in a variety of symbol systems in the Orient and the Occident, the historic religions are all hierarchial and universalistic. Both the earthly and the heavenly worlds are finally ordered by a sole creator or single principle that radically transcends the ordinary world of things and of persons. This profound dualism leads for the first time to the conception of a "core self" that is ultimately separable from all conditions of finite existence—from all ignorance, suffering, and death. This ultimate liberation underlies the religious ideal of "separation from the world" that pervades all the historic religions. In some instances, this ideal of world renunciation is extended to the entire religious community (Judaism, Islam), while in others it is limited to a monastic minority (Buddhism, Christianity). But all the historic religions demand of the pious some separation from ordinary worldlings.

These religious separations are, in turn, clearly reflected in the social order that accompanies historic religion. The emergence of a religious elite alongside of a political one creates a delicate balance of powers between political and religious leadership. This balance is complicated by a corresponding separation of the roles of the believer and the citizen among the masses. Given these tensions, balance often becomes imbalance between power elites, and separation often becomes opposition between social roles. To be sure, such imbalance and opposition are comparatively rare because the historic religions, like their earlier counterparts, typically sanction and stabilize the sociocultural order. But on occasion the historic religions have provided the ideology and inspiration for revolutionary changes in that order.

Unlike the previous stages, which embrace a wide variety of actual cases of religious symbolization and organization, early modern religion emerges only from the congeries of closely related cases known as the Protestant Reformation. This stage retains a dualistic separation of this world and the next, but collapses all hierarchical structuring of them. The Reformation represents a decisive break with all hierarchical legal and sacramental systems of salvation. Eternal life in the world to come can be sought in the midst of ordinary worldly affairs by persons of any station or calling.[5] All special ascetic and devotional practices are set aside as well as the monastic communities that specialize in them. In their place, service to God becomes a total demand to be realized in every walk of life. This early modern emphasis on the direct relation between the individual and God and on worldly life as an expression of faith opens the door to individual autonomy. Though that autonomy is still severely limited in religious and moral matters by rigid orthodoxy and ecclesiastical discipline, individuals assume increasing control over their own political and economic affairs. The resulting appearance of a variety of worldly organizations relatively free of any overarching ecclesiastical or governmental control multiplies the pressures and the possibilities for social change. Thereby early modern religion plays a key role in the full emergence of the multicentered, self-revising social order that characterizes today's democratic and voluntaristic societies.

Modern religion may in the long run turn out to be a transitional phase rather than a distinctive stage of religious development. But Bellah is sure that the religion emerging out of the last two centuries of intellectual, technological, and political change is already profoundly different from the religion of earlier stages. Modern religion's central feature is the elimination of all vestiges of the hierarchical thinking that was carried over from historic religion into the early modern stage. Modern religion is leaving behind all dualistic conceptions and authoritarian definitions of reality.

The modern search for new modes of religious symbolization and organization has produced an amazing variety of highly complex though essentially unitary worldviews. That search has by no means been confined to "officially" religious categories and thinkers. Indeed, the responsibility for making sense out of the ultimate conditions of human existence has, in the modern situation, shifted more and more to the individual. The Church as collective symbolization and communal embodiment of a religious perspective survives for many modern men and women, but with far greater fluidity of membership and flexibility of organization. The role of enforcing standards of doctrine and morality has been largely dropped, with the Church serving as a supportive community for those involved in the search for meaningful solutions to ultimate concerns. The underlying assumption of these trends and changes is that culture and personality are endlessly revisable. In the modern context, religion and life have become an "infinite-possibility thing" rather than a "one-possibility thing."

Bellah's descriptive analysis of the sweeping changes in religion, which have over the centuries led to the modern stage, throws considerable light on the new pluralism. Tracing out his five stages clearly shows that the new pluralism is no mere media creation or passing whim. Nor is it simply the result of "vocational crisis" or "academic professionalism" among today's theologians.[6] The new pluralism is obviously what Bellah has called "modern religion" and as such is firmly rooted in the modern world's self-understanding and social structure. Indeed, going somewhat beyond Bellah's descriptive analysis, a careful examination of that self-understanding and social structure will bring to focus what is genuinely new about the new pluralism. The modern world's self-understanding is deeply secular, and its social order is highly differentiated. These interdependent characteristics of modern thought and life have squeezed religion into the "private areas" of human experience and thereby forced religion into a "market place" of competing meanings. Precisely this privatization and commercialization are what makes the new pluralism a new religiosity.[7]

The historical causes and defining characteristics of secularization are topics of endless debate among interpreters of contemporary society. But all commentators essentially agree that secularization involves a dramatic shift in the modern era from "otherworldly" to "this-worldly" thinking. Traditional societies, from the primitive to the early modern, have been built on sacred worldviews. For them, religious representations and presentations of an "other" world have illumined and guided life in this world. But such traditional interpretive schemes and action plans have become increasingly problematic in the modern world as science, technology, and politics have concentrated new knowledge and power in human hands. Appeals to an extraordinary world alongside or above us have become less necessary as more has been learned about the ordinary world around and within us. Transcendental grounds and goals have increasingly given way to immanent explanations and controls of the natural and the human world.

This mounting secularization of the modern world's self-understanding is closely tied to the increasing differentiation of the modern world's social order. Ideological secularization and structural differentiation are, in fact, two aspects of a single process. An increasing fragmentation of overarching systems of religious

thought mirrors an increasing segmentation of institutional embodiments of human meaning. Religious worldviews have social "binding power" only when they are embodied in the primary public
institutions of a society.

In primitive and archaic cultures, the "official" worldview was
mediated through all the significant organizations and roles of the society. Historic cultures differentiated religious from nonreligious institutions but did not separate them. Indeed, specialized religious
institutions maintained their monopoly on reality definition and identity formation well into the early modern era. But the traditional preeminence of religious roles and organizations became increasingly
problematic in the modern era as the forces of industrialization and
urbanization spawned new tasks and new organizations. As social
structures became increasingly specialized, religious institutions became decreasingly authoritative. New political, economic, educational, military, and labor organizations appeared, with each
specialized institution generating its own goals of endeavor and ways
of proceeding and pressing that rationale on its membership. But
these specialized "performance demands" reached no further than
the particular interests served and obligations incurred within a
given group. As a consequence, life in the modern world is increasingly organized in segmented ways that neither call for nor receive
any overarching religious meaning. Correspondingly, religious institutions have become merely one among many specialized institutions
catering to a specialized clientele.

In this situation, religion has become deeply private. Faced with
the unrelenting advance of secular explanations and controls, religion
has retreated to the areas of residual mystery and complexity that still
defy purely secular analysis and competence. By and large, this retreat has moved in the obvious direction of personal and interpersonal experience. As such, this religious retreat is part of a larger
privatization of life within the culture. Much of what is billed as the
"new narcissism" or maligned as the "me generation" reflects this
culturewide narrowing of human meaning to the subjective domain
of self-realization and self-awareness and to the intersubjective circle
of family and friends. Not surprisingly, religion both inside and
outside the established traditions displays this convergence in the
personal and interpersonal. Certainly, this convergence can be seen
beneath the surface diversity of Eastern faiths, occult religions, esoteric sciences, self-realization movements, and body therapies that
populate the "Aquarian Frontier" of the religious counterculture. But
the same process is at work in the surge of experiential piety, devo-

tional mysticism, charismatic renewal, and spiritual healing in the mainline denominations. Religious beliefs and practices are confined to the essentially private realm of personal inwardness and interpersonal intimacy.

This "emigration" further and further into the private realm is encouraged and reinforced by the structural differentiation of modern society. Institutional segmentation leaves wide areas of life individually unstructured and culturally undetermined. The interstices between these functionally autonomous institutions create a "private sphere" of relatively autonomous action. Outside the areas that fall under the performance demands of those specialized institutions that regulate the legal and the economic orders, individuals are left to their own devices in choosing goods and services, careers and pastimes, friends and mates, morals and even religion. In point of fact, within the private sphere individuals are free to construct their own personal identity so long as that identity does not encroach on the freedom of others or disrupt the performance of public duty. Seen in this light, the widespread toleration and equivocation of modern religion is fully understandable. Since individuals are free to choose their own religion, the making of different choices or the changing of choices is to be expected and respected. Rather than internalizing any official or permanent religious system, modern individuals build their own private systems of ultimate significance out of the varied biographical and cultural resources that are available.

Paradoxical as it might sound, such privately practiced and personally constructed religion is subject to a high degree of commercialization. Wherever free choice and free competition prevail, a "consumer orientation" is inevitable. Although the private sphere described above allows great latitude in certain areas of choice, that freedom is not exercised apart from social pressures. A host of specialized institutions have appeared within the private sphere to supply that market with everything from leisure activities to religious experiences. Dating services, advice columns, and travel agencies are among the most obvious institutions catering to the private sphere. But churches, too, have been reduced to "merchandising" their religious products to prospective "buyers." As noted above, those products are primarily concerned with personal well-being and interpersonal success. Like other specialized institutions in the private sphere, churches depend on "product indentification" and "product satisfaction" on the part of their clientele. This dependence leads to a variety of strategies including "product variation" and "market expansion" in order to remain competitive. The churches survive by supplying what people want and need.

Still, in the final analysis, individuals must choose from among the variety of religious groups and goods that are available to them. Some remain loyal consumers of one group's religious beliefs and practices for a lifetime. Others exchange religious groups or interchange religious symbols with a great deal of ease. Indeed, in the religion marketplace, loyalties are being changed at an increasing rate, and religious organizations have for the most part adapted themselves to allow and even facilitate those changes. Open membership and ecumenical cooperation are but two of the most obvious signs of such adaptation. This fluidity and flexibility point to a deeper dimension of the commercialization of religion than the marketing techniques employed by modern religious groups. Religious beliefs and practices are increasingly being seen as something that we *use* rather than as something that we *are*. Creeds and liturgies are perceived as products of our own making and, like any other product, are subject to alteration or replacement when they no longer work for us or appeal to us. Thus, a person's religious identity is no longer bound up with one historic group or symbol system. The religion of the typical modern individual is an eclectic system of loosely held opinions and selectively followed practices subject to change without notice or fanfare.

Thus seen in historical perspective, the new pluralism reveals that the very shape of religion is undergoing radical change in our time. Institutionally specialized and socially objectivised forms of religion that establish and impose an "official" worldview are passing away. The monopoly on reality definition and personality formation long enjoyed by the biblical religions in Western culture has been broken up by the far-reaching changes in modern thought and life that are summed up in the umbrella terms "secularization" and "differentiation." The ensuing redistribution of the sources of human meaning and obligation among a variety of institutions and outlooks, some traditionally religious and some not, is altering both the form and the content of modern religion.

In this transitional situation, a variety of responses to the "official" religious systems of the past can be detected. At the extremes are unreflective affirmation and thoroughgoing rejection of these traditional sacred worldviews. There are those individuals, particularly in alienated and marginal groups, who still take the official model seriously and live with it more or less successfully. There are others, particularly in educated and advantaged circles, who have abandoned all traditional religious roles and representations in favor of a purely secular value system. But the majority of people neither uncritically accept nor categorically reject the interpretive schemes and action plans of the traditional religions. They search for ways of combining religious and secular sensibilities. One strategic move is to restrict the relevance of religious roles to domains that are free of secular jurisdiction. Another move is to loosen the connection between religious representations and domains of secular explanation. But, as we have seen, these delimiting and deliteralizing strategies "save" traditional religions at the price of their overarching coherence and social authority. Such strategies finally reduce modern religiosity to private and fragmented systems of ultimate meaning.

PLURALISM IN PROSPECT

If these trends continue—as they likely will since they are deeply rooted in the underlying assumptions and structures of contemporary life—religion will no longer be tied to any monolithic culture, community, or identity. Indeed, the growing pluralism of religious options in our time reflects a deepening pluralization of religious consciousness. This fundamental change is most visible in the symbolic promiscuity so typical of members of the religious counterculture, but it can be detected also in the private and commercial religion of the mainline traditions. The new pluralism, whether inside or outside the traditional religions, points the way to the emergence of a new "polysymbolic religiosity."[8] Precisely what this polycultural, polymorphic, polyvalent religiosity entails is far from clear in the scientific, historical, and philosophical literature that takes it seriously and normatively. But parties to the debate more or less clearly divide over two central issues that suggest radically different religious and human futures. They disagree over whether polysymbolic religiosity signals the culmination of the Modern or the initiation of the Postmodern Era. Paralleling this divergence, they also disagree over whether polysymbolic religiosity represents a new monotheism or a new polytheism.[9]

Polysymbolic Religiosity—Modern or Post-modern?
Historians of culture generally agree that the Modern Era began with the scientific and philosophical revolutions of the seventeenth and eighteenth centuries. The Enlightenment ushered in a revolutionary understanding of the natural and the human worlds that sharply broke with medieval civilization. That revolution is often en-

capsulated in epithets such as "autonomy" or "reason." While these descriptions are appropos of key thinkers (John Locke's "autonomous thinker") or discrete times (the eighteenth century as "The Age of Reason"), they do not embrace the entire sweep of the last three hundred years. They do not capture such distinctive affirmations of modernity as Pietism, Romanticism, or modern Christianity in its liberal or neo-orthodox forms. We need a broader characterization to appreciate all modernity's progeny. A more adequate summary characterization of the Modern Era is contained in the three terms subjectivity, universality, and immanence.[10]

The Modern Era rests primarily on the principle that personal self-consciousness is the indubitable foundation, the unrecognized presupposition of all else. From this principle, modernity's central problems have arisen—the conflict of nature and person, subject and object, fact and value, certitude and doubt. But from this principle also flow the modern world's distinctive achievements—experimental method, rational criticism, political freedom, individual autonomy, experiential religion. This individualism also sanctions those central institutions of the Modern Age—democracy, capitalism, and romantic marrige. The modern world's radical reconstructions of knowledge, morality, art, politics, and faith are rooted in the priority and trustworthiness of self-consciousness.

A second defining feature of modernity is the unshakable conviction of the unity of being and value, of truth and duty. On first glance, this stress on universality seems to be a concern shared by both the Classical and Modern ages since both assert this unity. But the harmony of the universe perceived by the new science proved incommensurate with the hierarchical visions of unity within classical theology and philosophy. The vertical and eschatological cosmos of the Classical Age gave way to a horizontally and temporally ordered universe. This ideal of a simple order entered into every field of human interest, resulting in new ways of understanding religion, mind, society, business, government, and international relations.

Finally, the modern world is shaped by a pervasive immanency. A. C. McGiffert describes this turn in thought and culture in these words:

> The dependence upon supernatural powers, the submission to external authority, the subordination of time to eternity, and of fact to symbol . . . the somber sense of the sin of man and the evil of the world, the static interpretation of reality, . . . the belief that amelioration can come only in another world beyond the grave—all of which characterize the Middle Ages—were widely overcome and men faced life with a new confidence in

themselves, with a new recognition of human power and achievement, with a new appreciation of present values.[11]

This love affair with humanity and earth gave birth to the technological, political, economic, and demographic revolutions still in process today. History-making and self-actualization became the birthright and duty of every citizen of the modern world.

Thus, the Modern Age stands for the triumph of subjectivity, universality, and immanence in every field of human endeavor. But there are claims on every hand today that the twilight of modernity "falls pitiless and sure." I will not rehearse these litanies of both weal and woe for the passing of our age.[12] That something of an epochal revolution in consciousness may be in the making seems obvious enough. More important for our purposes is to single out the driving force behind this culturewide upheaval that may mark the beginnings of a Postmodern Era. In that challenge, as I shall suggest below, we have the key to understanding both the cultural tumult and the religious revolution of our time.

But first, what brings on a revolution in consciousness serious and sustained enough to fashion a new cultural epoch? The end of an era comes with the exhaustion of its paradigmatic assumptions or generative ideas.[13] This exhaustion may come either when all answerable questions have been exploited or with the emergence of new, unanswerable questions. Paradigm shifts, to use Thomas Kuhn's terminology, begin in a culture when insoluable anomalies and violated expectations command the increasing attention of that culture. In such crisis circumstances, the search for and conversion to a new worldview can and does occur. Such a breakthrough depends upon finding some new organizing metaphor or shared paradigm through which to re-view and re-shape the world.

Given this reading of how epochal revolutions in consciousness occur, what has raised the question of a Postmodern Era? A number of the answers to this question being offered today seem off target because they do not contravene the foundational assumptions of modernity. For all the horrors visited upon modern life by technology, capitalism, or secularism, modernity need not fall under their weight since they are fundamentally compatible with the modern spirit. But something *has* arisen out of modernity that seems to call into question its very foundations. That something is pluralism. The discovery of the historical and linguistic nature of human existence has raised problems that may prove impossible to formulate much less to solve within the foundational assumptions of the Modern Era. The acknowledgement that all experience is conditioned upon and conditioned by particular historical and linguistic standpoints coupled with the manifest differentiation and fragmentation of standpoints within contemporary societies raises questions about all three principles of the Modern Age. In a world of pluralism, how can any human consciousness be a stable center, how can any human experience have a fixed horizon, and how can any human effort be a lasting achievement?

This radical questioning has provoked widespread discussion of a Postmodern Era. So far this possibility is expressed most frequently and forcefully as negations of the modern world's subjectivity, universality, and immanence. The abolition of autonomous selfhood, the abolition of integral worldviews, the abolition of history-making are the goals of a growing number of practical experiments and theoretical programs in human renewal. But those who are in the vanguard of this announced revolution in consciousness insist that there are affirmations concealed in these negations. They promise nothing less than the coming of a radically new sense of human life, space, and time freed from the anxiety and guilt, the repressiveness and uniformity, the futility and dread that have plagued humankind until the present day.

Seen in this light, the struggle between the modern and the postmodern is at depth a religious struggle. Precisely this struggle is mirrored in a sharp division among advocates of polysymbolic religiosity. Polysymbolists are divided over whether our cultural crisis is a purgation or a termination of the Modern Era. Some expressions of polysymbolic religiosity can only be understood as efforts finally to purge modernity of those carry-overs from the classical Christian past that always compromised its full subjectivity, universality, and immanence. These expressions claim to be post-Christian but not postmodern. Other versions of polysymbolism intend nothing less than a final break with all modernity's expressions of the autonomous and centered self, of the single universe and one humanity, of the success drive and work ethic. These expressions are thought to be not only post-Christian but postmodern as well. Not surprisingly, these very different assessments of the cultural situation are correlated with radically different accounts of polysymbolic religiosity. As we shall see below, these differences exhibit a monotheistic and a polytheistic form respectively.

In this context, the terms "monotheism" and "polytheism" are used in the generic sense employed in comparative discussions of religion since David Hume's *The Natural History of Religion*. Used generically or typologically, these terms denote worldviews that are monocentric and polycentric respectively.[14] They connote nothing per se about the particular nature or reality of these "centers"— whether they are thought to be personal or impersonal, supernatural or natural, transcendent or immanent, good or evil, real or illusory. Thus, in the discussion that follows, monotheistic forms of polysymbolism advocate a worldview of maximal unification, while polytheistic forms champion a worldview of maximal diversification.

Polysymbolic Religiosity—Monotheistic or Polytheistic?

The problem of pluralism is at the heart of the religious revolution as well as the cultural crisis of our time. The emergence of a new polysymbolic religiosity turns on the full and final acceptance of the radical historical and linguistic nature of human existence. For polysymbolic religiosity there is no single grammar, no single logic, no single symbol system, no single social structure, no single historic tradition for expressing the religious concerns and commitments of life. A new freedom to acknowledge the variety and tentativeness of every expression of human endeavor is the distinguishing feature of this new religiosity.

As such, polysymbolic religiosity is something quite different from similar-sounding attempts to accommodate pluralism within recent Christianity. Not surprisingly, the threat of skepticism and nihilism has kept many Christians within the pale of an authoritarian and unchanging orthodoxy. But a variety of contemporary experiments in Christian thought and life have sought to preserve Christianity while acknowledging pluralism. No two figures saw the decisive challenge of pluralism to Christianity more clearly than Ernst Troeltsch and Karl Barth.[15] Though they responded to this threat in very different ways—Troeltsch by immersing God in the realities of history, Barth by absorbing history in the reality of God—they both sought to affirm the finality of Christianity in the midst of a world of historical change and religious diversity. Their distinctive strategies have been refined and reformed in countless ways over the last half century of theological reflection. But none of these refinements has sounded the depths of the revolution in religious consciousness mirrored in the new pluralism. Precisely in their efforts to see the one God known *in Christ* within or beyond the many religions and cultures, these theological experiments reclaim with one hand the absolutism they have given away with the other.

By contrast, the polysymbolists categorically refuse to view the whole sweep of Western civilization (contra Troeltsch), much less the whole of reality (contra Barth) under the aspect of Christian faith. Indeed, this new religiosity is not only post-Christian but posttraditional as well. Though polysymbolic religiosity draws inspiration and direction from the myths and rituals, creeds, and practices of all the great world religions, no one tradition is given a definitive status. None of the traditions is to be embraced exclusively, though all may be used to give shape to the increasingly complex and variegated experiences of life.

Some polysymbolists draw on the many traditions to give expression to a religiosity that is distinctively monotheistic and modern. Their use of the traditions is "monotheistic" in the sense that they affirm a fundamental unity in, under, and beyond humankind's many piecemeal glimpses and symbolic systems of religious meaning. These polysymbolists are "modern" by virtue of their belief that modernity's search for an integral self, universe, and history can finally be realized by appreciating all of the particular and exclusive visions of that integral whole. Thus, these expressions of polysymbolic religiosity are, for the most part, monistic and mystical. They all strive to overcome the dichotomies that were carried over into the modern world from its classical Christian past—God versus self, mind versus body, humankind versus nature, individual versus community, contemplation versus activism, play versus work. They seek instead an organic harmony of humankind with the cosmos in subtle interaction. This rejection of the dominant traditions of biblical theism involves a protest against the historical particularity and the idealistic dualism of those traditions.

This modern-day, monotheistic polysymbolism has mushroomed in our time. It is reflected in such cultic movements as Theosophy, Eckankar, and Ontology; in such East-West syncretisms as Transcendental Meditation and Western Zen; and in a variety of parareligious self-realization therapies and disciplines. But it can also be seen in the spread of meditative disciplines, devotional mysticisms, and wholistic therapies within the mainline traditions. Monotheistic polysymbolism has its fair share of charismatic exemplars and opportunistic hucksters. But it also has a heritage of learned and honored spokesmen in the academy—from Max Müller and Sarvepalli Radhakrishnah to Mircea Eliade and Joseph Campbell.

A brief sketch of Joseph Campbell's thought will serve to illustrate this distinctive monotheistic form of polysymbolic religiosity.[16] Campbell approaches religion and culture in terms of myth-making and myth-meaning. In the past, connected stories of gods and heroes, of underworlds and afterlives were the means by which groups and individuals understood and ordered every domain of their existence.[17] Such comprehensive myth-systems, ritually enacted and socially imposed, patterned the thinking and living of all members within a given tribe or culture. But life and thought in the modern world have become increasingly secular and plural. As a consequence, the great traditional mythologies have lost their exclusive monopoly on world construction and personality formation.[18] Nevertheless, Campbell believes that deliteralized and deabsolutized mythologies can have a vital and permanent role in human life and thought.

Drawing on his encyclopedic study of myth from the archaic past to the creative present, Campbell finds that the fundamental themes of mythology are constant and universal. Stripped of their supernatural, literal, and historical posturings, the myths of humanity give expression and form to those two mysterious voids from which life comes and to which it returns—the unconscious self and the unlimited universe. More exactly, the "monomyth" in the many myths is the one story of each person's heroic journey of discovery that the two voids are one:

> Mythologies and religions are great poems and, when recognized as such, point infallibly through things and events to the ubiquity of a "presence" or "eternity" that is whole and entire in each. In this function all mythologies, all great poetries, and all mystic traditions are in accord: and where any such inspiriting vision remains effective in a civilization, every thing and every creature within its range is alive. The first condition, therefore, that any mythology must fulfill if it is to render life to modern lives is that of cleansing the doors of perception to the wonder, at once terrible and fascinating, of ourselves and of the universe.[19]

Though refracted through culturally rooted and relative symbols, the message of all mythology and the meaning of all religion center in the essential unity of the self and the universe.

Stated thus, Campbell's view of religion certainly reflects a monotheistic paradigm and connects with modern sensibilities of a universal order embracing one humankind. But can such a view, so reminiscent of the conventional wisdom of the East, do justice to modernity's concern for selfhood and history-making? Campbell is well aware of the self-negation and quietism of traditional Eastern and Western mysticisms, but he resolutely steers the new religiosity away from any flight from self and from history.[20] Campbell's "world-self" does not involve the extinction or the absorption of the self in the world process. Rather, the individual is viewed as a distinctive center and unique actualization of "Mind at Large."[21] Indeed, Campbell insists that individuals are the "eyes and mind, the seeing and thinking" of the universe. Thus, the unbounded sphere of the universe is centered everywhere in every person.

By the same token, Campbell does not sanction retreat from society and history. The heroic task of rejoining the unconscious self and the unlimited universe

> ... cannot be wrought by turning back, or away, from what has been accomplished by the modern revolution; for the problem is nothing if not that of rendering the modern world spiritually significant—or rather (phrasing the same principle the other way round) nothing if not that of making it possible for men and women to come to full human maturity through the conditions of contemporary life.[22]

To be sure, Campbell admits to a conservatism that eschews revolutionary and apocalyptic solutions to human ills and woes. He does counsel a greater tolerance for the world as it is, more "affection for the infirmities of life."[23] But he takes this stand as a rebuke against all utopian visions of fulfillment in some unreal future, against all nostalgic fantasies of perfection in some ideal past. He thereby calls on everyone to be the Creative Hero in every present time's struggle to elevate humankind to universal dignity and to fill the cosmos with personal meaning.

Thus Campbell sees in the new religiosity—properly tutored by the remythologization of consciousness—an integral self, universe, and history finally freed from the fragmenting dichotomies and partisanships of the past. The discovery and recovery of the essential unity of the self and the cosmos extends and enobles the self, reintegrates and resacralizes the cosmos, cools down and redirects history. For Campbell, only such a religious vision can retain the wisdom of ages past, purify and consolidate the gains of the present era, and open the doors to a barely imaginable future.

More difficult to document but no less real, still another organizing metaphor is at work in polysymbolic religiosity. It, too, celebrates the variety and many-sidedness of all expressions of culture and religion. But it decidedly rejects the monotheistic ideal of a fundamental unity underlying and integrating this heterogeneity. Thereby, it calls into question the Modern Era's sense of centered self, integral universe, and historical destiny. In short, this rival form of polysymbolic religiosity appears to be polytheistic and Postmodern.

This renascent polytheism is still more "lived out" than "thought out." Born of our time's historical dislocation, global awareness, and apocalyptic pessimism, it can be seen in its most spectacular forms in a worldwide counterculture and in a rising tide of occultism.[24] But it may also be detected in the remarkable fluidity of personal identities and social roles among many people in the culture at large. A number of commentators have seen a religious dimension in these challenges to established patterns of order.[25] Many have stressed the religious pathos of the countercultural world of drug trips, rock music, prolonged adolescence, sexual experimentation, and communal living. Others have discerned a serious revival of pagan religion beyond the faddish interest in astrology, witchcraft, alchemy, and divination. Still other commentators have seen revolutionary implications for religion as well as politics and art in the emergence of what Robert Lifton calls "protean man."[26] Despite an abundance of zany gurus, however, religious guides and philosophical interpreters are still few and far between. Nietzsche foresaw this polytheism, but he did not live to give it a lodestone and a language. Only a few able commentators such as Norman O. Brown, James Hillman, and David Miller are giving positive voice to the metaphysical intuitions and practical implications of this new form of religiosity.

Miller's recent book, *The New Polytheism*, explores the idea that we are undergoing an epochal revolution in consciousness.[27] Miller claims that our traditional Western theologies and psychologies are incapable of discerning and describing the true nature of our religious pluralism and cultural disassociation. But he does believe that the themes of these Nietzschean times can be found in the stories of Greek mythology and the insights of a new radical psychology. Both the ancient storytellers and such contemporaries as Brown, Hillman, and Ronald Laing recognize that deities and dreams are not about a fantasy world. Rather, they are ways of naming the contentious and creative powers and potencies in each of us, in societies, and in nature. But their naming is not one but many, not coordinated but diffuse. In short, the "public dreams" of our civilization's beginnings and the "private myths" of our personal imaginings reflect a pluralism and disassociation at the heart of reality as well as in the midst of experience.

Unfortunately, Miller complicates and even obscures his notion of a "deep polytheism" by a muddled discussion of monotheism and polytheism.[28] He suggests that polytheism can contain a "monotheism of sorts" by combining a monotheistic faith with a polytheistic theology. This language sounds very much like the monotheistic religiosity discussed above, or even like recent Christian acknowledgments of the perspectival and polysemous character of religious language.[29] But a closer reading of Miller dispels both of these associations.

For one thing, Miller's "monotheism of sorts" fully acknowledges and approves the death of God as the obituary for "a single center holding things together."[30] The demise of a monotheistic way of speaking and living opens the way to radically new and varied dimensions of reality and definitions of existence. Furthermore, Miller explains the faith of this "monotheism of sorts" as the worship of one deity *at a time* in a large pantheon of deities.[31] This explanation rests on his conviction that the Gods and Goddesses are the names of those structures and forces, always unharmonized and often unrecognized, which give shape to social and personal existence.[32] Thus, "worshipping one God at a time" means that all the shaping structures and forces of existence must be given their due, though this fidelity means the loss of a single centered self, bounded universe, and historical destiny. In Miller's own words:

> Some may think the point of all this talk about polytheism is an attempt to "get it all together" in the name of some new monotheism which happens to be called by the name of "polytheism." The contrary is the case. Polytheism in this book is the name given to disparateness in symbolic explanation and in life, and if it is a viable description of where things are and where they are going, it should have the function of keeping it all apart.[33]

"Monotheism," in Miller's ill-advised use of this term, envisions no fundamental unity in reality or in experience.

Miller, then, sees polytheism as the root metaphor of our exploded cultural sphere. Socially, polytheism is a situation in which varied patterns, values, and principles sometimes mesh harmoniously but more often war with one another. Such a situation is saved from sheer anarchy and chaos by the possibility of identifying a limited coherence within each of the many orders. Psychologically, polytheism is the radical experience of equally real but mutually exclusive aspects of the self.

> The person experiences himself as many selves each of which is felt to have autonomous power, a life of its own, and without regard to the centered will of a single ego. Yet surprisingly this experience is not sensed as a pathology. One gets along quite well in reality; in fact, the very disparateness of the multifaceted self seems to have survival power.[34]

Philosophically, polytheism is the recognition of multiple realities and multiple truths. No coherent explanations or unifying systems are possible precisely because we live in a "pluriverse" rather than a universe.

Thus, Miller believes that our exploded horizons have shattered the circles of both monotheism and the Modern Era. But he heralds a way of confirming self, society, and cosmos in their radical disparateness through the rebirth of the Gods and Goddesses. "Their stories are the paradigms and symbols that allow us to account for, to express, and to celebrate those multiple aspects of our reality that otherwise would seem fragmented and anarchic."[35]

In conclusion, while all polysymbolists are prepared to make a virtue of our time's cultural fragmentation and religious pluralism, they hear very different messages sounding through the cacophony of these clashing perspectives. Some hear the sounds of a new Pentecost—our religio-cultural diversity is leading to that "planetization" that lies at the heart of the modern vision of reality. These monotheistic polysymbolists contend that a thoroughgoing relativizing of all symbol systems can produce a unified world culture freed from despotic control and conformity. A world empire without emperor can happen only when universal order and meaning is mediated through all native soils and symbols but contained by none. By contrast, other polysymbolists hear the sounds of a new Babel— our religio-cultural diversity is a welcome reversal of all human efforts, ancient and modern, to unify all perspectives and peoples around a single center. These polytheistic polysymbolists argue that human freedom and creativity require differentiation and diversification. Only the thoroughgoing pluralizing of all symbol systems can support an interdependent world culture free for creative idiosyncrasy and productive conflict. A world community without cult can occur only when symbols and visions of an all-embracing order and meaning are relinquished once and for all.

What then of polysymbolism with its conflicting visions of the future of religion and culture? The polysymbolists are moving us closer to understanding the true nature of the cultural tumult and religious revolution of our time. They have seen that radical pluralism is somehow both cause and consequence of this ferment. But they leave us with the tantalizing question unresolved: Pentecost or Babel? The polysymbolists leave us waiting for a barely imaginable Pentecost or Babel that is yet to come.

Notes

Chapter One

1. For a discussion of pluralism making use of a different typology and broader time frame than this study's, see David Tracy, *Blessed Rage for Order* (New York: Seabury Press, 1975).

2. Roger L. Shinn, "The Shattering of the Theological Spectrum," *Christianity and Crisis*, 30 September 1963, pp. 168–71.

3. The era of "modern theology" began with the scientific and philosophical revolutions of the seventeenth and eighteenth centuries. Modern theologies are those interpretations of the Christian faith that are formulated in explicit relation and accommodation to the prevailing scientific and philosophical knowledge of the times. This constructive relation may not, however, always involve overt synthesis of Christian and cultural forms. Thus, Neo-orthodoxy is every bit as modern as the old liberalism and the new pluralism in theology.

4. For extended discussion of the crucial role of science in the history of modern theology, see John Dillenberger, *Protestant Thought and Natural Science* (Nashville: Abingdon, 1960); Alan Richardson, *The Bible in the Age of Science* (London: SCM Press, 1961); Ian G. Barbour, *Issues in Science and Religion* (Englewood Cliffs, N.J.: Prentice-Hall, 1966); Kenneth Cauthen, *Science, Secularization and God* (Nashville: Abingdon, 1969); Langdon Gilkey, *Religion and the Scientific Future* (New York: Harper & Row, 1970).

5. For a useful historical survey of these theological adjustments, see James C. Livingston, *Modern Christian Thought* (New York: Macmillan Co., 1971).

6. The classic statement for this relocation of miracle is Friedrich Schleiermacher's "universalizing" of miracle: "Every finite thing, however, is a sign of the Infinite, and so these various expressions declare the immediate relation of a phenomenon to the Infinite and the Whole. But does that involve that every event should not have quite as immediate a relation of the finite and to nature? Miracle is simply the religious name for event. Every event, even the most natural and usual, becomes a miracle, as soon as the religious view of it can be dominant. To me all is miracle." *On Religion: Speeches to Its Cultured Despisers* (New York: Harper & Row, Torchbooks, 1958), p. 88.

7. Paul Ricoeur, *Freud and Philosophy* (New Haven: Yale University Press, 1970).

8. For an illuminating discussion of the social construction of reality and of the displacement of traditional religious institutions from the center of this process in the modern world, see Peter Berger, *The Sacred Canopy* (Garden City, N.Y.: Doubleday, Anchor Books, 1969).

9. Some measure of doubt lies at the bottom of all theological reformations. Usually those doubts are limited to the intellectual formulations of faith. Seldom has theological reflection taken place amid doubts about the spiritual realities of faith. Such radical doubt—doubt that touches the very roots of faith—is the cultural context and even the existential standpoint for the new theologies under review in this book. One of the distinguishing features of many of the new theologies is that they are more an inquiry into the possibilities of faith than a confession of the certainties of faith. For a particularly poignant expression of this theological stance, see Van Harvey, "The Alienated Theologian," in *The Future of Philosophical Theology*, ed. Robert A. Evans (Philadelphia: Westminster Press, 1971), pp. 113–43.

10. The development of a morality of knowledge and its negative impact on traditional faith have been persuasively argued by Van Harvey, *The Historian and the Believer* (New York: Macmillan Co., 1966).

11. The problem of evil as a decisive cause of radical doubt was underscored in the "death of God" literature. For a succinct statement, see John A. T. Robinson's essay, "Can a Truly Contemporary Person Not Be an Atheist?" in *The New Reformation?* (London: SCM Press, 1965), pp. 106–22. That this obstacle to theistic faith is still insurmountable to many is suggested by James W. Woelfel's essay, "The Death of God: A Belated Postscript," *The Christian Century*, 29 December 1976, pp. 1175–78.

12. Albert Camus, *The Plague* (Middlesex, England: Penguin Books, 1966), p. 178.

13. Contrary to the claims of many commentators on the movement, the persistence of religion does not refute all notions of the "death of God." The radicals never proclaimed the death of religion. What they heralded was the dissolution of that form of religion that had shaped and sustained Western culture for more than a thousand years—the belief in a transcendent problem-solving and need-fulfilling God. Indeed, each of the radi-

cals explored new ways of being religious without *that* God. These experiments are still going on inside and outside the Church in the new theologies and the new religions. The recent explosion of intensely private and pluralistic religiosity is, as Nietzsche foretold, the expected consequence of the "death" of God. See Andrew Greeley, *Unsecular Man: The Persistence of Religion* (New York: Delta Books, 1973).

14. This requirement of "objective uncertainty" is reflected in all neoorthodox conceptions of faith, e.g., Barth's *sola Christus*, Bultmann's authentic existence, Tillich's courage to be, Reinhold Niebuhr's justification by grace, and H. Richard Niebuhr's radical faith.

15. Though I do not agree with his analysis at certain crucial points, Ian Barbour offers the best analysis in detail of the two-fold challenge of scientific theories and scientific methods to contemporary theological reflection. See *Issues in Science and Religion*, especially pp. 137–463.

16. This way of characterizing the essentials of scientific thinking is drawn from Ernest Gellner's important "decoding" of the modern epistemological debate in *Legitimation of Belief* (London: Cambridge University Press, 1974).

17. A number of commentators have shown how Neo-orthodoxy was the theological precipitate of the "death of God" movement. Langdon Gilkey offers the most lucid account in *Naming the Whirlwind* (Indianapolis: Bobbs-Merrill, 1969), especially pp. 3–147.

18. Seen in this light, Bonhoeffer's call for a theology appropriate to a "world come of age" belongs with Neo-orthodoxy rather than with the "death of God" theologies where it is often assigned. Bonhoeffer's prison notes actually summoned Neo-orthodoxy to become fully consistent with its own methodological assumptions and thereby develop a truly "secular" theology without covert appeals to biblical or inward authority. We shall return to this issue in the next chapter. See Dietrich Bonhoeffer, *Letters and Papers from Prison*, rev. ed. (New York: Macmillan Co., 1967), pp. 139–47, 162–64, 167–72.

19. For source materials and interpretive essays on the new mysticisms, see Robert S. Ellwood, Jr., *Religious and Spiritual Groups in Modern America* (Englewood Cliffs, N.J.: Prentice-Hall, 1973), and on the "death of God" theologies, see Lonnie D. Kliever and John H. Hayes, *Radical Christianity: The New Theologies in Perspective* (Anderson, S.C.: Droke House, 1968).

20. The present study is limited to theological experiments in the renewal of Christian theism, albeit a theism quite different from traditional or classical theism. There is a parallel literature that starts from the same problematic of radical doubt but explores nontheistic forms of religiosity, including that informed by Christian symbols. Obviously, the "death of God" theologies are prime examples of such new forms of religion. But there are nontheistic counterparts for each of the new types of theology explored in this book. For example, on secularity see William Hamilton, *On Taking God Out of the Dictionary* (New York: McGraw-Hill, 1974);

on process see Julian Huxley, *Religion Without Revelation* (New York: Mentor Books, 1957); on liberation, Joachim Kahl, *The Misery of Christianity* (Middlesex, England: Pelican Books, 1971); on hope, Ernst Bloch, *Atheism in Christianity* (New York: Herder & Herder, 1972); on play, David Miller, *Gods and Games* (New York: Harper & Row, 1973); and on story, see Sam Keen, *To a Dancing God* (New York: Harper & Row, 1970).

21. For surveys and bibliography covering this "linguistic turn" in philosophical theology, see Frederick Ferré, *Language, Logic and God* (New York: Harper & Row, 1961), and William T. Blackstone, *The Problem of Religious Knowledge* (Englewood Cliffs, N.J.: Prentice-Hall, 1963).

22. Efforts to give thematic expression to the religious dimensions of ordinary experience can be distinguished from attempts to validate the truth of such thematizations. Of course, questions of the interpretation of experience and of the criteria of interpretation are finally not separable, but, as Stephen Toulmin has shown in his *The Uses of Argument* (Cambridge: Cambridge University Press, 1964), "experience" can enter argument as the data from which inferences are drawn or as the backing which legitimates the criteria by which such inferences are made. In the latter case, the appeal to experience goes beyond empirically accessible information to a construal of reality experienced from a certain point of view. The new theologies of experience are broadly concerned with furnishing experiential backing for theological claims.

23. This move from theology to experience is especially clear in the hybrid "theologies of culture" inspired by Neo-orthodoxy which mine art, drama, literature, philosophy, and the social sciences for the existential questions to which Christian theology alone gives answer. For an example of this kind of apologetics, see William A. Johnson, *The Search for Transcendence* (New York: Harper & Row, Colophon Books, 1974).

24. Such concerns are not entirely ignored in the new theologies of experience. For example, see Raymond Panikkar, *Worship and Secular Man* (Maryknoll, N.Y.: Orbis Books, 1973), Schubert M. Ogden, *The Reality of God* (New York: Harper & Row, 1964); and Donald E. Miller, *The Wing-Footed Wanderer* (Nashville: Abingdon, 1978).

25. "Foundational" theology precedes theological construction proper by establishing through philosophical or phenomenological means the possibility of faith in God. Consideration of specific formulations of faith do not enter into foundational theology. For example, see Gilkey, *Naming the Whirlwind;* Tracy, *Blessed Rage;* and Peter Berger, *A Rumor of Angels* (Garden City, N.Y.: Doubleday, 1969).

26. A "root metaphor" is some feature of ordinary experience that is employed analogically to explain the whole of experience. This approach proceeds by elucidating the distinguishing attributes of some ordinary experience, then generalizing those attributes by applying them to the whole of experience, and finally reinterpreting ordinary experience in the light of this new slant on both the whole and its parts. For the classic

statement on root-metaphor analysis, see Stephen Pepper, *World Hypotheses* (Berkeley: University of California Press, 1961).

27. "Whatever Happened to Theology?" *Christianity and Crisis* 35 (May 1975): 108, 111, 115, 113.

28. For important theological statements developed in close relation to science, see Barbour, *Issues in Science and Religion;* Cauthen, *Science, Secularization and God;* and Gilkey, *Religion and the Scientific Future.* On theology and technology, see Gabriel Vanhanian, *God and Utopia* (New York: Seabury Press, 1977).

29. For recent apologetic theologies modeled on the experience of beauty, see Roger Hazelton, *Ascending Flame, Descending Dove* (Philadelphia: Westminster Press, 1975); and on fantasy, see Morton T. Kelsey, *Dreams: The Dark Speech of the Spirit* (Garden City, N.Y.: Doubleday, 1968).

30. I tell my students, only half-jokingly, that they can complete a crash course in new types of contemporary theology by reading all the works of Harvey Cox in chronological order. Cox has contributed an important volume to almost every new type of contemporary theology: *The Secular City,* rev. ed. (New York: Macmillan Co., 1966); *On Not Leaving It to the Snake* (New York: Macmillan Co., 1964); *God's Revolution and Man's Hope* (Valley Forge, Pa.: Judson Press, 1965); *The Feast of Fools* (New York: Harper & Row, Colophon Books, 1969); and *The Seduction of Spirit* (New York: Simon and Schuster, 1973). True to form, Cox's latest book, *Turning East: The Promise and the Peril of the New Orientalism* (New York: Simon and Schuster, 1977), explores the latest experiment in religious studies—a polymorphic religiosity that takes pluralism itself as a constructive principle for reflection. Cox has often been charged with following the fads in theology. He explains that, to the contrary, these forays constitute a series of experiments in solving the one problem of how to speak of God in a secular fashion. "The Secular City—Ten Years Later," *The Christian Century,* 28 May 1975, pp. 544-47. See also Cox, "God Sets the Agenda," *The Christian Century,* 29 August 1978, p. 742.

Chapter Two

1. Martin E. Marty, *The Modern Schism* (New York: Harper & Row, 1969).

2. For the classic statement on the thoroughgoing acculturation of American religion, see Will Herberg, *Protestant-Catholic-Jew* (Garden City, N.Y.: Doubleday, Anchor Books, 1955).

3. Marty insists that the Continent's "utter secularism," England's "mere Christianity," and America's "controlled secularity" are present in some degree throughout the Western world. They are thereby elements in a single ongoing episode of the secularization of Western culture. *Modern Schism,* p. 144.

4. For the history of the term "secular," see Ronald Gregor Smith, *Secular Christianity* (London: Collins, 1966), pp. 141–49.

5. Especially see Bonhoeffer's *Letters and Papers from Prison*, rev. ed. (New York: Macmillan Co., 1967); and idem, *Ethics* (New York: Macmillan Co., 1955).

6. John A. T. Robinson, *Honest to God* (Philadelphia: Westminster Press, 1963).

7. A sampling of the public furor that surrounded the publication of this book can be gained from David L. Edwards, ed., *The Honest to God Debate* (London: SCM Press, 1963). The way was prepared for Robinson to become a cause célèbre by the paperback publishing explosion and the expansion of religious studies as an undergraduate academic discipline in the fifties.

8. Robinson, *Explorations into God* (Stanford: Stanford University Press, 1967,) and idem, *The Human Face of God* (Philadelphia: Westminster Press, 1973).

9. Robinson, *Honest to God*, pp. 29–44, and idem, *Explorations into God*, pp. 41–57.

10. See Robinson, *Honest to God*, pp. 45–63; idem, *Explorations into God*, pp. 58–73; idem, *Human Face of God*, pp. 180–211.

11. Robinson, *Explorations into God*, pp. 97–117.

12. "Panentheism" rendered literally means "all-in-God." In this modern alternative to theism (God-above-all) and pantheism (all-as-God), God is in everything and everything is in God though God is more than the mere sum of all things.

13. See Robinson, *Honest to God*, pp. 64–83, and idem, *Human Face of God*, pp. 212–44.

14. See Robinson, *Honest to God*, pp. 84–104, and idem, *The New Reformation?* (London: SCM Press, 1965), pp. 9–105.

15. See Robinson, *Honest to God*, pp. 105–21, and idem, *Christian Morals Today* (Philadelphia: Westminster Press, 1964).

16. Harvey Cox, *The Secular City*, rev. ed. (New York: Macmillan Co., 1966).

17. The "secular city" is more than a casual metaphor for society in Cox's thought. Echoing Comte's three ages of man, Cox divides Western culture into three epochs—tribal, town, and technopolitan societies. The latest cultural epoch, which has ushered in a whole new species of human community and cognitive style, results from a fusion of technological and political components of modern culture. Ibid., pp. 1–13.

18. For the "shape" and "style" of life in the secular city, see ibid., pp. 43–73.

19. Ibid., pp. 15–32. Cf. Gabriel Vahanian's discussion of Christianity and secularity in *The Death of God* (New York: George Braziller, 1961), pp. 60–78.

20. Cox, *Secular City*, pp. 213–17.

21. Ibid., pp. 217–25, and Harvey Cox, "The Death of God and the Future of Theology," in *The New Christianity*, ed., William Miller (New York: Delacorte Press, 1967), pp. 382–83.

22. Cox, *Secular City*, pp. 225–35.

23. Ibid., pp. 230–32.

24. Cox, "Death of God," pp. 384–89; idem, "Afterward," in *The Secular City Debate*, ed. Daniel Callahan (New York: Macmillan Co., 1966), pp. 197–203; idem, "Why Christianity Must Be Secularized," in *The Great Ideas of Today: 1967* (Chicago: Encyclopedia Britannica, 1967), pp. 19–21.

25. Cox, *Secular City*, pp. 108–42.

26. Cox illustrates these tasks of the Church through discussions of work, play, sex, and education "in the secular city." These chapters gave a certain notoriety to Cox's secularized Christianity at the time of their publication but now they seem rather tame. Ibid., pp. 145–208.

27. Paul van Buren, *The Secular Meaning of the Gospel* (New York: Macmillan Co., 1963), pp. xiii–xiv.

28. Paul van Buren, *The Edges of Language* (New York: Macmillan Co., 1972).

29. Van Buren repeatedly disclaimed affiliation with the "death of God" movement, since he believes the problem of God is a question of linguistic usage rather than ontological reality. See *Secular Meaning*, pp. 81–106, and *Edges of Language*, pp. 3–5.

30. Van Buren, *Secular Meaning*, pp. 1–20, 57–106.

31. Ibid., pp. 135–56.

32. Ibid, pp. 135–92.

33. Ibid., pp. 23–55, 157–71.

34. Ibid., pp. 173–92.

35. This shift was clearly signaled in essays by van Buren on "William James and Metaphysical Risk" and "Is Transcendence the Word We Want?" republished in *Theological Explorations* (New York: Macmillan Co., 1968), pp. 133–81. But the philosophical underpinnings of this move were only barely indicated there.

36. Van Buren, *Edges of Language*, pp. 14–77.

37. Ibid., pp. 78–114.

38. Ibid., pp. 115–31.

39. Ibid., pp. 132–50.

40. Ibid., pp. 123–31.

41. Ibid., pp. 151–66.

42. For similar theologies of secularity, see James E. L. Newbigin, *Honest Religion for Secular Man* (London: SCM Press, 1966); Ronald Gregor Smith, *Secular Christianity;* John MacQuarrie, *God and Secularity* (Philadelphia: Westminster Press, 1967); Colin W. Williams, *Faith in a Secular Age* (New York: Harper & Row, 1966); Robert L. Richards, *Secularization Theology* (New York: Herder and Herder, 1967); and Edward Schillebeeck, *God and the Future of Man* (New York: Sheed and Ward, 1968).

43. Cf. Alistair Kee, *The Way of Transcendence* (Middlesex, England: Penguin Books, 1971). Most secular theologies in this vein have only been sketched out in essays, e.g., R. B. Braithwaite "An Empiricist's View of the Nature of Religious Belief," in *The Existence of God*, ed. John Hick (New York: Macmillan Co., 1964), pp. 229–52; John Wisdom, "Gods," in *Philosophy and Psychoanalysis* (Oxford: Blackwell, 1953); Ronald Hepburn, "Scepticism and the Naturally Religious Mind," in *Christianity and Paradox* (New York: Pegasus, 1966).

Chapter Three

1. Alvin Toffler, *Future Shock* (New York: Bantam Books, 1970).

2. For a fuller discussion of modern humanity's experienced sense of change, see Langdon Gilkey, *Naming the Whirlwind* (Indianapolis: Bobbs-Merrill, 1969), pp. 31–71.

3. A short history of process models in culture, philosophy, and theology introduces a useful anthology of process thinkers. Ewert H. Cousins, ed., *Process Theology* (New York: Newman Press, 1971), pp. 3–35.

4. Cousins recognizes the broader lineaments of process theology as do many of the process theologians. Cousins's anthology reflects this broader view of process thought and includes several essays comparing the process theologians discussed in this chapter to one another.

5. John B. Cobb, Jr., *Living Options in Protestant Theology* (Philadelphia: Westminster Press, 1962), pp. 316–17, and idem, *Christian Natural Theology* (Philadelphia: Westminster Press, 1965), pp. 14–15, 270–71.

6. Cobb, *Living Options*, pp. 312–23. Cf. *Christian Natural Theology*, pp. 11–15.

7. Cobb, *Living Options*, p. 50n, and idem, *Christian Natural Theology*, pp. 259–67. Implicit in the notion of Christian theology is an acknowledgement of the historical relativism of all philosophical and theological understanding. Cobb finds this same final acquiescence to relativism in Whitehead. Idem, *Christian Natural Theology*, pp. 271–77.

8. For a beginner's introduction to Whiteheadian metaphysics as a context for Christian faith, see Eugene H. Peters, *The Creative Advance* (St. Louis: Bethany Press, 1966).

9. As we shall see below, "enjoyment" does not always imply consciousness or pleasure. Whitehead uses the term "enjoy" to emphasize that every actual occasion has an inner reality and a contextual reciprocity with the environing world *in and of itself.* In this sense, every dynamic unit of the entire process of reality has its own existence and value.

10. Cobb, *Christian Natural Theology,* pp. 160–68, 268–70.

11. John B. Cobb, Jr., *God and the World* (Philadelphia: Westminster Press, 1969); idem, *The Structure of Christian Existence* (Philadelphia: Westminster Press, 1967); idem, *Christ in a Pluralistic Age* (Philadelphia: Westminster Press, 1975); idem with David Ray Griffin, *Process Theology* (Philadelphia: Westminster Press, 1976).

12. Cobb, *God and the World,* p. 20.

13. Ibid., pp. 42–66.

14. Cobb, *Christian Natural Theology,* pp. 48–91, 176–214, and Cobb and Griffin, *Process Theology,* pp. 78–79.

15. See Martin E. Marty's description of the "utter secularity" of the "God-killers" in the French Enlightenment in *The Modern Schism* (New York: Harper & Row, 1969), pp. 21–34.

16. Teilhard published more than 200 articles on geological and paleontological subjects in scientific journals. By their very nature, most of the findings in these articles have been superseded by later scientific discoveries.

17. Pierre Teilhard de Chardin, *The Divine Milieu* (New York: Harper & Row, 1960); idem, *Hymn of the Universe* (New York: Harper & Row, 1961); idem, *The Future of Man* (New York: Harper & Row, 1964); idem, *Science and Christ* (New York: Harper & Row, 1965); idem, *The Phenomenon of Man* (London: Collins, Fontana Books, 1959); idem, *Man's Place in Nature* (New York: Harper & Row, 1966).

18. Teilhard, *Phenomenon of Man,* p. 32. Whether Teilhard's "hyperphysics" is truly scientific or not is, of course, a matter of great debate among scientific and philosophical commentators on Teilhard's evolutionary thought.

19. Ibid., pp. 35–40, 328–39.

20. Ibid., p. 241.

21. Ibid., pp. 328–30; Teilhard, *Man's Place,* pp. 17–36. This "law" is an instrument of measurement and valuation for Teilhard. Quantity and quality vary directly.

22. Teilhard, *Phenomenon of Man,* pp. 43–81.

23. Ibid., pp. 67–72.

24. Teilhard is convinced that evolutionary and life scientists have been unable to exclude teleological principles from their explanations of

growth and progress. They have simply disguised these principles as purely mechanistic and random variations.

25. Teilhard, *Phenomenon of Man*, pp. 114–55. Teilhard recognizes a certain randomness and wastefulness in the evolutionary process, but he believes these "evils" are always contained and ultimately redeemed within God's "personalizing" of the universe.

26. Ibid., pp. 181–318, and idem, *Man's Place*, pp. 79–121.

27. Teilhard, *Man's Place*, pp. 94–95.

28. Ibid., pp. 79–82; idem, *Future of Man*, pp. 124–39; and idem, *Phenomenon of Man*, pp. 279–99.

29. Teilhard admits that he would have never ventured to envisage the universe fulfilling itself around a "Center of centers" had he not found its speculative model and living reality in Christian dogma. *Phenomenon of Man*, p. 322.

30. Teilhard, *Future of Man*, p. 304.

31. "Planetization" does not naturally produce "Pleromization" for Teilhard. Final fulfillment is ultimately God's action not humankind's achievement. But the "Parousia" is the fulfillment of a *prepared* earth. That preparation comes only through human struggle and sacrifice. Not surprisingly then, "death" is both the metaphor and the means of the final "ex-centration" and "re-creation" required for entrance into the Kingdom of God. See *Phenomenon of Man*, pp. 300–18.

32. Teilhard, *Divine Milieu*, p. 42.

33. John B. Cobb, Jr., ed., *The Theology of Altizer: Critique and Response* (Philadelphia: Westminster Press, 1970), p. 14.

34. Thomas J. J. Altizer, *The Descent into Hell* (Philadelphia: Lippincott Co., 1970), pp. 179–81.

35. Thomas J. J. Altizer, *Oriental Mysticism and Biblical Eschatology* (Philadelphia: Westminster Press, 1963).

36. Thomas J. J. Altizer, *Mircea Eliade and the Dialectic of the Sacred* (Philadelphia: Westminster Press, 1963).

37. Thomas J. J. Altizer, *The Gospel of Christian Atheism* (Philadelphia: Westminster Press, 1966); idem, *The New Apocalypse* (East Lansing, Mich.: Michigan State University Press, 1967); idem, *The Self-Embodiment of God* (New York: Harper & Row, 1977).

38. Altizer, *Christian Atheism*, pp. 21–54, 112–20.

39. Altizer, *Descent into Hell*, , pp. 179–92.

40. In his latest book, *The Self-Embodiment of God*, Altizer develops this same theme on the analogy of speech. God "othered" the world into being by breaking his self-contained and self-sufficient Silence through speaking the Word.

41. Altizer, *Descent into Hell*, p. 190.

42. Altizer, *Mircea Eliade*, pp. 81–92, 117–200; and idem, *Christian Atheism*, pp. 76–84, 102–22.

43. Altizer, *Christian Atheism*, pp. 62–69; and idem, *Descent into Hell*, pp. 97–132.

44. Altizer, *Descent into Hell*, p. 214.

Chapter Four

1. Christopher Lasch, *The Culture of Narcissism* (New York: W. W. Norton, 1979).

2. Thomas Hanna, *Bodies in Revolt: A Primer in Somatic Thinking* (New York: Holt, Rinehart & Winston, 1970). Somatic comes from the Greek word *soma* which means "body."

3. Walter Rauschenbusch, *A Theology for the Social Gospel* (New York: Macmillan Co., 1917); Marabel Morgan, *The Total Woman* (New York: Simon and Schuster, Pocket Books, 1975).

4. Rosemary Reuther has proposed a similar thesis. She suggests that all social oppression is modeled on body-mind dualism. White males identify themselves with mind's superiority and authority. Accordingly, their "natural" opposites—women and blacks—are identified with the body. Thus, women and blacks are routinely treated as instruments of the white male because of their "inherent" inferiority and subjugation. *Liberation Theology* (New York: Paulist Press, 1972), pp. 16–22.

5. For examples of this variety, see Thomas M. McFadden, ed., *Liberation, Revolution and Freedom* (New York: Seabury Press, 1975); and Gerald H. Anderson and Thomas F. Stransky, eds., *Mission Trends No. 3: Third World Theologies,* (New York & Grand Rapids, Mich.: Paulist Press and Eerdmans Publishing Co., 1976).

6. The 1975 Detroit "Theology in the Americas" Conference brought together black, feminist, and Third World theologians for the first time. For a report, see Robert M. Brown, "Reflections on Detroit," *Christianity and Crisis*, 27 October 1975, pp. 251–56.

7. For a summary and a response to such critiques of liberation theology, see Robert M. Brown, *Theology in a New Key: Responding to Liberation Themes* (Philadelphia: Westminster Press, 1978), pp. 101–31.

8. James H. Cone, *Black Theology and Black Power* (New York: Seabury Press, 1969), p. 1.

9. James H. Cone, *A Black Theology of Liberation* (Philadelphia: Lippincott Co., 1970), and idem, *God of the Oppressed* (New York: Seabury Press, 1975).

10. Cone, *Black Theology of Liberation*, p. 6.

11. Cone, *Black Theology and Black Power*, p. 123. Cf. *Black Theology of*

Liberation, pp. 223–49. Cone severely criticizes post-Civil War black religion for its otherworldliness and spirituality though he attributes such escapist ideas to the influence of the white masters. Though Cone has no sympathy for notions of a future life that "drug" people against the pains of present misery, he does acknowledge that the promise of ultimate victory over death sometimes does motivate revolutionaries who struggle against great odds. Idem, *Black Theology of Liberation*, pp. 225–27.

12. Cone, *Black Theology of Liberation*, p. 23.

13. Ibid., pp. 112ff.; idem, *Black Theology and Black Power*, pp. 130ff.

14. Cone, *Black Theology of Liberation*, pp. 25–27.

15. Ibid., p. 18.

16. Ibid., pp. 197, 227.

17. Ibid., pp. 79–80.

18. Cone, *Black Theology and Black Power*, p. 151.

19. Cone, *Black Theology of Liberation*, p. 229.

20. Ibid., p. 183.

21. Ibid., p. 29.

22. Cone, *Black Theology and Black Power*, p. 145.

23. Ibid., p. 41; idem, *Black Theology of Liberation*, p. 185.

24. Feminists regularly draw a sharp line between "women's liberation" and the "sexual revolution," charging that the latter simply makes it easier and more acceptable for men to prey on women.

25. Betty Friedan, *The Feminine Mystique* (New York: Dell Publishing Co., 1963).

26. Kate Millett, *Sexual Politics* (Garden City, N.Y.: Doubleday, 1970).

27. Simone de Beauvoir, *The Second Sex*, trans. H. M. Parshley (New York: Alfred A. Knopf, 1953).

28. Mary Daly, *The Church and the Second Sex* (New York: Harper & Row, 1968). In her most recent book, *Gyn/ecology: The Metaethics of Radical Feminism* (Boston: Beacon Press, 1978), Daly clearly moves beyond the circle of "Christian theologian." But *The Church and the Second Sex* and her *Beyond God the Father* (Boston: Beacon Press, 1973) belong to women's liberation theology and continue to exercise enormous influence in that movement.

29. Daly, *Beyond God the Father*, pp. xi–xii.

30. Ibid., p. 98.

31. Ibid., p. 19.

32. For an interdisciplinary discussion of the role of symbols in personal and social existence, see Ernest Becker, *The Birth and Death of Meaning* (New York: Free Press, 1971).

33. Daly, *Beyond God the Father*, pp. 6–11.

34. Ibid., pp. 83–87.

35. Ibid., pp. 13–43.

36. Ibid., p. 29.

37. Ibid., p. 94.

38. Ibid., pp. 82–97.

39. Ibid., p. 97.

40. Ibid., pp. 44–68.

41. Ibid., pp. 69–97.

42. Ibid., pp. 98–131.

43. Ibid., pp. 132–54.

44. Ibid., pp. 155–98.

45. Ibid., p. 174.

46. Gustavo Gutiérrez, *A Theology of Liberation* (Maryknoll, N.Y.: Orbis Books, 1973). For a briefer statement of Gutiérrez's thought, see "Freedom and Salvation: A Political Problem," in *Liberation and Change*, by Gustavo Gutiérrez and Richard Shaull (Atlanta: John Knox Press, 1977), pp. 3–94.

47. Gutiérrez, *Theology of Liberation*, p. 10.

48. Ibid., pp. 25–37.

49. Ibid., p. 177.

50. Ibid., pp. 235–39.

51. Ibid., pp. 181–99.

52. Ibid., pp. 232–39.

53. Ibid., pp. 101–31, 255–85.

54. Ibid., pp. 108–19.

55. Ibid., pp. 101–31. The most notable indication of such transformations was the Conference of Latin American Bishops, held at Medellin, Colombia, in 1968. This conference was to Latin American Catholics what Vatican II was to Roman Catholicism around the world.

56. Ibid., p. 139.

57. Ibid., pp. 116–17, 269–70; idem, "Freedom and Salvation," pp. 57–77.

58. Gutiérrez, *Theology of Liberation*, pp. 265–79.

59. Ibid., p. 267.

60. Ibid., p. 270–72.

61. Ibid., p. 235.

62. Ibid., pp. 287–306.
63. Ibid., pp. 194–208; idem, "Freedom and Salvation," pp. 65–67.
64. Gutiérrez, *Theology of Liberation*, p. 66.
65. Ibid., pp. 262–65.
66. Ibid., p. 265.
67. Ibid., p. 307.
68. For a theology of liberation "for oppressors," see Brown, *Theology in a New Key*. For a theology of liberation "beyond partisanship," see Schubert M. Ogden, *Faith and Freedom: Toward a Theology of Liberation* (Nashville: Abingdon, 1978).

Chapter Five

1. For a useful introduction, see Lois and Stephen Rose, *The Shattered Ring* (Richmond: John Knox Press, 1970).
2. Isaac Asimov, *Foundations* (New York: Avon Books, 1964).
3. For an introductory theological engagement with futurology, see Ted Peters, *Futures—Human and Divine* (Atlanta: John Knox Press, 1978).
4. Herman Kahn and Anthony Weiner, *The Year 2000* (New York: Macmillan Co., 1967).
5. John R. Platt, *The Step to Man* (New York: John Wiley, 1966).
6. Robert Heilbroner, *An Inquiry into the Human Prospect* (New York: W. W. Norton, 1974).
7. Gabriel Marcel, *Homo Viator: An Introduction to a Metaphysics of Hope* (New York: Harper & Row, Torchbooks, 1962).
8. Karl Menninger, *The Vital Balance* (New York: Viking Press, 1963); Erich Fromm, *The Revolution of Hope* (New York: Harper & Row, 1968).
9. Peter Berger, *The Sacred Canopy* (Garden City, N.Y.: Doubleday, Anchor Books, 1969); Clifford Geertz, *The Interpretation of Cultures* (New York: Basic Books, 1973).
10. William Lynch, *Images of Hope* (London: Helicon Press, 1966); Frank Kermode, *The Sense of an Ending* (New York: Oxford University Press, 1967).
11. For a discussion of Bloch, see Harvey Cox, "Ernst Bloch on the 'Pull of the Future,'" in *New Theology No. 5*, ed. Martin E. Marty and Dean G. Peerman (New York: Macmillan Co., 1968), pp. 191–203.
12. There are obvious similarities between Bloch and such process philosophers as Hegel, Bergson, and Whitehead. Similarly, as we shall see, there are remarkable parallels between process theology and theology of hope. The similarities are due to both approaches taking seriously

man's historicity and nature's evolution rather than to direct borrowing. For an instructive comparison of process and hope thinkers, see Walter A. Capps, *Time Invades the Cathedral* (Philadelphia: Fortress Press, 1972), pp. 95–97.

13. The following phenomenological sketch of hope is indebted for its major points to Josef Pieper, *Hope and History* (New York: Herder & Herder, 1969), pp. 13–28.

14. For example, see Roger Garaudy, *From Anathema to Dialogue* (New York: Herder & Herder, 1966), and Vitezslav Gardavsky, *God Is Not Yet Dead* (Harmondsworth, England: Penguin Books, 1972).

15. Especially influential is the work of Ernst Kasemann in New Testament studies and Wolfhart Pannenberg in historical theology.

16. Moltmann's reflection introduces M. Douglas Meeks, *Origins of the Theology of Hope* (Philadelphia: Fortress Press, 1974), pp. ix–xii.

17. Jürgen Moltmann, *Theology of Hope* (New York: Harper & Row, 1967); idem, *The Crucified God* (New York: Harper & Row, 1974). For a shorter statement of Moltmann's theology of hope, see his keynote paper delivered to the 1968 Duke University Consultation on the Task of Theology Today: "Theology as Eschatology" in *The Future of Hope*, ed. Frederick Herzog (New York: Herder & Herder, 1970), pp. 1–50.

18. Moltmann's primary foils are liberal and neo-orthodox theologies. He seldom finds it necessary to engage directly scholastic or orthodox theologies.

19. Moltmann's writings are suffused with acknowledgments of the positive contributions of Feuerbach and Marx to a proper understanding of the Gospel and the world. Not surprisingly then, Moltmann has been a leading figure in establishing a vigorous "Christian-Marxist dialogue." For an example, see his *Religion, Revolution and the Future* (New York: Charles Scribner's Sons, 1969), especially pp. 63–82. For a fuller discussion of the Christian-Marxist dialogue, see Thomas W. Ogletree, ed., *Openings for Christian-Marxist Dialogue* (Nashville: Abingdon, 1969).

20. Moltmann, *Theology of Hope*, pp. 37–94.

21. In the "Preface" to *Theology of Hope*, Moltmann cautions that his method of critical engagement does not imply rejection or condemnation of the views he contests. He stresses that critical questions are "a sign of theological partnership" (p. 10). Nevertheless, he leaves no question but that proper theological formulations are of great importance.

22. Ibid., p. 16.

23. Moltmann, "Theology as Eschatology," p. 10. Also see idem, *Religion, Revolution*, pp. 177–99.

24. Moltmann, "Theology as Eschatology," p. 10.

25. Moltmann, *Religion, Revolution*, pp. 200–20.

26. Moltmann, *Theology of Hope*, p. 41. For his brief phenomenology of "promise," see pp. 102–6. For the relation of "promise" to specific themes, see pp. 95–148.

27. Ibid., pp. 139–229; idem, *Religion, Revolution*, pp. 3–18.

28. Moltmann, *Theology of Hope*, pp. 22–26.

29. Ibid., pp. 17–19.

30. Ibid., p. 179.

31. Ibid., p. 17.

32. Ibid., pp. 230–303.

33. Ibid., pp. 304–38.

34. Moltmann, *Religion, Revolution*, pp. 19–42; idem, *The Experiment Hope* (Philadelphia: Fortress Press, 1975), pp. 101–18, 147–57.

35. Moltmann, *Religion, Revolution*, pp. 40–41.

36. Moltmann is fond not only of stressing the prefix "pro-" by setting it off by a hyphen, but also of substituting "pro-" for the more normal prefix "re-" as a way of seeing the present in light of the enacted future ("pro-") rather than the recollected past ("re-"). Thus, he changes reformation, revolution, renewal, restoration, and even religion to pro-formation, pro-volution, pro-newal, pro-storation and pro-ligion. For Moltmann, "pro-" is the prefix of motion into the future and of advocacy. See *Religion, Revolution*, pp. 19–41.

37. Ibid., p. 34.

38. Carl E. Braaten, *The Future of God* (New York: Harper & Row, 1969); idem, *Christ and Counter-Christ* (Philadelphia: Fortress Press, 1972); idem, *Eschatology and Ethics* (Minneapolis: Augsburg, 1974).

39. Braaten, *Eschatology and Ethics*, p. 122.

40. Braaten, *Future of God*, pp. 17–32; idem, *Eschatology and Ethics*, pp. 7–42.

41. Like Moltmann, Braaten directs most of his criticism against neo-orthodox reductions of eschatology to a present realization of God's eternity and man's freedom. Braaten, *Future of God*, pp. 19–23; idem, *Christ and Counter-Christ*, pp. 2–7.

42. Braaten, *Future of God*, pp. 58–108; idem, *Christ and Counter-Christ*, pp. 40–55.

43. Braaten, *Future of God*, p. 59.

44. Ibid., p. 91.

45. Ibid., pp. 155–60; idem, *Christ and Counter-Christ*, pp. 101–18.

46. Braaten, *Christ and Counter-Christ*, p. 103.

47. Braaten, *Future of God*, p. 160.

48. Braaten, *Christ and Counter-Christ*, pp. 7–19.

49. Braaten, *Future of God*, pp. 29–30.

50. Carl E. Braaten with Robert W. Jensen, *The Futurist Option* (New York: Newman Press, 1970), pp. 4–5.

51. Braaten, *Future of God*, pp. 107–40; idem, *Eschatology and Ethics*, pp. 85–104.

52. Braaten, *Future of God*, p. 119.

53. Ibid., pp. 133–40; idem, *Christ and Counter-Christ*, pp. 135–48.

54. Braaten, *Future of God*, pp. 141–66; idem, *Eschatology and Ethics*, pp. 105–87; idem, *Christ and Counter-Christ*, pp. 101–34.

55. Braaten, *Eschatology and Ethics*, p. 165.

56. The slogan came, of course, from Vahanian's book *The Death of God* (New York: George Braziller, 1961). For a trenchant criticism of the later movement, see "Swallowed up in Godlessness," which was published in *The Christian Century* in 1965 and republished in *The Death of God Debate*, ed. Jackson Lee Ice and John J. Carey (Philadelphia: Westminster Press, 1967), pp. 143–49.

57. Gabriel Vahanian, *God and Utopia* (New York: Seabury Press, 1977), p. 7.

58. Vahanian seems to exempt Moltmann from his general criticism of the hope theologians for removing God and the Kingdom too far into the future. Ibid., p. 60n.

59. Vahanian metaphorically assigns the year "2000" as the full dawning of "technological civilization." Ibid., p. 28.

60. Vahanian, *Wait Without Idols* (New York: George Braziller, 1964).

61. Vahanian, *No Other God* (New York: George Braziller, 1966).

62. Vahanian, *God and Utopia*, pp. 27–56, 77–92.

63. Ibid, p. xviii.

64. Ibid., p. xvii.

65. Ibid., pp. 1–3. Vahanian does not intend the word "religiosity" to carry any pejorative weight. Religiosity refers to the "fullness of religious sensibility." That fullness includes "the conditions of credibility of any religion as well as those of its intelligibility. It is what makes religion both credible and intelligible." Vahanian's more technical definition of religiosity is "the utopian relationship to God grasped . . . as nexus or articulation of the interpersonal structure of the human reality." Just what the latter definition involves will become clear in the discussion to follow. Cf. Gabriel Vahanian, "Religion and Technology," in *Introduction to the Study of Religion*, ed. T. William Hall (New York: Harper & Row, 1978), pp. 236–37.

66. Vahanian, *God and Utopia*, p. xvi.

67. Ibid., pp. 36–47, 112–25. See especially the entire essay entitled, "The Word of God and the Word of Man," in *No Other God*, pp. 37–63. In my judgment, this essay is the hermeneutical key to a proper reading of Vahanian's thought.

68. Vahanian, *No Other God*, p. 55.

69. Vahanian, *God and Utopia*, p. 83.

70. Vahanian nowhere gives an account of his understanding of the normativeness that he attributes to the biblical faith. He does not, for example, turn his own schematic analysis of different types of religiosity on the biblical materials themselves in any systematic way. The implication of his appeals to the biblical faith, however, is that the biblical perspective is normative because it does indeed structurally reflect the dimensions of authentic humanization and renders it possible.

71. Vahanian, *God and Utopia*, p. 17.

72. Ibid., pp. 1–3.

73. Ibid., pp. xxviii, 20–30, 44–55. Vahanian's use of the word "technique" in *God and Utopia* requires the utmost attention to the context of use. Sometimes he uses the word to denote *any* cultural mode of religiosity or "art of living." At other times, he intends only the specific cultural form of religiosity and humanism that is emerging in the new technological civilization now dawning. Matters are complicated still further by the fact that Vahanian believes that the latter "technique" is implicit in every earlier technique of the human as their true structure and intention. Thus, he can speak of the technique now emerging in technological society as "the technique of techniques." Ibid., p. 85.

74. The following account of Vahanian's comparative and critical analysis of alternative techniques and changing vectors of utopian faith is a reconstruction drawn from the whole of *God and Utopia* and from his crucial article on "Religion and Technology." Because Vahanian defines and redefines his terms always in the process of argument and always turns the argument first this way and then that, very few clear and extended passages dealing with a specific theme or problem are to be found. The schematic structure and essential elements of his analysis must be gleaned in lexical fashion and then arranged in a summary way for purposes of description and criticism. For this reason, I will footnote only those passages in the book where the discussion concentrates on a specific theme or problem.

75. Vahanian, *God and Utopia*, pp. 17–30.

76. Vahanian also regularly refers to this orientation as a "sacral" mode of transcendence. True to form, in other contexts, he sees the "sacral" as coterminous with all forms of soteric religiosity. These reference ranges for the word sacral are worth noting because they clarify his oft-made distinction between the desacralization of modern culture and religion (which he acknowledges) and their secularization (which he condemns). The secularization of culture and religion excludes all forms of religiosity

while their desacralization excludes only one form—the soteric forms.

77. Vahanian, "Religion and Technology," p. 243.

78. Vahanian, *God and Utopia*, p. 5.

79. Ibid., pp. 9–30.

80. Ibid., p. 19.

81. Ibid., pp. 13–17.

82. Ibid., pp. 57–92.

83. Ibid., p. 29.

84. Ibid., p. 28.

85. Ibid., pp. 98, 100–126.

86. Ibid., pp. 128–38.

87. Ibid., p. 84.

88. Ibid., p. 112.

89. Ibid., p. 85.

90. Ibid., p. 93.

91. Ibid., p. 137.

92. Ibid., pp. 38–45.

93. Ibid., pp. 145–54.

94. Ibid., p. 154.

95. Moltmann has moved in both directions, especially in the direction of a revolutionary politics of faith. See his *Theology of Play* (New York: Harper & Row, 1972) and *The Gospel of Liberation* (Waco: Word Publishers, 1973).

Chapter Six

1. This paraphrase of the Pledge of Allegiance was suggested by Michael Novak's title "One Nation Under Sports" in his enlightening study of sports as a "natural religion," *The Joy of Sports* (New York: Basic Books, 1976), p. 1.

2. For an excellent survey of the scholarship on play and its relevance to a contemporary understanding of religion, see David L. Miller, *Gods and Games* (New York: Harper & Row, 1973), pp. 17–117.

3. Johan Huizinga, *Homo Ludens* (Boston: Beacon Press, 1955).

4. Ibid., p. 28.

5. Ibid., p. 211.

6. It is worth noting that the Latin term *ludus* reflects this aspect of play

since this term means both "play" and "school."

7. Cited in Erik Erikson, *Childhood and Society* (New York: W. W. Norton, 1950), p. 222.

8. For example, Michael Novak argues that sports are a universal "natural religion." Though they are not like creedal or civil forms of religion, Novak does regard sports as an authentic form of religion. See *Joy of Sports*, pp. 18–34, 341–42.

9. Miller draws a clear distinction between "theologies of play" and "play theologies." For the first group, the Christian faith is applied to play as a way of making that play religiously meaningful. For the latter group, human play is applied to the Christian faith as a way of making that faith humanistically meaningful. This is a contrived distinction that does not hold up when specific play thinkers are assigned to one or another group. The distinction that can and should be made among theories of play and religion is the distinction between theistic and nontheistic treatments of play and religion. Our concerns in this book are limited to the former. See *Gods and Games*, pp. xvi–xxii.

10. Hugo Rahner, *Man at Play* (New York: Herder & Herder, 1972).

11. Ibid., pp. 3–6.

12. Ibid., p. 65.

13. Ibid., p. 7.

14. Ibid., p. 8.

15. Ibid., p. 68.

16. The three forms of play that Rahner invokes most often are games, drama, and especially dance. These choices are understandable since they embody so well his ideas of play—lightness and freedom of spirit, instinctive command of the body, nimbleness of mind, and movement. Ibid., p. 11.

17. Ibid., pp. 17–25.

18. Ibid., p. 18.

19. This summary formula is the essence of all play in Rahner's view.

20. Ibid., pp. 26–45.

21. Ibid., pp. 26–27.

22. Ibid., p. 27.

23. Ibid., pp. 2, 91–105.

24. Ibid., pp. 27–29.

25. Ibid., pp. 46–64.

26. Ibid., pp. 53–61.

27. Ibid., pp. 65–90.

28. Rahner quotes this passage from Hippolytus. This image of the Logos dancing was frequently cited in mystical theologies throughout the Middle Ages. Ibid., p. 77.

29. Rahner describes the medieval Easter ritual of a "sacral ball game" played by the bishops and clerks in the cathedral of Auxerre. They moved through a carefully regulated dance order over the pattern of a labyrinth painted on the floor of the church. As they gracefully moved through the labyrinth, they threw the Easter ball to one another rejoicing like children because as the rising sun blazes its way across the earth so the Risen Son lights the way through the labyrinth of the world. Ibid., pp. 84–86.

30. Harvey Cox, *The Feast of Fools* (New York: Harper & Row, Colophon Books, 1969).

31. This is certainly Cox's own view of his work: "I consider all my books to be a part of a pattern, perhaps of a ministry. I consider all of them to be works of 'pastoral theology.' In each I have tried to center on a particular issue currently vexing the communities of faith and to discover what the churches should do and say in light of the larger working of the spirit in the world." "God Sets the Agenda," *The Christian Century*, 29 August, 1978, p. 742.

32. Cox, *Feast of Fools*, p. vii.

33. Ibid., pp. 3–6.

34. Ibid., pp. 21–55.

35. Ibid., pp. 27–30.

36. Ibid., pp. 30–47.

37. Ibid., p. 46.

38. Ibid., pp. 59–97.

39. Ibid., p. 59.

40. Ibid., p. 62.

41. Ibid., pp. 70–81.

42. Ibid., p. 70.

43. Ibid., pp. 82–97.

44. Ibid., p. 87.

45. Ibid., p. 94.

46. Ibid., pp. 131–38.

47. Ibid., pp. 139–57.

48. Ibid., p. 150.

49. Ibid., pp. 49–57.

50. Ibid., p. 144.

51. Ibid., p. 142.

52. Robert E. Neale, *In Praise of Play* (New York: Harper & Row, 1969). For an illuminating vignette of Neale's position, see his published response to the long essay on theology of play by Jürgen Moltmann, "Crucifixion as Play" in *Theology of Play* (New York: Harper & Row, 1972), pp. 76–86.

53. Neale, *In Praise of Play*, pp. 19–41.

54. Ibid., pp. 25–41.

55. Ibid., p. 22.

56. Ibid., p. 23.

57. Ibid., p. 24.

58. Ibid., p. 25.

59. Ibid., pp. 42–69.

60. Ibid., pp. 44–56.

61. Ibid., p. 48.

62. Ibid., p. 56.

63. Ibid., pp. 56–69.

64. Ibid., p. 83.

65. Ibid., pp. 98–125.

66. Ibid., pp. 111–25, 137–46, 157–62.

67. Neale suggests that the sacred might well be defined as "The Surprising." Ibid., p. 166.

68. Ibid., p. 114.

69. Ibid., p. 114.

70. Ibid., pp. 126–63.

71. Ibid., pp. 126–27.

72. Ibid., p. 145.

73. Ibid., pp. 157–62.

74. Ibid., pp. 166–72.

75. Neale contends that our society is as prudish about death as the Victorians were about sex. Both our censorship and pornography of death express a deep distance and disgust of death. Ibid., pp. 167–69.

76. Ibid., pp. 172–78.

77. Ibid., p. 163.

78. For a similar theological sketch—but from a neo-orthodox rather than an orthodox point of view—see Joseph C. McLelland, *The Clown and the Crocodile* (Richmond: John Knox Press, 1970).

Chapter Seven

1. For a discussion of these interlocking functions of myth in primitive cultures, see Joseph Campbell, *Myths to Live By* (New York: Viking Press, 1972), pp. 214–15, and idem, *The Masks of God: Creative Mythology* (New York: Viking Press, 1970), pp. 608–24.

2. John Donne, "An Anatomy of the World," in *John Donne: The Complete English Poems*, ed. A. J. Smith (London: Allen Lane, 1974), p. 276.

3. For a most helpful discussion of the historical development of the narrative tradition as this development is reflected in formal and functional analyses of story, see Robert Scholes and Robert Kellog, *The Nature of Narrative* (London: Oxford University Press, 1966).

4. Frank Kermode, *The Sense of an Ending* (London: Oxford University Press, 1977).

5. Formal comparisons between stories and life have generally stressed only the inherent temporality of both. Recently some commentators have begun to lay equal stress on the narrative character of human spatiality. For a summary discussion of story and temporality, see Stephen Crites, "The Narrative Quality of Experience," *Journal of the American Academy of Religion*, 39 (September 1971):291–311. For story and spatiality, see Lonnie D. Kliever, "Story and Space: The Forgotten Dimension," *Journal of the American Academy of Religion*, 45 Supplement (June 1977):529–63.

6. For an annotated bibliography of these various uses of "story," see George W. Stroup III, "A Bibliographical Critique," *Theology Today* 32 (July 1975):133–43.

7. John S. Dunne, *Time and Myth* (Garden City, N.Y.: Doubleday, 1973), p. 113.

8. John S. Dunne, *A Search for God in Time and Memory* (New York: Macmillan Co., 1969), pp. ix–xi, 4–8; idem, *The Way of All Earth* (New York: Macmillan Co., 1972), pp. ix, 151–55, 220–32.

9. John S. Dunne, *The City of the Gods* (New York: Macmillan Co., 1964); idem, *The Reasons of the Heart* (New York: Macmillan Co., 1978).

10. See Dunne's "A Note on Method" appended to *Reasons of the Heart*, pp. 147–52. Dunne leaves the clear impression in this reflection on his authorship that the unity of his work was not by design but by discovery.

11. In *City of the Gods*, Dunne contrasts the "mythological" and the "mystical" approaches to the problem of death. The former promises some form of unending life on earth, while the latter abandons the hope to extend life on earth indefinitely in favor of acquiescence to mortality or belief in immortality (p. 223). This rather specialized definition of myth, embodying as it does from Dunne's viewpoint a wholly inadequate understanding of life and death, does not carry over as the meaning of

myth in Dunne's later writings. In those writings, the wider conceptions of myth indicated above prevail.

12. Ibid., pp. 1–80.

13. Ibid., pp. 1–15.

14. Ibid., pp. 16–28.

15. Ibid., pp. 29–80.

16. Ibid., pp. 81–159.

17. Ibid., pp. 162–81.

18. Ibid., pp. 217–28.

19. Ibid., pp. 110–36, 223–24.

20. Ibid., pp. 140–59, 228–31.

21. Dunne, *Search for God,* p. ix.

22. Ibid., pp. 1–31.

23. Ibid., pp. 33–37.

24. Ibid., p. 215.

25. Ibid., pp. 75–168.

26. Ibid., pp. 75–117.

27. Ibid., pp. 119–68.

28. Ibid., pp. 169–209.

29. Dunne, *Way of All Earth,* pp. 4–26.

30. Ibid., pp. 1–106.

31. Ibid., pp. 109–218.

32. Ibid., pp. 220–21.

33. Dunne sees this dialectical truth exemplified explicitly in Jesus and implicitly in Gotama and Mohammed. He sees Gotama's emphasis on the "no self" and Mohammed's emphasis on "God's otherness" as over-emphases which nevertheless imply and require their opposites. On Gotama, pp. 27–65, and on Mohammed, pp. 109–34, in *Way of All Earth.*

34. Ibid., pp. 135–87.

35. Ibid., pp. 189–218.

36. Dunne, *Time and Myth,* p. 5.

37. Ibid., pp. 5–46.

38. Ibid., pp. 47–83.

39. Ibid., pp. 84–120.

40. Dunne, *Reasons of the Heart,* pp. 1–16.

41. Ibid., pp. 17–92.
42. Ibid., pp. 93–129.
43. Ibid., p. 151.
44. James Wm. McClendon, Jr., *Biography as Theology* (Nashville: Abingdon, 1974).
45. Ibid., pp. 13–38.
46. Ibid., pp. 28–38.
47. Ibid., pp. 31–33.
48. Ibid., p. 31.
49. Ibid., pp. 34–38. For a systematic and detailed study of religious convictions, see James Wm. McClendon, Jr., and James M. Smith, *Understanding Religious Convictions* (Notre Dame, Ind.: University of Notre Dame Press, 1975).
50. McClendon, *Biography as Theology*, p. 34.
51. Ibid., pp. 35–38.
52. Ibid., p. 35.
53. Ibid., pp. 87–111.
54. Ibid., pp. 37–38.
55. Ibid., pp. 99–102.
56. Ibid., p. 40.
57. Ibid., pp. 93–99.
58. Ibid., pp. 192–95.
59. Ibid., pp. 39–86.
60. Ibid., pp. 112–68. Clarence Jordan was the founder of Koinonia Farms in Americus, Georgia, and authored the *Cotton Patch Version* of the New Testament. Charles Ives was the great American composer who combined a radical departure from traditional harmony and tonality with the unique sounds of America—rural nature, city streets, marching bands, gospel hymns—to achieve a distinctively American and modern music.
61. McClendon, *Biography as Theology*, p. 99.
62. Ibid., pp. 99–108, 171–79.
63. Ibid., pp. 107–8.
64. Ibid., pp. 190–92.
65. Ibid., pp. 192–95.
66. Ibid., pp. 197–202.
67. Ibid., pp. 204–15.

68. Ibid., p. 203.

69. Sallie McFague, *Speaking in Parables* (Philadelphia: Fortress Press, 1979), p. 1.

70. Ibid., pp. 1, 24, 63, 82.

71. For a brief overview of McFague's position, see her "Parables, Metaphor, and Theology," *Journal of the American Academy of Religion*, 42 (December 1974):630–45.

72. McFague, *Speaking in Parables*, pp. 2–3.

73. Ibid., p. 4.

74. Ibid., p. 8.

75. Ibid., pp. 26–30.

76. Ibid., pp. 43–65.

77. Ibid., pp. 56–72.

78. Ibid., p. 81.

79. Ibid., p. 6.

80. Ibid., pp. 4, 45, 51, 66, 87, 91.

81. Ibid., pp. 2–6, 13–17, 66–89.

82. McFague cites the work of A. T. Cadoux, Amos Wilder, Norman Perrin, Dan Via, Robert Funk, and John Dominic Crossan as especially important. Ibid., p. 72.

83. Ibid., pp. 72–88.

84. Ibid., p. 71.

85. Ibid., pp. 83–88.

86. Ibid., p. 86.

87. Ibid., pp. 92–118.

88. Ibid., p. 115.

89. Ibid., pp. 119–44.

90. Ibid., pp. 127–38.

91. Ibid., pp. 138–43.

92. Ibid., pp. 145–76.

93. Ibid., pp. 146–56.

94. Ibid., pp. 157–74.

95. Ibid., pp. 165–66.

96. Ibid., pp. 175–76.

97. Ibid., p. 94.

98. Ibid., pp. 177–78.

99. Ibid., pp. 80–88.

100. Ibid., p. 83.

101. Ibid., pp. 180–81.

Chapter Eight

1. For example, see Jacob Needleman, *The New Religions* (Garden City, N.Y.: Doubleday, 1970); Robert S. Ellwood, Jr., *Religious and Spiritual Groups in Modern America* (Englewood Cliffs, N.J.: Prentice-Hall, 1973); Irving I. Zaretsky and Mark P. Leone, eds., *Religious Movements in Contemporary America* (Princeton, N.J.: Princeton University Press, 1974); Charles Y. Glock and Robert N. Bellah, eds., *The New Consciousness* (Berkeley: University of California Press, 1976).

2. Robert N. Bellah, "Religious Evolution," in *Reader in Comparative Religion*, ed. William A. Lessa and Evan Z. Vogt (New York: Harper & Row, 1965), pp. 36–50.

3. Ibid., p. 39.

4. Ibid., p. 40.

5. Bellah sees similar breaks with mediated systems of salvation in other traditions such as Shonin's version of Pure Land Buddhism and certain tendencies in Islam, Buddhism, Taoism, and Confucianism. But he believes these breakthroughs were only successfully institutionalized in the Protestant Reformation. Ibid., pp. 40–41.

6. Cf. Van Harvey, "The Alienated Theologian," in *The Future of Philosophical Theology*, ed. Robert A. Evans (Philadelphia: Westminster Press, 1971), pp. 113–43.

7. The following analysis draws heavily on Thomas Luckmann's account of what is happening to religion within urbanized and industrialized society: *The Invisible Religion* (New York: Macmillan Co., 1967). For comparison, see Peter Berger, *The Sacred Canopy* (Garden City, N.Y.: Doubleday, 1967), and Bryan Wilson, *Contemporary Transformations of Religion* (London: Oxford University Press, 1976).

8. The phrase "polysymbolic religiosity" is taken from William C. Shepherd, "On the Concept of 'Being Wrong' Religiously," *Journal of the American Academy of Religion* 22 (March 1974): 66–81. I agree in the main with Shepherd's argument that historic theism, though irrefutable, is irrelevant to our cultural context and that a new polysymbolic religiosity is emerging which does fit that context. But Shepherd does not mark the distinction between monotheistic and polytheistic forms of polysymbolic religiosity as I do below. Cf. William C. Shepherd, "Religion and the Counter-culture—A New Religiosity," in *Religion American Style*, ed. Robert H. McNamara (New York: Harper & Row, 1974), pp. 348–58.

9. The remaining material in this chapter appeared earlier in a slightly different form in my article "Polysymbolism and Modern Religiosity," in *The Journal of Religion,* 59 (April 1979):169–94, and is herein used by permission of the University of Chicago Press. For a related treatment, see my "Authority in a Pluralistic World," in *The Search for Absolute Values in a Changing World* (New York: The International Cultural Foundation, 1978), pp. 157–73.

10. This brief construction of the modern era is my own, but it is heavily indebted to John Herman Randall, Jr., *The Making of the Modern Mind,* rev. ed. (Boston: Houghton Mifflin, 1940).

11. A. C. McGiffert, *The Rise of Modern Religious Ideas* (New York: Macmillan Co., 1921), cited in James C. Livingston, *Modern Christian Thought* (New York: Macmillan Co., 1971). p. 2.

12. For example, see Nicholas Berdyeav, *The End of Our Time* (London: Sheed and Ward, 1933) and idem, *The Fate of Man in the Modern World* (Ann Arbor, Mich.: University of Michigan Press, 1961); Pitirim A. Sorokin, *The Crisis of Our Age* (New York: E. P. Dutton, 1946); Northrup Frye, *The Modern Century* (Toronto: Oxford University Press, 1967); Karl Jaspers, *Man in the Modern Age* (Garden City, N.Y.: Doubleday, Anchor Books, 1957); Herman Kahn and Anthony J. Wiener, *The Year 2000* (New York: Macmillan Co., 1957); Peter F. Drucker, *The Age of Discontinuity* (New York: Harper & Row, 1969); Romano Guardini, *The End of the Modern World* (Chicago: Henry Regnery Co., 1968); John Lukacs, *The Passing of the Modern Age* (New York: Harper & Row, 1970); Robert J. Lifton, *Boundaries* (New York: Random House, 1969); Paul Goodman, *New Reformation* (New York: Random House, 1970); Theodore Roszak, *The Making of a Counter Culture* (Garden City, N.Y.; Doubleday, 1969) and idem, *Unfinished Animal* (Harper & Row, 1975); and Allen Wheelis, *The End of the Modern Age* (New York: Harper & Row, Torchbooks, 1973).

13. This reading of revolutions in epochal consciousness is based on Susanne K. Langer, *Philosophy in a New Key* (New York: Penguin Books, 1942),chapter 1, and on Thomas S. Kuhn, *The Structure of Scientific Revolutions,* 2d ed., rev. and enl. (Chicago: University of Chicago Press, 1970).

14. I had considered using only the terms "monocentric" and "polycentric" to distinguish these very different versions of polysymbolic religiosity in deference to those who might mistakenly identify this new religiosity with traditional forms of monotheism and polytheism. I have, however, retained the generic terminology of monotheism and polytheism because it is already in use in the literature on polysymbolism.

15. For an instructive study of Troeltsch and Barth in this regard, see Thomas W. Ogletree, *Christian Faith and History* (New York: Abingdon, 1965).

16. The clearest one-volume statement of Joseph Campbell's position is *Myths to Live By* (New York: Viking Press, 1972).

17. In the past, according to Campbell, mythological systems served four functions: the metaphysical function of linking the individual to the mystery of the universe as a whole, the cosmological function of furnishing an intelligible and heuristic image of nature, the sociological function of articulating and enforcing a specific social and moral order, and the psychological function of marking a pathway to carry the individual through the stages of life. See representative discussions in Campbell, *Myths to Live By*, pp. 214–15; idem, *The Masks of God: Creative Mythology* (New York: Viking Press, 1970), pp. 608–24.

18. See Campbell, *Myths to Live By*, pp. 3–20, and idem, *Masks of God*, pp. 573–624.

19. Campbell, *Myths to Live By*, p. 257. Campbell's classic study of the "monomyth" is his *The Hero with a Thousand Faces*, (Princeton, N.J.: Princeton University Press, 1972).

20. See Campbell, *Myths to Live By*, pp. 61–81.

21. Campbell does believe that the unconscious self and the unlimited universe share a common structure. This structure is mirrored in the standard repertoire of archetypes that recur in the dreams and myths of all humankind and in the coming together of explanatory concepts in the natural and life sciences. But Campbell stresses that only the forms of archetypes and laws are set. The *content* is taken from individual experience and thereby bears the indelible stamp of a particular locus and focus. See Campbell, *Myths to Live By*, pp. 44–60, and "A Conversation with Joseph Campbell" in Sam Keen, *Voices and Visions* (New York: Harper & Row, 1974), pp. 76–81.

22. Campbell, *Hero with a Thousand Faces*, p. 388.

23. Keen, *Voices and Visions*, pp. 81–86.

24. See Lifton, *Boundaries*, for a discussion of these features of contemporary life as contributory to the emergence of "protean man."

25. For example, see Goodman, *New Reformation*; Roszak, *Making of a Counter Culture*; Jonathan Eisen, "The Rock Rebellion: Anarchy as a Lifestyle" in *The National Catholic Reporter* 24 September 1969; Benjamin DeMott, "Rock as Salvation," in *Supergrow* (New York: E. P. Dutton Co., 1969); Leslie Fiedler, "The New Mutants," in *Partisan Review* 32 (Fall 1965): 505–25; Charley D. Hardwick, "The Counter Culture as Religion: On the Identification of Religion," *Soundings* 61 (Fall 1973): 287–311.

26. For example, see Ellwood, *Religious and Spiritual Groups*, and idem, "Polytheism: Establishment or Liberation Religion?" in *Journal of the Academy of Religion*, 42 (June 1974):344–49; Shepherd, " 'Being Wrong' Religiously"; James Hillman, "Psychology: Monotheistic or Polytheistic," in *Spring 1971* (New York: Spring Publications, 1971), pp. 193–208 and idem, *Revisioning Psychology* (New York: Harper & Row, 1975); Kenneth Gergen, "Multiple Identity: The Healthy, Happy Human Being Wears Many Masks," *Psychology Today*, 5 (May 1972): 31–35; Ronald Laing, *The Politics of Experience* (Middlesex. England: Penguin Books,

1967); Robert A. Dahl, *Polarchy* (New Haven: Yale University Press, 1971).

27. David L. Miller, *The New Polytheism* (New York: Harper & Row, 1974).

28. Ibid., pp. 5–30.

29. For example, see Van Harvey, *The Historian and the Believer* (New York: Macmillan Co., 1969), and Ray L. Hart, *Unfinished Man and the Imagination* (New York: Herder and Herder, 1968).

30. Miller, *New Polytheism*, p. 3.

31. Ibid., p. 30.

32. Ibid., pp 6–7, 55–56.

33. Ibid., p. 76. Emphasis added.

34. Ibid., p. 5.

35. Ibid., p. 7.

Index of Subjects

Index of Persons